T0323790

THE GOD WHO COMES

THE GOD WHO COMES
Dionysian Mysteries Revisited

Rosemarie Taylor-Perry

Algora Publishing
New York

ISBN: 0-87586-213-6 (softcover)
ISBN: 0-87586-214-4 (hardcover)
ISBN: 0-87586-230-6 (ebook)

Library of Congress Cataloging-in-Publication Data

Taylor-Perry, Rosemarie.
  The God who comes : Dionysian mysteries revisited / Rosemarie
Taylor-Perry.
     p. cm.
Includes bibliographical references and index.
  ISBN 0-87586-214-4 (alk. paper) -- ISBN 0-87586-213-6 (pbk. : alk.
paper)
  1. Eleusinian mysteries. 2. Religions. I. Title.

  BL795.E5T25 2003
  292.3'6--dc22
                          2003015837

Printed in the United States

TABLE OF CONTENTS

To reconstructionist pagans everywhere.

Acknowledgements

I would like to thank Tim White of *Shaman's Drum*, for editorial inspiration, excellent artwork, and encouragement; Gemma Dubaldo, for never wavering in her faith or friendship; numerous Reconstructionist Hellenes, for advice; Kevan Taylor-Perry and Serena Perry, for love and for putting up with "those boring times when Rosemarie needs to write"; and the staff at Algora Publishing, for working through the many mysteries of my manuscript with me.

INTRODUCTION

This book began nearly ten years ago, from the desire to determine — as accurately as historically possible — exactly how ancient and Classical adherents of Hellene Mystery Deities performed their worship. I understood why they should wish to worship these Deities, as I myself shared that impulse: What I did not understand, and proposed to amend with *The God Who Comes...*, was how the rituals were related chronologically; why it seemed that many aspects of ritual action were unclear or appeared transposed; and why no scholar intent upon probing the hows and wherefores of ancient Mystery rites had ever presented them in any sort of chronological, easily-understood manner. The writing of this book has ended in the same spirit in which it has begun, but I now have a much deeper understanding of both how and why our Hellene forebears worshipped as they did — based upon archaeological, scholarly, and iconographic evidence, as opposed to prevailing New Age fictions. In this book I have attempted to share the easier understanding of these deeper meanings with all who are interested in them.

I have also attempted to describe how each ritual was performed. However, I have avoided a cookbook-type "do this, then do that" format, as such a format ultimately confuses more than it enlightens, and imposes an author's own strictures upon material which, by its very nature, is open to various levels of interpretation. As Kerenyi noted in *Dionysos*, (350): "Only where there was no set place for the mysteries — no setting hallowed from time immemorial as was the Boukoleion in Athens — a place had to be sought and the setting created."

CHAPTER ONE: HELLENIC MYSTERY DEITIES

Prior to taking part in ancient Greek Mystery ceremonies, initiates were required to gain some understanding of the nature of the Deities which were believed to appear, in one form or another, during the sacred rites.[1] Such an understanding is no less necessary for the readers of this book, which attempts to give a detailed glimpse into the specifics of those Hellenic rites of passage and initiation that sought to unveil the *mysterum tremendum*.

Lady of Much Bounty

The most thoroughly documented of the Hellene Mystery ceremonies is that of Demeter at Eleusis, known in ancient times as the "Greater Mysteries," or *Eleusinia*. Demeter, an agricultural goddess, evolved from earlier, pre-agricultural Mother goddesses similar to Gaia, Rhea, or Meter.[2] She was known in the Hellene world as the spirit of the unripe fruit, whereas her virgin daughter Kore was considered to be the spirit of flowering.[3]

Linking Demeter to Kore is Persephone, that goddess known in the ancient teachings of Eleusis as "Savior."[4] Persephone is an archetype of unifying force. She stands on the threshold between crone and maiden, death and life, virginity and childbirth, winter and summer; she acts as the nexus around which the ancient Greek wheel of life revolved. In this sense, she is similar to Dionysos, to whose sacred Infant form she gives birth in the Mysteries of Eleusis,[5] and in whose initiation ceremony — *Agrai*, or "The Lesser Mysteries" — she takes an active role.[6]

Kerenyi, in his book *Eleusis: Archetypal Image of Mother and Daughter*, noted that the unifying force of Persephone bound the Demeter/Persephone/Kore triad into a single goddess, a maiden, mother, and crone archetype not unlike the Hellenic Hecate, from whom Hecate may actually have evolved.[7] Mythically, as the Homeric *Hymn to Demeter* points out, it was Hecate — goddess of caves, dung, the moon, and darkness — who helped Demeter ascertain the exact whereabouts of her abducted daughter, Kore.[8]

Mallory, author of *In Search of the Indo-Europeans* (130-135) noted that the tendency to impute a sacred, purifying, or divine nature to the number three — or items in groups of threes — was a religious trait of the Indo-European forebears of the European people; this divine tripartite archetype continues intact today in the Christian image of Deity consisting of Father, Son, and Holy Spirit. The Christian message, too, is a promise taken directly from pagan Mystery religions: Eternal life based upon the death and resurrection (*palingesia*) of Deity.[9]

Hades, the abductor of Kore, also has a tripartite nature, which defines his archetype. As the underworld lord of the dead, Aidoneus — an appellation of Hades, which is derived from an ancient root word meaning "father"[10] — he abducted the maiden, as described in the Homeric *Hymn to Demeter*:

> The earth gaped open and Lord Hades, whom we will all meet, burst forth with his immortal horses onto the Nysian plain. Lord Hades, son of Cronus who is called by many names. Begging for pity and fighting him off, she was dragged into his golden chariot. She screamed the shrill cry of a maenad, calling father Zeus, Zeus the highest and the best...[11]

As Sky God, or Zeus, this tripartite Deity allows, even hallows, the abduction of his own daughter, who is also his paramour.[12] The dual nature of Zeus as lord of the dead is exemplified by the appellation *Zeus Mielichos*, the sacred snake-god of the ancient Hellenes, who housed the spirits of departed ancestors.[13] The taking of Kore by Hades is the act which allows the conception and birth of a second integrating force: Iacchos, also known as *Liknites*, the helpless infant form of that Deity who is unifier of the dark underworld (*cthonic*) realm of Hades and the Olympian ("shining") one of Zeus; this integrating force is the Mystery archetype *par excellence*, Dionysos.[14]

The Dionysian Archetype among Various Cultures

Dionysos, the most thoroughly studied of all Hellenic godforms, is an old and complex Deity whose worship in Attica was composed almost entirely of initiatory Mystery rites. His archetype possesses many configurations, which this section explores. At the Mysteries of Demeter at Eleusis, he was best known as the sacred Child, of whom Christ ("Anointed One") is a syncretistic form.[15]

Syncretistic Deities are those which vary in little more than name from culture to culture, or in which there is cultural alteration of superficial aspects, but little or no variation in the archetype's underlying ritualistic or mythological framework. As Danielou noted in *Shiva and Dionysos: Gods of Love and Ecstasy* (26): "The legends surrounding a particular divine aspect in the various civilizations only differ in the indigenous names given to the heroes and gods." The study of syncretism by comparative mythologists — particularly in combination with comparative linguistic analysis — has aided anthropologists in tracing immigration and emigration patterns of preliterate social groups.

Dionysos himself admits, in Euripides' *Bacchae*, to having wandered the whole world, spreading his worship as he traveled:

> I was in Phrygia before I came here, and Lydia, where the earth flows gold. I passed the broiling plains of Persia, and Bactria's walled towns. The Medes then, their freezing winters, then opulent Arabia and down along the bitter, salt-sea coasts of Asia...[16]

Considering the number and the surprisingly far-flung locales of Dionysos-syncretistic godforms, this is not an idle boast.

Dionysos-syncretistic archetypes display consistency in two aspects, which tend to appear together regardless of secondary, cultural traits. The first of these constants is *shapeshifting*, imparting a "trickster" aspect to such Deities, generally utilized for evasion or as a test of the faithfulness of a worshipper. Such godforms as the Greek Hermes and the Native American animistic forms Raven and Coyote exhibit this tendency.[17] The second Dionysian constant is *rebirth from death*, the promise of which is conveyed upon adherents. (It might be successfully argued that rebirth itself is a form of shapeshifting, meaning that there is really only one major constant among Dionysian-syncretistic divinities). Dionysos is the only Hellenic godform who can instill life as well as take it away: Among various cultures, such an archetype is usually portrayed as some form of vegetation Deity, perhaps because of the seemingly miraculous and endless regenerative ability of plant life.[18]

Consistency between Dionysos-type godforms is also demonstrated in five minor attributes, which fluctuate in degree depending upon the particular norms, standards, and values of a given culture. These attributes are:

1. Unsurpassed viciousness toward those who would harm the followers of the god. When this aspect of Dionysian godforms is aroused, they are what has been termed "Hunters of Men."[19]

2. These Deities are lawgivers who, very often, figure in literal or symbolic acts of human sacrifice, whether this sacrifice occurs because of the breaking of laws, as part of worship, or for the granting of special favors to a community at large. Paradoxically, these same godforms ultimately do away with all requirements for human sacrifice.[20]

3. Such archetypes are portals between upper, lower, and middle worlds: Bridges between the realms of life and death, they are gatekeepers, or the companions of gatekeepers, and masters of altered states of being. This is a natural outgrowth of the vegetation-Deity persona of these archetypes, many of which are allied with one or more entheogenic substances.[21]

Perhaps for this reason, myths which describe Dionysos-syncretistic gods usually declare that these Deities are capable of making their presence felt *within* the hearts or minds of their followers, and even that worshippers or clerics of such divinities are coeval with their god.[22]

4. Godforms of this type are often portrayed as adherents or defenders of the divine feminine, and can often be found in the company of female worshippers, goddesses, or their own mates, without whom they are incomplete, and upon whom they rely in order to fulfill their multiple roles of Divine Child, Bridegroom, Father, Savior, and Reborn One.[23] Sensuality, too, is a Dionysian trademark: This is usually a paradoxical sensuality, at once childlike and ravaging, remarkably androgynous yet undeniably masculine in its expression.[24]

5. *Bewitching* is an acceptable description of Dionysos-syncretistic Deities; many are unsurpassed in the powers of discrimination, response, wisdom, healing, fertility, prophecy, and magic in general. When Dionysos was invoked or worshipped by the ancient Greeks for his command of the powers listed above, he was considered *agathos daemon*, or "the good demon": Demons, to the pagan Hellenes, were not necessarily wholly evil forces of the kind espoused by the Christian faith. They were seen as demigods capable of bringing either wealth and happiness or pain and suffering to mankind, of appearing in any sort of theriomorphic form — including no form at all — and of interceding between the supreme godhead and mankind.[25]

In ancient Greece, Dionysos was known as "serpent of a thousand heads" or "(he of) the thousand names." Many scholars believe that the numerous appellations by which Dionysos was known in Europe are proof that the godform we know today as Dionysos originated elsewhere, arriving in Greece as an exotic, Homeric-era latecomer. Danielou and others suggest that the "original" Dionysian godform may have been the Dravidian Deity Shiva,[26] whose religious relics have been found even among pre-Harappan, preliterate Indus cultures. Several distinct aspects of Shiva do indeed reflect Dionysos as the ancient Hellenes knew him, for instance Shiva Nataraja (lord of the dance which simultaneously creates and destroys), Shiva Ardhanari (lord in lady, or divine androgyne), and Shiva Linga (lord of the phallus, that organ symbolic of regeneration from death in numerous ancient cultures). Willamowitz theorized that the template for Dionysos was the Egyptian god of eternal life, Osiris.[27] However, both the Egyptians and the Dravidians attributed the aforementioned five minor Dionysian traits to a majority of their godforms: Thoth and Horus, Anubis and Min, and the Dravidian Kartikeya all have Dionysian features — a cultural religious preference, not the origination of an Hellenic god.

Physical archeological evidence demonstrates that the Deity name *Dionysos* is first found among ancient Mycenaean shard fragments that bear traces of a language known as Linear B, that language which took over from the earlier Linear A after one or more successful regional influxes of new cultural groups with innovative ideas and ideologies. Such finds lead me to agree with the hypothesis supported by Nilsson, Burkert and Campbell, namely: Dionysos was "born" within the locale which we call Greece at about the same time as Linear B,[28] out of an amalgam of spiritual traits native to certain godforms of both the indigenous people — most likely Minoan — and the immigrants. I would add to this a theory of my own, which is that, among Homo Sapiens humankind as a whole, there has *always* been a "Dionysos-type" Deity securing the portals between life, death, and rebirth. Furthermore, if the knowledge revealed by the efforts of comparative mythologists — such as Campbell — is correct, it is that very Deity whose worship in most societies is primary, since it revolves around the issues and innate meanings of the here and hereafter.

Archaeologists agree that a nomadic plains people, similar to later Scythian or Mongol tribesmen, emerged from the vast Eurasian grasslands in successive waves to unite either forcibly or peacefully with the settled peoples of numerous archaic civilizations including those in India, Egypt, and the Greek mainland. With the nomads came the domestic horse, the agile light chariot and spoked wheel, highly tensile recurved bows, advanced metallurgy, a god- and light-oriented religion, hallucinogenic mushrooms and herbs, the sweat bath, and the worship of fire. Those with whom they merged were ancient city-dwellers wise in the ways of agriculture, writing, large-scale engineering, economics and mathematics. Modern Western culture hails from the powerful combination of just such divergent groups. Similar to pre-Aryan cultures found in Egypt and the Indus, the Minoan civilization encountered by the nomads was a goddess-revering fishing culture, one that held the snake and the moon and the horns of the bull to be most holy, and that utilized opium gum in healing and religious rites.[29] *Centaurs*, and the mythologies surrounding these creatures, may be mythopoeic recollections of the first men on horseback ever seen by the Minoans.[30]

Dionysos-syncretistic godforms from other cultures include:[31]

> *Adonis* (Greco-Roman derivative of *Attis*)
> *Agao-Wedo* (*Ellegua* to the practitioners of vodoun: "Soul-father")
> *Attis* (Phrygian derivation from *Tammuz*)
> *Cernunnos* (also *Herne*. Celtic/Britain: "the Hunter [of men...?]")
> *Dinné-altsó-natlehi* (Navajo: Dinéh aspect of Coyote, "He who changes into everything")
> *Enki* (also *Ea*. Sumerian: "Law giver")
> *Gwyn* (Welsh derivation from *Herne*)
> *Hainuwele* (Polynesian/West Ceram: "He who sprouts and grows")
> *Hyakinthus* (Late Classical Greek: Lover of Apollo)
> *Katagama* (Modern Hindu Dionysian incarnation of *Krishna*)
> *Krishna* (Aryan Vedic Hinduism: "The pure [one]")
> *Masau'u* (Hopi vegetation katchina/ancestor spirit: Also *mudman* and *clown* katchinas)
> *Maui* (Polynesian/Hawaii: "Trickster")
> *Mir Susne-kum* (Siberian/Ostyak: "[the] Sevenfold one")
> *Ochosi* (also *Osain*. African/Yoruba vegetation Deity)
> *Odin* (Scandinavian: "Mad or ecstatic one," also "Lord of souls" and "Wanderer")
> *Skanda* (Tamil Hindu derivation from *Kartikeya*: "Jet of sperm or fire")
> *Tammuz* (also *Dumuzi*. Babylonian: "Father/lord")
> *Tlaloc* (Huichol god of paradisical visions)
> *Wodan* (also *Wotan*: Germanic derivative of *Odin*)
> *Xochipilli* (Aztec vegetation Deity: "Prince of flowers")

Alternate Names (*Who* he is)[33]

> Bacchos (Phrygian: "Shoot/sprout")
> Bassareus (Lydian: "Fox")
> Dolichenus/Herlichenus (Hittite/Semite: "Storm-bringer")
> Dusares (Arabian: "Tendril")
> Fufluns (Arcadian/Etruscan: "God of Wine")
> Gestin (Sumerian: "God of Wine")
> Liber (Roman: "Freedom")
> Sabazios (Cretan: fusion of Dionysian and Jovian qualities, as are many epithets of Dionysos)
> Thyionidas (Rhodian: "Of the phallus")

The following titles are those given primarily to the Hellenic aspects of Dionysian manifestation.[32] The name *Dionysos* itself most likely means "lord of wine" (*Deo-œnos-os*).[33]

Titles (*What* he is)[34]

> Amphietes (God of Two Years)
> Bromius (Fire-Born God)
> Charma Brotoisin (God of Many Joys)
> Choreios (God of the Dance)
> Dimetor (God of Dual Mothers/Wombs)
> Dimorphos (God of Two Forms)
> Dithyrambos (God of Two Births)
> Epaphios (God Who Inspires Frenzy)
> Erectheus (God Conceived in the Underworld)
> Erikipeos (The Androgynous God)
> Iacchos (God of Resounding Cries/Lord of Cries)
> Kissos (God of Ivy)
> Lenaios (God of the Vats [*pithoi*])
> Liknites (God of the Winnowing Basket)
> Melpomenos (God of the Joyful Song)
> Musagetes (God of the Muses: an epithet which equates Dionysos and Apollo)
> Pelekys (God of the Axe)
> Philopaigmos ("Goatfoot God"/"Lover of Satyrs")[35]
> Phytalmios (God of Growth)
> Polymorphos (God of Many Forms)
> Sphaleotas (God Who Causes Stumbling [*or*, God Who is Lame])
> Thyoneus (Raging God)

Trieterikos (God of Alternating Festival Years)
Zagreus (Horned/Hunting God)[36]

Appellations (preceded by a name: dependent on what ritual is being performed)[37]

Agrionos (Savage)
Aigobolos (Goat Killer)
Aisymnetes (The Masks)
Antheros ([of] flowers)
Anthrophorestes (Man-Destroyer)
Arsenothelys (Androgyne)
Bakcheutos (Loud One)
Bougenes (Calf)
Braites ([winter/ice?] Breaker)
Cthonios (Subterranean: Zeus, Hades, and Hermes also share this epithet)
Dendrites (Of the Trees [*Dendreus/Endendros*])
Dissotokos (Of Two Origins)
Dusales (Hybrid)
Eiraphiotes (Sewn In)
Eleutherius [also *Eleutheros*] (the Greek form of *Liber*, god of freedom)
Enorches ([having] Testicles)
Eriboas (Howler)
Erikapaios (Eternal Singer)
Eriphos (Kid [goat])
Euboleus (Good Counsel[or])
Evius (Echoing Cry)
Gynnis (Girlish)
Hugiates (Dispenser of Health: an epithet shared with Aesclapios)
Iatros (Delight)
Ignigena (Conceived of Fire)
Isodiates (Divider of the Sacrifice)
Iyngies (of the Wryneck bird: possible derivation of the word *Jynx*)
Katharsios (Purifier [katharzasthai: catharsis/transmutation])
Kadmeios ([pertaining to] Hermes)
Kechenos (Valor) [It also seems to mean "golden-yellow; saffron or grain-colored"; this color is often connected to Dionysian worship.]
Kouros (Boy/Youth)
Lampter (Light)
Laphystios (Glutton)
Limnaios (Marsh-Born)
Lyseus (Releaser, Destroyer, Deliverer)
Maenomenos (Mind-Expander: Master of Maenads)
Melanaigis (Black Goatskin)

Merotraphes ("seam-splitter" would be a modern rendition of this epithet)
Mielikos (Benevolent Sweetness [honey or figs]*, also spelled *meilikos*)
Mitrephoros (Crown/Circlet)
Morychos (Dark One)
Nyktypolos (Night Prowler [*Nyktelios*])
Œnos (Wine)
Orthos (Erect/Rampant)
Omestes (Eater of Raw Flesh)
Omphakites (Unripe [prob. refers to grapes])
Pergethes (Benefactor)
Phales (Phallus)
Phanes (Winged*)[38]
Phloios (Regeneration: of a vegetative nature [*Phleus/Phleon*])
Ploutos (Wealth [also referent to *Iacchos*, son of Hades Plouton and
    Demeter])
Polygethes (Joy Bringer [*Charma Brotoisin*])
Polyeides (Many-formed One)
Protogonos (Firstborn)
Pyrigenes (Fire-Born)
Perikionos (Of the Pillar)
Pseudanor (Falsely Virile)
Sisopolis (City's Savior*)
Staphylos (Grape)
Sykites (Fig: referent to *Thyionidas Phallon*)
Tauromorphos (Bull-Formed)
Taurophagos (Bull-Eater)
Telagios (of the Sea [*Aktaios*])
Thesmophoros (Law Giver)
Triptolemos (Sower)
Trigonos (Thrice-Born)

One method of using these titles, names, and appellations would have been the equivalent of first, middle, and last names, e.g.: *Bassareus Zagreus Staphyloi*, literally "the fox who stole (captured) the grapes," a lighthearted combination of names that sheds new light on all fox-inhabited fables — Dionysos-syncretistic godforms are constantly linked to the fox, as Robert Graves notes in *Difficult Questions* 101-102. Other titles known to have been used include *Dionysos Trieterikos Katharsein*: "Lord of Wine who Purifies (the Triennial Feasts)," an appellation appropriate to Dionysian rites held once every three years; or play-on-word titles such as that commonly used during the Classical Katagogia festivals and ceremonial processions: *Phales Phanes*, "The Winged Phallus," a raunchy Greek double-entendre for the god who really gets around. Statuary of winged phalli are common in museums which preserve ancient and Classical iconography, serving to confound and embarrass the general public. These names, titles, and appellations could be combined and recombined in limitless ways, exemplifying once more the boundless forms in which the great Shapeshifter might manifest.

The Dionysian Archetype Over Time

> A bull be, Bacchus,
> or a serpent many-headed be,
> or a radiant lion be:
> hunt the hunter, Bacchus...[39]

I conjecture that the worship of the god who has been named so many things by so many people is the oldest and most continuous form of worship in the world, aside from the worship of the Great Mother, to which it is complimentary.[40] To begin to fully understand the complex, ambivalent and paradoxical godform known as Dionysos requires a lengthy journey through time; this section explores the probable antiquity of the Dionysian archetype.

First, however, the basic Classical Greek nature of this Deity should be clarified, in order to separate out demoralizing misconceptions purposely attached to his worship.

The five major clarifications that follow appear to be paradoxical: They are supposed to be. Not springing from a Zoroastrian-type duality — in which a good god is opposed by an evil one — this most ancient of pagan godforms *is* duality; more accurately, the archetype is polar in nature. Human minds tend to register inseparable polarities as paradox.[41]

Primary dualities that characterize the Dionysos godforms are as follows:

(1) Dionysian godforms are often presented in literal, animistic terms (e.g.: To be "washed in the Blood of the Lamb"), but they are generally experienced by humans as part of the self, making them concurrently anthropomorphic. Lord of plants and animals, yet innately more than either, such a god is also the reaper and the hunting animal master — the hunter of humankind.[42] The Dionysos portrayed in Euripides' *Bacchae* is just such a Deity.

(2) Perhaps as an offshoot of the preceding characteristics, Dionysos was anciently known to be the fierce and merciless protector of that which merits mercy: The unborn, the possible, the serendipitous — of any helpless, voiceless being.[43]

(3) Shapeshifter in both space and time, he is both sacrificer and sacrifice, crushed grape and dancing winetreader, simultaneously. A myth exists of the infant Dionysos delighting in killing small creatures in order to bring them back to life, even as the murderous Titans crept up to slaughter the oblivious child god. This myth springs from just such an archetype and its related rituals.[44]

(4) He is the archetype of endless life through death *ad infinitum*, neither one of which is given as "reward" or "punishment" as is the case in certain forms of Buddhism (see Campbell's *Masks of God: Oriental Mythology* for an excellent treatise on the different forms this religion has adopted over time). Rather, both act as partners in a balanced cycle to create the universe as we perceive it, filled with the complimentary opposites of light and darkness, motion and stillness, conflict and harmony.[45] As the rituals in this book will demonstrate, all Mystery rites depend upon a framework of complimentary opposites, which may be why Persephone herself was equated with Pandora — the Greek first woman — who introduced the play of opposites into the world.[46]

(5) Lord of both upper and lower worlds, he is the ithyphallic god of fertility and the eunuch god of sterility, the giver of laws and the breaker of chains, at one and the same time. Many of the Classical Greek titles given to Dionysos, such as *Eleuthereus, Thesmophoros, Katharsios, Lyseus,* and *Trigonos* illustrate this point.[47]

For various socio-political reasons, the Pagan Dionysian archetype has fallen under the burden of numerous misconceptions. Let's look at five misconceptions, including the origins of those misconceptions and their revision, so that the true nature of the Dionysian archetype is clarified:

(1) *Lecherous.* One of Dionysos' classical roles was god of fidelity in marriage.[48] To modern English speakers, this stands in bemusing opposition to the ancient Greek word for ritual worship of Dionysos, which is *orgazein.* A common mistake made by people whose primary language is English is to translate this word as "(sexual) orgy" — meaning that half of the word is entirely passed over, causing the loss of a complex spiritual concept; though the simple translation of *orgazein* is "celebration," there is more to it than that.

"Zein" is a form of the word "zöe." The most simplistic translation of *zöe* is "eternal life"; a more accurate one is that used by Kerenyi to describe the Dionysian archetype: *Indestructible Life*. More than simply describing the immortal nature of the soul, *zöe* infers the very energy which animates the soul to make it immortal — "life of the soul." It implies, too, the constant drive of the soul for incarnation.

This is the point at which the "Org-" prefix of the word comes in. "Celebration of the physical expression of that energy which animates the soul" is the nearest English approximation of *orgazein* that I can come up with. Christianity encapsulated the idea of this energy in the concept of the Holy Spirit, or *hagion pneuma* ("pure breath of life"). It is understandable that early Christian bishops — a title created by Diocletian, equivalent in meaning and authority to the word "judge"[49] — wished to strip a concept as spiritually riveting as *orgazein* away from the worship of Dionysos: Thyiades performed Lenean midwinter rites on Parnassos well into the sixth century of the first millennium, and as late as 691 CE ecstatic cries of "Dionysos!" were heard throughout the Byzantine empire during festivals associated with wine. Stern measures needed to be taken by anyone wishing to stamp out this particular worship — even Rome never managed to quell the Bacchanalia. Although it had been brutally outlawed by the Republic in 186 BCE, Bacchic worship flourished under the Roman empire, and in Byzantine Roman Britain the rites of Dionysos were Christianity's primary competitor for religious dominance.[50]

For these reasons, those Dionysian festivals and rites not appropriated wholesale by Christianity over time were altered in meaning to appear nefarious or spiritually deadening; this includes altering the concept of *orgazein* into "orgy." It is also interesting to note that the modern image of Satan ("an adversary") has horns and hooves like a satyr or silenus, as the ancient god Dionysos himself does at times, especially in the aspects of Sabazios, Zagreus, Iacchos, and Dusares. As noted earlier, one of Dionysos' Hellenic titles was *agathos daimon*, or "the good demon." Under the influence of a young theocracy violently opposed to any other religion which could conceivably undermine the relative stability of their power, "good" was stripped from this aspect of Dionysos.[51]

Dionysian worship was neither one big swingers' club, nor gang rape, nor an endless self-gratification carnival: It was the worship of instinct, intuition, and necessity — of life, and death, and life again, the very bedrock of all Mystery religions, including Christianity.[52]

(2) *Filthy.* This concept was a Levite and Zoroastrian anti-Dionysian tactic. Aryan Vedics, though unrelated to Semitic peoples, incorporated a comparable method in order to damper worship of Shiva, implying that this god of eternal life was a necrophiliac, a baneful spirit obsessed with decay and the smoke of pyres.[53] (I theorize from this that one or more waves of Indo-European immigrants whose ideology influenced the godforms and worship of ancient cities may have been followed by one or more waves of Semitic peoples, who

attempted to overlay the influence of the earlier nomads with their own. For an interesting treatise on the striking similarities of Semitic godforms with Dionysos, see Graves' *The White Goddess*.) Similarly, it is commonly — though erroneously — believed that Hebrew kosher laws are cleanliness ("health") laws. They are not. They are religious dietary laws. Such laws historically act to physically separate believers, lifting the former to an allegedly higher moral, spiritual — and often, authoritarian — plane. Such religious dietary strictures exist or have existed among Hindu Brahmins, Pythagoreans and Orphics, Muslims, orthodox Catholics, and others.

For example, Exodus 23:19, 34:26 and Deuteronomy 14:21 state: *"Thou shalt not seethe a kid in its mother's milk."* It is known that the stewing of a young animal in the milk of its mother was a form of sacrament to ancient Dionysian worshippers; inscriptions found on thin gold plates in the tombs of such individuals read: θεοϳ εγενοι ανΘρωποι ˜ επιφοϳ εζγαλα επετεϳ, or: "From man (thou hast) become (a) god; (a) kid (thou hast) fallen into milk."[54] Any combination of meat with milk products is forbidden in the Orthodox Jewish faith, which is a modern derivation of the class-structured creed brought to the ancient Canaanite people by Levite overlords.

Similar sacramental meals involving piglets were prepared by Hellenes for the feast following the Eleusinia, which gave honor to Demeter and Persephone: Proscriptions against eating or even touching the flesh of swine may be a tacit proscription against goddess worship. Alternatively, since the Levite Hebrews and later the Arab people from among whom Islam arose were originally nomadic tribes, the proscription could simply be an outgrowth of the impossibility of raising the unmilkable, independent-minded pig in large, fast-moving herds; the same porcine traits which made the pig a treasured source of protein in a settlement would make the pig an alien and unpleasant creature to nomads.[55]

Eating raw meat (*omophagy*) was another Dionysian sacramental act, perhaps symbolic of the power of "raw" nature over civilization and the power of Deity over that of self-proclaimed holy men. It is known that in Classical times, the eating of raw meat by Greco-Roman citizens was an act of defiance against State-sanctioned sacrifice and the State-sanctioned rules of worship that went along with it, as was the choice made by some to take recourse by some to lifelong vegetarianism.[56] Even today, most forms of omophagy are implicitly forbidden because they are inherently uncivilized, a tacit sacrament to the undomesticated, visceral nature of humankind and the power of the old gods.[57] Anciently, however, plants as well as animals were included in the sacrament of "raw-eating," particularly those mind-expanding plants of which Dionysos is patron.

Classical plays which speak of a mother tearing and eating her child may not have been in reference to some literal, inhuman cannibalistic act. Instead, they may allude to a priestess — a modern, catch-all term the historical pagan Greeks did not possess — crushing and imbibing the entheogenic herbs sacred to Dionysos, which maenads would gather in the ends of their thyrsoi. The *thyrsos*, that Dionysian staff of legend, was made of a chambered narthex (fennel) stalk, which could hold water to keep cut plants fresh for transport. Since plants were considered to be living representations of the god, and the priestesses of Dionysos were also known as his "mothers" or "nurses," the allegory of the dismembered and devoured child comes clear in this context.[58]

Also, I theorize that many of the small animals which female devotees of Dionysos carry in Classical artwork may, in fact, represent *symbols* of animals — children's toys, which are a typical thing for any child's nursemaids to carry; and toys were some of the characteristic contents of the Dionysian *liknon*, or sacred basket. Symbolically, the "tearing apart" of animals by Dionysians may be considered to survive in such diverse cultural rituals as the rending of a piñata on a child's birthday.

(3) *Vengeful*. Neither life nor death nor rebirth, as natural processes, deals vengeance. Vengeance, like strip mining or vaccination, is a human invention. The cycle of death and rebirth implicit in all Mystery rites is learning, not retribution — a gift, not a curse. Generally, people receive from life that which they choose to receive.

This is illustrated in the myth of Midas. A rich king, Midas succors the mythic stepfather of Dionysos, Silenus. In return, a grateful Dionysos offers Midas whatever he wishes in the world; allowing avarice free reign, Midas requests that everything he touches be turned to gold. Knowing this to be the prayer of a fool — whence modern Americans derive the saying: "Be careful what you wish for, you just might get it!" — the god posed the question a second time, to give the king an opportunity to change his mind. Midas insisted, and spent a miserable period unable to eat or drink, divesting his loved ones of life by turning them into gold with any gesture of physical affection.[59] The myth ends when Dionysos allows Midas to wash away in a river this horrid gift of the king's own choosing.

(4) *Patriarchal*. A neo-pagan friend innocently inquired, "He's sort of a patriarchal god, isn't he?" I gave a deep sigh. Then, I laughed!

"Patriarchy," as popular culture defines it — a sort of wholesale misogyny driven purely by spite, jealousy, and a sense of insecurity within a male population, whose intent is to denigrate women through a continuous, heavy-handed application of physical and mental stricturing — is a term designed to fit a preconceived and largely erroneous belief structure; an equivalent ideology has never been conclusively proven to have existed anciently, and though certain fundamentalist societies currently exist which may be arguably said to possess such a gender-based system of purposeful cruelty, these societies are for the most part relatively modern institutions. Such a structure would have little patience with androgynous gods who sacrifice their maleness on occasion, out of respect for and love of the Great Mother, or who fiercely defend and love human females so much that at least occasional freedom from demands, bondage, or conditioning is a prerequisite to worship.[60]

Greek myth relates that Dionysos was allowed to bring his mortal mother, Semele, back to her original earthly state, and furthermore to grant her eternal life as a goddess (*Thyone*) — but the price he paid to be allowed to do this was an effeminate demeanor, which is why Dionysos is typically portrayed with long hair and, often, wearing women's garments; as shapeshifter he occasionally appears to his worshippers in female form.[61]

Related to Dionysian polarity, androgyny, and numerous dual traits is the singular spiritual form that the worship of Dionysian-syncretistic godforms often takes. As Campbell clearly points out in *Masks of God: Primitive Mythology* (pp. 229-242), there are two main human conduits of divine force found in all cultures: the shaman, and the priest. Though these terms are sometimes used interchangeably, in fact the two roles are mutually exclusive, standing in direct conflict with one another.

Shamanic spiritualism is the trademark of nomadic peoples. It is the realm of the vision quest, of unwritten oral knowledge, of Deity as a shapeshifter who appears in varying guises to different individuals. This religious convention grants worshippers immense creative freedom in their spirituality, but little in the way of religious comfort or security. I hypothesize that when a nomadic people alters its spirituality to conform to the priestly pattern, a shaman must first take on the role of prophet, spurred to this role through the desire of his people to change their nomadic way of life to a settled one. Such appears to have been the case with both Judaism and Islam.

Priestly spiritualism is a development of settled communities, whose class structures are more markedly differentiated than those found in nomadic societies. It is the realm of direct revelation from select archetypes whose form is static, via clerics specially chosen for this role. Individual visionary epiphanies are generally downplayed in such a religious atmosphere, which strictures an individual's religious creativity but offers great peace of mind and soul in the secure promises of its tenets, which are usually put into written format in order to maintain the agreed-upon archetype's traits within the community's successive generations in as unmodified a form as possible.[62]

The myths and rituals of Dionysos contain elements native to the milieu of both agrarian priest-kings and nomadic shaman-warriors, reflecting and mythically maintaining a period of homogenization between a settled society and a nomadic one. The Classical Hellene civilization with which we are familiar hails from just such a combined culture, and this is the source of the paradoxical nature of Dionysos that gives his worship such allure.[63]

(5) *Cruel.* Dionysian sacraments were sometimes heavily mind-altering, and some entheogens — such as the datura beloved of the Dravidian godform Shiva, as well as its more potent relative, brugmansia — can cause irreversible insanity, and even death, when used without proper knowledge of their growth habits, toxic properties, reactivity, and correct preparation. Such facts were known to ancient Mystery clerics, and were undoubtedly the reason for the restrictive, heavily ritualized formats of Hellenic Mystery rites. The use of

substances which could possibly cause harm to those not privy to their ways was surely a great help to those who desired to forbid and demonize Mystery rites using entheogens.

This leads into the next classification of this chapter, those things that Dionysos is known to loathe:

(1) Greed and avarice: False gain.
(2) Arrogance and conceit: False modesty.
(3) Tyranny and oppression: False piety.
(4) Pomposity and lip service: False promises.
(5) Self-hatred and codependency: False image, false virtue.

The reason the ancients considered these things to be distasteful to a god such as Dionysos is relatively easy to understand: This archetype cannot easily penetrate such emotions or their consequent actions, because such emotions and actions stand at odds with the urge to life, which must by its very nature reach out to envelop everything that lives.

Instead of the Dionysian impulse of ecstasy, individuals harboring such mindsets perceive only an impulse of madness — not because "the god is angry!," but because the physical laws of cause and effect (which may be considered to have been created by divine force) ensure that madness is precisely what such attitudes turn life into.

When the great Athenian comedies, such as Aristophanes' *Frogs*, were written, Dionysos himself was often portrayed as having traits detestable to gods of the Dionysian archetype. This allowed Dionysos' worshippers to poke fun at those traits through himself: Since Dionysos was experienced in his worshippers as part of themselves, this enabled them to see the ridiculous quality of such behaviors, if need be giving them impetus to discard them as offensive personal characteristics. This was recognized anciently as part of Dionysos' cathartic nature. Antipater of Thessalonika summed it up in the fifth century BCE as follows:

> These are Aristophanes' marvelous plays,
> so often crowned with ivy from his Deme.
> What Dionysian pages, and how clear
> that ringing voice of comedy edged with charm.
> Heroic dramatist fit to take on Greece,
> hating the bad, and making fun of it![66]

Prehistoric Dionysian Forms

The mythic god of wine, Dionysos, was born on the fabled island of Nÿsa; another derivation of "Dionysos" might be *Dio-nÿsa* or *Theo-nÿsa*, which translates as "the Zeus — *Theos* — of Nÿsa."[67] It is with wine that a Dionysian journey through time must begin and, in true labyrinthine style, spread outward in several directions, only to ultimately end back where it began.

Dionysos, and many of the syncretistic forms of Dionysos, are generally considered to be, primarily, "gods of wine." The earliest purposeful human alteration of a non-alcoholic liquid into an alcoholic one has been tentatively proposed to have occurred during the Chalcolithic era, a period of transition between the hunter-gatherer practices of the Mesolithic and the farming communities of the Neolithic.[68] Not yet agricultural, the Chalcolithic ancients did not utilize sugar, which wasn't widely used even in its native environment of India until sometime after the first Aryan incursions of approximately 2000 BCE.[69]

For the fermentation of liquid to occur, sugars are the most important ingredient after yeast. Grape juice — the basis of all Classical Greco-Roman wines — is the only fruit juice both sweet and liquid enough to allow fermentation to take place without further addition of cane, corn, beet, or malt sugars, none of which stone-age man used (though a rare treat of maple or birch sap may have been enjoyed). There is one liquid more sugary than grape juice, however, and this the ancients did use: Honey.

People of the late Mesolithic and early Neolithic were, by and large, still hunter-gatherers. Modern aboriginal hunter-gatherer and nomadic communities utilize a clever method for cooking liquids, such as soups or teas: A leather sack is suspended over the radiant heat of coals, and as long as the leather is kept moist by the cooking sack's contents, which seep very slowly through the skin's natural pores, it will not burn. Honey, a ubiquitous modern tea sweetener which surely performed the same role anciently, was perhaps added to tonics of otherwise unpalatable, vitamin-rich herbs steeped in hot water. Honey usually carries within it pollen from the flowers that the bees collected nectar from, as well as fungus, mold, and yeast spores which spontaneously cause fermentation when honey is mixed with water and left to sit.[70] Caves have been discovered in which there is extensive rock art depicting people collecting honey, and apparently preparing mead, by just this method. Similar honey-wine rock art, known as *araña*, is widespread, and has been discovered in locations as diverse as Greece and Belgium.[71]

In one mid-Neolithic Cretan cave can be found the araña of "the honey thieves," a preliterate "recipe" for mead-making which lived on orally to ultimately become the Homeric myth of the Cave of Light and Honey, where a great sacrificial Bull was born and slain by a serpent during the time of radiant heat (summer solstice or *opora*, the ancient Greek New Year), its hide magically transforming into a skin of mead.[72] The Cretan *araña* is the first appearance of this mythos in either the Aegean or Mediterranean areas, and it is a myth of life through death.[73] Its metaphor survives to this day in the words we use to speak of the divine, as noted by Danielou: "The French word 'Dieu' comes from the (Indo-European) root 'Div', which means 'radiant'. The Germanic 'Gott' and English 'God' come from another Indo-European root, 'Go', which surprisingly means 'the Bull'."[74]

In the great Paleolithic Auragnacian temple-caves, which date from 20,000 to 12,000 years ago, remain the artful renderings of the sacrificial bulls of the summer hunt. In winter, however, the wild cattle and other ruminants would migrate away over the plains, and people whose wintertime survival depended upon the secure warmth of permanent dwellings — usually built beneath deep rock overhangs, but never in actual caverns, which were the abode of ritual only — could hardly follow. What animal was there left to hunt in the depths of winter; did hunters struggle through deep snow to chase fleet game?

Not when a large animal existed which, in winter, was sluggish and generally somnolent, a dangerous animal given by providence to relatively weak humankind as sustenance — an animal which fattens preferentially on honey prior to its winter hibernation and often lives in a cave — the bear.[75]

In this section, I will attempt to link these apparently varying themes together in a great Paleolithic-to-Neolithic mythological progression without sounding like some sort of deranged stock market report, though I find it more than a little bemusing that these two animals, bull and bear — which meant food and life to our prehistoric ancestors — continue on as economic symbols. (The word "economics" involves how sustenance is obtained, stored, or traded, whether one is dealing in concrete sustenance, such as wheat; abstract sustenance, such as shares of a stock in a wheat processing plant; or the money which can be used to purchase bread).

To modern-day Ainu tribes, the bear is revered as a god in stone-age style. Taken from its hibernating mother in winter, as Dionysos was torn from

Semele's womb by Zeus' lightning,[76] it is nursed by the tribe's women, the way wild animals were mythically nursed by Dionysos' maenads.[77] Once the bear is weaned, it is given a place of honor in the northernmost corner of the chief's dwelling, and grows through the summer in a cage of plaited grapevine — that most Dionysian of plants — prior to its sacrificial death the following winter. This ritual is a living Paleolithic reenactment of life's rebirth from death: The young bear is believed by the Ainu people to be a journeying god, who will intercede with the universe in their favor and who, through the midwinter sacrificial death which frees its soul, will live forever, ultimately enabling them to do likewise.[78]

According to Campbell, many ancient and modern aboriginal peoples have revered a similar "journeying god" mythos, hailing from Paleolithic hunter-gatherer societies, in which the symbolic animals so revered may be (depending upon geographic locale) the bear, lion, or panther — the latter ultimately finding its place in Classical Greek myth as the familiar of Dionysos.[79] There is, in fact, a myth in which Dionysos is captured by greedy pirates intent on ransom, who believe the god to be the youthful son of some king because of his rich saffron and purple raiment. To strike terror into the hearts of his captors, the Deity turns first into a panther, then into a lion, then into a bear, and converts the ship's masts into grapevines:[80]

> Little slender lad, lightning-engendered,
> Grand master of magicians:
> When pirates stole you at Icaria
> Wild ivy gripped their rigging, every oar
> Changed to a serpent, panthers held the poop,
> A giant vine sprouted from the mast crotch
> And overboard they plunged, the whey-faced crew!
> (Robert Graves *Difficult Questions...* 111-112, verses 6-12)

In the beautiful book *The Cave of Lascaux: The Final Photographs*, by Mario Ruspoli, a tiny bear is seen, painted in one corner of the vast, rambling cavern. It is difficult to see, because it is hidden *within the heart of a bull*. It is the only bear to be found anywhere within the temple-cave of Lascaux.[81] The great Bull of Life, of Cretan myth and the Lascaux caverns where the painted bulls are pierced and bleeding, must die to provide not only food and raiment but a leather flask for honey wine. In the heart of this bull who brings all boons and surfeit is hidden the bear, who intercedes with the great Bull on behalf of mankind and who, as "honey bear," magically becomes honey wine, reborn from death within its leather flask, bringing euphoria and relief from pain to mortal mankind.

The sacred message behind this ancient and pervasive epiphany is that *life and death are one and the same,* a *mysterion* of complimentary opposites: Paleolithic and modern sacrifice-and-intercession rituals, which imply that birth and death are portals that open upon immortality, relay exactly the same message as the one found in the myths and rituals of Dionysos and his changeful father, Zeus. The Greeks knew and recorded the mysterious circumstance that Dionysos was a "second Zeus," even as Zeus was a "second Kronos" — a god continuously rebirthed and slain, even as animals and plants must be in order to sustain mankind.[82] All Deities of the ancient Hellenic Mystery initiations shared in this epiphany, and transmitted the same message — Kore and Demeter of the fallen flower and unripe fruit, Hecate of the shadowed cavern, Hades the dark reflection of shining Zeus, and Dionysos, whom Kerenyi so appropriately termed *Archetype of Indestructible Life.*

In a cavern not unlike the labyrinthine Cretan ritual-fermentation caves, where honey-water may have been ceremonially sewn into the hide of a sacrificial bull, is the Animal Master of Trois Freres, etched and painted some fourteen thousand years ago; ears and antlers of a stag, eyes of an owl, paws of a bear, phallus of a big cat, tail of a horse (bringing to mind the *sileni* of Dionysian myth), beard and legs of a man — the great Shapeshifter, Hunter of hunters — dancing.[83]

Dionysos is also the dancer (*Choreios*), the masked and costumed one (*Aisymnetes*), the horned or antlered hunter (*Zagreus*) who was known in Greece as the one sewn in: sewn into the thigh of that god mythically known as the Great White Bull born in a Cretan cave — Zeus.[84] Dionysos is Bougenes "bull's son" and Dithyrambos "twice-born." And, of course, he is Polymorphos, *god of many forms.*

The Most Modern Dionysian Form

As previously noted, Christ, like so many of the beliefs and rituals underpinning Christianity, is syncretistic with Dionysian forms and ceremonies. Indeed, during Europe's Dark Ages, when literacy was the privileged right of the few, and the many spent their lives fighting tooth and nail against seemingly endless waves of invaders including the Franks, Saxons, Angles, Jutes, Goths, Vandals, Burgundians, Huns and Mongols, it was the Christian Church that preserved fragments of ancient Mystery rites which, in pagan fashion, had never been written down. In medieval Europe, the church did not attempt to hide this fact; rather, it was exaggerated to the point of parody in such activities as the Midwinter Fool's Mass, an undoubtedly entertaining spectacle followed by a feast:

> Introibo ad Itare Bachi —
> Ad eum qui letificat cor hominis...
> Potemus. Aufer a nobis, quesumus, Bache,
> Cuncta vestimen'ta nostram, ut ad taberna
> poculorum nudis corporibis mereamur
> introire. Per omnia pocula poculorum. Stramen.
>
> (Let us go up to the altar of Bacchus —
> to him who gives joy to man's heart...
> Let us drink. Take from us, we beseech thee, Bacchus,
> all our clothes, that we may be worthy,
> with naked bodies, to enter into the
> tavern. Unto us all, drink without end.)[85]

Dionysian rites, from which both the Greek Orthodox and Roman Catholic branches of the early Church borrowed heavily, include the rite of baptism, the concepts of sacramentalism and transubstantiation, and the observance of the Lenten period. Baptism, either via immersion or by sprinkling, was a common form of purification in pagan ceremonies.[86] In the Dionysian *Agrai* (lesser Mystery) rite, an initiate was daubed with chalky clay or lime in memory of his Titanic — fallen or sinful — nature at the outset of the ceremony.

Ultimately, the initiate would have the white chrism removed by immersion in a bath: His subsequent cleaned condition symbolized his new oneness with the god Dionysos, whom the cannibalistic Titans could not destroy. In Christian baptism, the initiate is immersed first, to symbolize a promised resurrection in imitation of Christ, whom men could not kill: The Christian daubings come after immersion rather than before, and are done with sanctified oil, rather than ochre; this chrism marks a new Christian's unity with the Holy Spirit (*hagion pneuma*),[87] a force of *orgazein*, that celebratory vigor which animates the human spirit.

To differentiate their religious practices from pagan ones, early Christians simply resorted to altering the order of ceremonial acts. This tended to keep events familiar and comfortable enough so that individuals could adopt the new faith without psychological discomfort, while adding new dimensions to rituals which, over millennia, may have become rote, dry, and in many instances, meaningless. Such was the case with the Christian observance of Lent, a word and observance taken directly from the ancient Hellenic late-midwinter ceremony of *Lenaia*.

Lenaia, also known as the lesser or rural Dionysia, celebrated the beginning of the "Dionysian time" in mainland Greece, a roughly forty-day-long period which would end with the feasting and mummery of *Anthesteria* and the lesser Mystery rites of Agrai, the observances of which were required to be preceded by an extended abstinence-fast. Lent is also a forty-day span during which abstinence-fasting is performed. Although Lenten mummery and feasting — ushered in by Carnivale, Mardi Gras, or related festivities on Fat Tuesday — precedes the Christian abstinence period rather than following it, it was and is nevertheless customary to baptize Christian initiates during the Easter celebrations which mark the end of Lent, again equating the Christian immersion rites of baptism with the cleansing rites of Agrai.

Christian titles, too, were taken from pagan clerical and — more commonly, since such titles tended to bear a more far-reaching authority — political roles. *Bishop*, as previously noted, was Diocletian's own title for diocesan judges, a *diocese* being a number of cities under the management of one *vicar* — previously called a *basileus*, in Athens — who was responsible to the Roman prefect in charge of that part of the Empire.[88] The Christian titles "Pope" and "Pontiff" once had, respectively, lowly sacerdotal and high political meanings in Rome, but both were originally pagan titles: A *popa* was a sacrificial butcher who apportioned the parts of an animal to those present during sacrifice and saw to its preparation, and the *pontifex* was the head priest of Jupiter Magnus Maximus, an ancient role held, during Imperial times until the reign of Gratian, by the Roman emperor himself.[89]

Portions of myths relating to Dionysian-syncretistic godforms of several cultures may be noted in the Christian mythos. The date of December 25th as the time of Christ's nativity was almost certainly adopted from the cult of Mithras, a Persian godform of unity between the divine and mortal realms, as were the rites of sacramental bread and wine, the Christian tradition of being a "soldier" for Christ to fight against darkness, and the belief that the Christ, like Mithras, was resurrected and ascended into heaven with a promise to return in the fullness of time;[90] the jubilant cry "He is risen!," and its attendant concept, were part of the resurrection ceremony of Attis,[91] and the mythos of Christ's return and subsequent reformation of the world is a tale as ubiquitous as that of the Great Flood, spanning cultures as diverse as Babylonian (the triumphal return of Enkidu) and Norse, whose ancient *Ragnarok* myth promises that Balder, the treacherously slain son of Odin, will arise to bind the Fenris wolf — the Norse symbol for evil — away from the world forever.[92] However, of Jesus and Dionysos specifically, there are no fewer than a dozen — and possibly more — exact mythological equivalencies. These are:

1. The semi-divine births of both were celebrated with late midwinter nativity festivals: Christ's birth was not originally given as December 25th, but as January 6th ("Epiphany"), the date on which it is still celebrated by the Eastern Orthodox church and certain groups of American immigrants.[93]

2. Both claim a divine as well as a human lineage consisting of famous and heroic ancestors, as gods of eternal life.[94]

3. There is a desire in the tales of both Deities for spontaneous, unprompted recognition as Sons of God (e.g.: "Who say you that I am?")[95] in combination with a denial of their divinity by their own societies (e.g.: "I would have gathered you beneath my wings as a hen gathers her chicks, but you would not...")[96]

4. Women tend to be the first witnesses to miracles and epiphanies of these godforms.[97]

5. Both are called by the appellations "bridegroom" and "savior,"[98] and spoke of perfect oneness with their followers.

6. Both Jesus and Dionysos are symbolically correlated to the vine.[99]

7. The turning of water into wine was a yearly Dionysian epiphany in Greece, reflected in the tale of Jesus' acts at the Marriage in Cana.[100]

8. The roles and titles of infant sacrificial animals were applied to both Jesus and Dionysos sacramentally.[101]

9. The riding of donkeys as a form of triumphal entry was common to the mythos of both archetypes.[102]

10. Both were identified as grantors of eternal life through similar symbols: The phallus, as previously noted, was a Dionysian symbol of life eternally regenerating itself; the fish symbol used by both early and modern Christians to distinguish themselves is symbolic of the phallus. According to most mythographers, the fish, the phallus, and the snake are interchangeable symbols of that force which gives life to the soul, or *orgazein*.[103]

11. In Hellenic Greece, as well as elsewhere in the ancient world, the pig was believed to have the ability to absorb evil from humans like a sponge. In Hellenic Mystery rites, the pig was used in just this manner. The Greek authors of the original New Testament may have had this ancient practice in mind when they wrote of Jesus transferring evil spirits from humans into a group of pigs.[104]

12. Both Dionysos and Jesus were capable of traveling from the underworld to the heavenly realm; both were considered sacrificial gods whose worship made blood sacrifice obsolete: As Nonnus related in pre-Christian writings, "The Lord Bacchus wept to still the tears of mortals" — reminiscent of Jesus' experience in the garden of Gethsemane.[105]

Because of these similarities of worship, archetype, and form, it would not have been terribly difficult to graft the worship of Christ onto the worship of any Dionysian-syncretistic Deity, one reason for the success of the spread of the Christian religion. The primary reason that early Christians were hounded and proscribed by some Roman emperors[106] was not because they worshipped a non-Roman godform: Gods and goddesses as diverse as the Egyptian Isis and Osiris, the Persian Mithras, and the Celtic Sequana and Nodens were honored in Rome.[107] The dogmatic tendencies of many early Christians (who believed that their god would literally be returning to remake the historical world, which made it unnecessary for them to follow certain imperative societal conventions such as honoring the emperor, taking part in State festivals or, in the case of extremists such as the Stylites and *parabolani*, working, bathing, or using sanitary facilities[108]) represented a destabilizing rather than unifying religious force — a potential danger to the existence of any society in which politics, power, education, and religion are intertwined. In such a governmental system, such destabilizing forces must be put down, because they endanger the existing regime.

A destabilizing force similarly arose to challenge the ruling political, religious, and educational power structure of the Catholic Church shortly after the bubonic plague killed over a quarter of the inhabitants of Europe in the thirteenth century CE. The Renaissance represented a shift in the class structure of the people of Europe, due to wealth and educational opportunities left behind by the vast number of individuals destroyed by the plague. Much of this wealth was put to use to increase global exploration, with the intent of gaining more wealth via mercantilism; one unintended result of this was the broadening of the average European's horizons. Venturers to Arabia and Asia, such as Marco Polo, brought back two innovations that revolutionized European life irrevocably: the compass, and the knowledge of movable-block printing. A new wave of compass- and sextant-guided exploration made the average citizen aware of previously unknown places, such as the Americas; the new ease of printing reading material made the written word accessible to individuals who had never dared hope to own a book. The Protestant religious revolution of Martin Luther occurred during this same period.

By the middle of the fourteenth century, it was obvious to the vast majority of middle-class Europeans that the past was more far-reaching than they had been led to believe, that the future held more options than they had dreamed of, and that the earth was not a forbidding flat plane set upon a field of darkness inhabited by demons. All of this represented a loss of political and social control to the Church, and culminated in the hysteria and murderous intent of the Inquisition in Europe and the "witch trials" of America[110] — the Christian power structure's response to social destabilization, just as the purges of Christians by Diocletian was the pagan power structure's hysterical and murderous response to social destabilization. I theorize that just such a response is the natural urge of any human power structure — especially the theocratic — in the face of what it perceives to be a threat to that structure. Dionysos and Dionysos-syncretistic godforms, and their methods of worship, often manifest as instruments of change and potential destabilization. As Martha Nussbaum notes in C. K. Williams' translation of Euripides' *Bacchai* (xlii): "Where, with pity, terror, and a peculiar awe, a community pieces itself together from the fragments of limbs torn in ecstatic rage, Dionysos presides."

Titles Held by Athenian Worshippers of Dionysos[111]

What the followers of Dionysos were called, anciently, depended upon what action they were performing and what emotion they were (ritualistically supposed to be) experiencing at a given time in a given ritual. The duties of "priest" or "priestess" were not, by and large, lifelong covenants among the ancient Hellene people;[112] the *hosioi* ("unifiers...") were an exception. However, as Luck notes (204), the famous Plutarch was himself a *hosios* of Delphi: Such an important clerical position obviously did not stand in the way of a man pursuing other interests in Classical Greece.

The titles, ritual symbolism, ritual actions, responsibilities, and ostensible emotions of Dionysian clerics are summarized in the following chart. Scholars tend to mix up Hellenic Mystery clerical titles (e.g.: "Thyiad", "Maenad" and "Bacchante" are often used interchangeably, which would be roughly equivalent to using the Christian titles of "monk," "pontiff" and "cardinal" all to mean "priest," when in fact these are all markedly different clerical positions). The chart first gives the Athenian, Eleusinian and Delphic titles of each class of cleric. In the Hellene Mystery religions, there were complementary male and female clerics (e.g., the Maenadic role was complementary to the role of Kourete or Korybant, and both were considered both literal and mythic functions). Except at Eleusis in the Telesterion, men and women *did not ever* undergo religious experience "co-ed"; they even ate in different areas after a sacrifice and, in some instances, ate different parts of the animal according to stricture. The ancients would have considered anything else shameful.

As in modern Christian Catholicism, each type of cleric was associated with different symbols and implements. These are given at the top of each section of the chart (e.g., the Pope is associated with pontifical attire, a priest with sacramental dishes, etc.). Finally, each Mystery cleric, male or female, was associated with particular actions and emotions. In Pagan religion, *your action is your emotion*, or to borrow from Christian phraseology (albeit backwards) "Works overshadow faith." Each Hellenic cleric had particular actions to perform which symbolized the emotional state that the worshipper was expected to display; behavior derived from that.

Hiera and Hierus were the highest titles obtainable in the ancient Greek clerical system; Bacchai and Bacchoi were famously known as reciters of sacred prayer, players of sacred music, and "displayers of the sacred." These combined traits link these divergent titles to the *Hierophant* role. Anyone who states that, "men cannot be followers of Dionysos" is quite mistaken; I am not at all sure where this belief came from, though it is prevalent among early twentieth-century archaeologists and late twentieth-century neo-pagans. Male followers of Dionysos did have a penchant for dressing up as animals, however (*Dionysiacchoi Thiasoi Satyron*, or, loosely translated: "Dionysian Priesthood of Satyrs"), so I suspect that they might be mistaken for the legendary satyrs or sileni on the artistic artifacts which make up the vast bulk of Dionysian ritual relics; similarly, male followers of Dionysos occasionally dressed as women. Also, male Dionysians sometimes used a spear as a thyrsos and a shield as a Liknon: The myth of the Kouretes/Korybantes and the festival of *Katagogia* as a festival of Dionysos may have derived from this practice.[12]

Table 1: Athenian, Eleusinian and Delphic titles of each class of cleric

FEMALE	MALE	EMOTION/ACTION
symbolism: scourge/thyrsos/alteration of mind THE THIASOS MAENAD ("*phoibad*"?)[113]	KOURETE or KORYBANT ("*keres*"?)[114] [Roman: Lupercai]	(fierce) / "Thanatos" [DEATH] — Sacrificial rituals (*ambivalent adoration/sacrifice frenzy*) Emotions/actions which exemplify the regret *and* anticipation felt as the Wheel of Life turns...as new gateways open.
symbolism: *Liknon/swing(ing)/washing or anointing* *CONSECRATION* THYIADI[115] (vegetarianism was a trademark of these worshippers)[117]	HOSIOS[116]	(tender)/ "Thyein [Zein]" (REBIRTH) — Awakening/renewal/offering or rectifi- cation rituals (*nurturant, limitless, and dynamic recognition of the god Dionysos*) Emotions/actions which exemplify (com)passion toward all Being and the need to identify oneself with it. (*The movement from Thyein to Heros and back again is entirely spontaneous: this movement may be termed ENTHOUSIASMOS*)
symbolism: *wine jar/phallic pillar/Shapeshifting* *COMING OF AGE RITUALS* GERAIRA or LENAI[118] (Lenaia...)	THESPIAN or KOMOI[119] (also *epheboi*: Katagogia)	(evocative) / "Phallophoros" [LIFE] — Ladies/Lords of Tragedy and Comedy (*During rituals of mythic rite-reenactment, processions and/or in the theatre.*) Emotions/actions which exemplify or emphasize a common bond.
symbolism: *wreath/torch/Great Rite or snake* TELETAI BACCHANT (HIERA) ("*baccai*")[120]	HIEROPHANT (HIERUS) or BOUKOLOI ("*baccoi*")[121]	(invocative)/ "Heros" [GODHOOD] (*That state during which worshipper and Deity — or dead loved one — unite/commune*) Emotions/actions which exemplify recognition of "The God Within"

CHAPTER TWO: BRIEF OVERVIEW OF ALL MAJOR ATHENIAN FESTIVALS

In ancient and Classical Attica, there were over 25 yearly state-run festivals (*heortai*) open to all eligible Athenians, and up to ten times as many rituals directed toward the Deities of the ten to twelve specific tribes (*phratrae*)[1] of Athens, all of which were made up of certain guilds (*demes*).[2] This book focuses on four Mystery festivals of primary importance — Lenaia, Anthesteria, Agrai, and Eleusinia. However, there were other Hellenic festivals in which actions, implements, or symbology relating to Mystery worship can be found; they include the ceremonies of Arrhephoria, Dioskodion, Haloa, Katagogia, Skiraphoria, and Thesmophoria.[3] These festivals are less well-documented than the four I have chosen to focus on, therefore their inclusion in this book is of necessity more brief. In this outline, I present most of the state-directed festivals that Classical Athenians might have attended. In chronological order, beginning with the first festival of the Attic New Year, these were: [4]

Festivals and Their Segments in Chronological Order

Celebration(s): Segments	Classical Greek Lunar-Month Name	Relative Dates in Modern Solar Calendar
Hecatombia[5]		
Kronoia		
Synoikia and Diisoteria	*Hecatombion*	July/August
Metageitnia	*Metageitnion*	August/September

Genesia		
Boedromia		
Eleusinia	*Boedromion*	September/October
Oschophoria		
Thesmophoria: [6]		
Stenia		
Anodos and Kathodos		
Nesteia		
Kalligenia		
(Pleurosia and Kalamaia?)		
Khalkeia		
Pyanepsia	*Pyanepsion*	October/November
Maimakteria		
Dioskodion	*Maimakterion*	November/December
Poseidia		
Haloa		
Lenaia		
Gamelia	*Poseidon-Gamelion*	December-February[7]
Anthesteria: [8]		
Chytrogia		
Chöes, Apatouria & Limnaia		
Pithogia		
Diasia		
Agrai	*Anthesterion*	February/March
Katagogia (*ultimately replaced by*: Dorpia, Anarrhysis, Koureotis, and Epibda)		
and Pandaia		
Elapheibolia	*Elaphebolion*	March/April
Munychia		
Athens' Olympia		
Delphinia	*Munychion*	April/May
Thargelia		
"Vestalia":		
Kallynteria		
Plynteria	*Thargelion*	May/June
Panathenaia: [9]		
Skiraphoria		
Arrhephoria		
Bouphonia & *pannychis*		
Dipolia & Diomedia	*Skiraphorion*	June/July

Phratrae-directed festivals were often known only by the name of the Deity(ies) or *demes* in question.[10] I use the Attic festival calendar in this book because it appears to predate Ionian culture and therefore to retain its more ancient Mycenean roots, while still allowing for Ionian influence.

Festivals and Their Segments, in Alphabetical Order

AGRAI: A place-name which has come to signify the lesser Mysteries of Dionysos and Persephone, held by the ancient and Classical Hellenes in the early spring each year, seven months prior to the Greater Mysteries of Demeter at Eleusis. See pages 81-102.

ANARRHYSIS: "Sacrificial remembrance"; see *Apatouria*.

ANODOS: "Lowering"; see *Thesmophoria*.

ANTHESTERIA: A festival whose name reflects the Hellenic love of words with dual meanings, *Anthesteria* means both "festival of souls" and "festival of flowers," an innuendo of the promise given by the Mysteries — that the human soul could be reborn like a flower out of the mud. See pages 69-80.

APATOURIA: (February-March) "Rites of Deception." This odd-sounding ritual was part of the ceremonies of *Anthesteria*. It entailed giving children gifts and sleep-inducing wine in order to divert their attention. In Imperial times, there was a second *Apatouria* each year, whose purpose was to fulfill the civic necessities once undertaken at the democratic *Katagogia* (see pages 40-45). The Imperial Apatouria, according to Parke (88-92), was held in the autumn, and was a four-day-long festival during which new ephebes were given their panoply and trimmed their forelocks prior to beginning Imperial service. Brides were entered into the records of their new *phratrae* at this time as well. The names of the four days that made up the Imperial *Apatouria* were *Dorpia* (introductory suppers), *Anarrhysis* (sacrificial remembrances), *Koureotis* (youth's day), and *Epibda* (following day — *Epibda* also infers "being hung over"). See *Katagogia* for information on the methods by which these things were performed in the Periclean (democratic) period.

ARRHEPHORIA: (June-July) Part of the large New Year's festival of *Panathenaia*, this festival was also known as "the Thesmophoria of the unmarried girl."[11] *Arrhephoria* means "(the carrying of) that which is forbidden," and was sometimes also referred to as the *Arrhetophoria*, "(the carrying of) that which is ineffable."

Classically, this festival involved the weaving of a new robe (*peplos*) for the city's statue (*xenon*) of Athena Polias, as well as the carrying of sacred, veiled baskets to and from hallowed chasms beneath the Acropolis, in all likelihood a visit to the underground chasm (*megara*) of the Temple of Demeter, which may have housed sacred snakes. One of the species known to have been kept and revered by the Greeks was the Cyprian catsnake, a lovely dun-yellow creature mottled with purplish-brown, whose venom — otherwise harmless to humans — is reputed to be psychoactive; the venom of the African purple-glossed snake is said to have a similar effect. All Mystery festivals which appear to have utilized serpents, such as the *Agrai*, *Thesmophoria*, and *Arrhephoria* ceremonies, may have been feeding times for just such sacred reptiles which, as opposed to eating the piglets and cereal products lowered into the *megaron* in these ceremonies, were probably sustained by the vermin and insects attracted by edible votive offerings. According to the *Scholia to Lucian* (Dialogues Meretrobius II;1):

> The Thesmophoria, a festival of the Greeks, includ(es) mysteries, and these are called also Skirrophoria. According to the more mythological explanation they are celebrated (in that) Kore, when she was gathering flowers, was carried off by Plouton. At the time a certain Eubouleus, a swineherd, was feeding his swine on the spot and they were swallowed down with her in the chasm of Kore. Hence in honour of Euboleus the swine are thrown into the chasms of Demeter and Kore. Certain women who have purified themselves for three days and who bear the name of "drawers up" bring up the rotten portions of the swine that have been cast into the *megara*. And they descend into the inner sanctuaries and having brought up (the remains) they place them on the altars, and they hold that whoever takes of the remains and mixes it with his seed corn will have a good crop. And they say that in and about the chasms are snakes which consume the most part of what is thrown in; hence a rattling din is made when the women draw up the remains and when they replace the remains by those well-known images, in order that the snakes which they hold to be the guardians of the sanctuaries may go away.
> The same rites are called Arrhetophoria (carrying of things unnamed) and are performed with the same intent concerning the growth of crops and of human offspring...They employ also fir-cones on account of the fertility of the tree, and into the sanctuaries called *megara* these are cast and also, as we have

already said, swine — the swine, too, on account of their prolific character — in token of the growth of fruits and human beings, as a thank-offering to Demeter, inasmuch as she, by providing the grain called by her name, civilized the human race. The interpretation then of the festival given above is mythological, but the one we give now is physical. The name Thesmophoria is given because Demeter bears the title Thesmophoros, since she laid down a law or Thesmos in accordance with which it was incumbent on men to obtain and provide by labor their nurture.

The girls chosen for the sacred duties of the *Arrhephoria* underwent three days of purificatory rituals — including sacrifices, abstinence fasts, and ritual bathing — prior to the rite itself.[12] As all New Year's rituals were Athenian (either in nature or via funding for their yearly performances), it stands to reason that Athena, patron goddess of Athens, who mythically rescued the remains of the sacred Infant in a basket so that Persephone might give him new birth, was the primary deity honored in these rituals.

ATHENS' OLYMPIA: (April-May) This celebration was utterly unrelated to the festival held in the city-state of Olympia, from which our own modern *Olympics* has been derived. Little is known of the Athenian *Olympia*, save that it consisted of equestrian events and sacrifices, perhaps linking it to worship of Poseidon.[13]

BOEDROMIA: (September-October) Ceremony in honor of "(Apollo) the helper." No detailed information is available for this festival.

BOUPHONIA: (June-July) "Voice (or sound) of the bull." This festival was a large-scale ox sacrifice, ostensibly a remembrance of the original act of homage from Athena to her father, Zeus, in thanks for her panoply. The literal translation of this festival's name implies that oracles may have been taken from the sounds the bulls made at the time of their sacrifice. The simplicity and straightforwardness of this portion of the *Panathenaia* suggests that it springs from archaic roots — perhaps a paleolithic rite honoring the Animal Master who brings food, to which mankind must make restitution via a "sacred king." In the *Bouphonia* ceremony of Classical Athens, a sacred king was indeed honored; the mythic Erectheus, "the earth-born one" — an epiphany of Dionysos, the Indestructible, who was also honored in the *Pandaia* ceremony.[14] Well before the Classical Hellenic period, animals were considered perfectly acceptable surrogates for human sacrifice, hence the equation of the wholly anthropomorphic gods of Classical Greece with particular sacrificial animals.[15]

At the end of the *Bouphonia*, a peculiar ritual was publicly held by the priestesses of Athena and the priests of Erectheus. Aristophanes relates this ceremony in *The Clouds*, a rite known to scholars of ancient religions as "the comedy of innocence," in which all those who must kill to eat attempt to lay the guilt for the killing upon one another until, finally, it is adjudicated that the true culprit of the crime must be the weapon with which the animal was killed. In the *Bouphonia* ceremony of Athena and Erectheus, the sacrificial weapon used for slaughtering the bulls was punished by being cast into the sea.[16]

CHOËS: (February-March) "(Day of) wine pitchers." This portion of the three-day-long festival of *Anthesteria* is also referred to as "(The Day of) Pollution"; see *Anthesteria*.

CHYTROGIA: (February-March) "(Day of) pots." This is the oblation of mixed grains which marks the end of the *Anthesteria* festival; see *Anthesteria*.

DELPHINIA: (April-May) "Festival of Delphi." This festival of Apollo's advent at Delphi occurred on the 7th day of the Athenian month of Munychion, which was called "Bysios" in Delphi. It was a day of oracular pronouncements, when the priestess dedicated to the Delphic Apollo — the *Pythia* — would mount the tall, covered tripod in the center of the temple in order to receive visions in response to posed questions. Devereux (46-48) suggests that the visions received on this day were caused by inhaling a vapor of laurel leaves mixed with the psychoactive seeds of the henbane plant, both of which were sacred to Apollo.[17]

DIASIA: (February-March) "Feast of banishment,"[18] probably a continuation of the "driving-out" ceremony which took place after the Anthesteric *Chytrogia*. According to Parke (120-123), this ceremony was a combination of *nephalia* and *holocaust* rites in honor of Zeus Cthonios or Zeus Mielichos.

Modern Greek expressions derived from the ancient Greek root of *Diasia* all have ghostly implications of noise, disturbance, and enforced separation between alternate dimensions, an indication that the banishment performed by worshippers in this ancient ceremony may have been executed using percussion instruments — bells, drums, cymbals, et al. A belief in the power of sound to drive away demons still exist among various cultures, and the modern use of firecrackers at festivals and wind chimes on doorsteps hails from the ancient practice of scaring off unwelcome spirits with the use of sound.

Alternatively, this ceremony may have been similar to the Roman *Lemuria* ritual, in which less than well-meaning spirits were sent away by the spitting-out of beans, and the litany "with these beans I redeem me and mine."[19]

DIISOTERIA: (July-August) Festival of "Zeus the Savior," held at year's end, was one of the festivals which reinstituted community law and daily life after the topsy-turvy ceremonies of *Kronoia* were over. New city magistrates and other figures of authority were given their "keys of office" at this festival.[20]

DIOMEDIA: (June-July) Also called *Diomeia* by some scholars, this was the great feast which signaled the end of the *Panathenaia*; see *Panathenaia*.

DIOSKODION: (October-December) "Festival of Zeus' sacred fleeces." Zeus Mielichos, whose symbol was an enormous but benign snake — a metaphor for the still-common Attic belief that the souls of dead loved ones could reappear as snakes[21] — was worshipped at this festival, which entailed the purification of storerooms and fields using the sacred fleeces of rams sacrificed so that their blood might fructify the next year's harvest.[22] Sacred fleeces were commonly used in the ancient Hellene world as ceremonial purifiers in sacrifices, after certain ritual baths, and during the enthronement portions of the greater and lesser Mysteries; and they were considered to be capable of purifying those guilty of killing.[23] Rational human beings can neither perform sacrifice nor eat without the knowledge of guilt for the act of killing, and the *Dioskodion* ceremony was a tacit acknowledgment that mankind gains its life only through death.

Storage rooms themselves were consecrated, purified, and granted symbolic protection during the festival of *Dioskodion*. As Harrison (642) quotes from Harpocration and Athenaeus:

> They set up Zeus Ktesios in storerooms...It (the *kadiskos*) is the vessel in which they consecrate the Ktesian Zeuses, as Antikleides says in his "interpretations," as follows: The symbols of Zeus Ktesios are consecrated as follows: "the lid must be put on a new *kadiskos* with two handles, and the handles crowned with white wool...and you must put into it whatever you chance to

find and pour in ambrosia. Ambrosia is pure water, olive oil and all fruits. Pour in these."

It appears that the *kadiskos* vessel itself, "enlivened" by whatever it contained, was a primitive *xoanon* (idol) designed to guard storage rooms.

Wool's ritual cleansing capability may have derived from the facts that it can be taken *without* killing and that it is continuously restored. Milk and honey appear to have had similar purifying functions.

DIPOLIA: (June-July) The meaning of the name of this portion of the *Panathenaia* festival — "the two cities" — undoubtedly refers to the *agon*, or competition portion, of the New Year's festivals proper. Members of Hellenic city-states that were invited to take part in the Athenian *Panathenaia* competed in both athletic events, including such competitions as chariot racing, and non-athletic events such as theatrical and poetic contests.

DORPIA: "Suppers..."; see *Apatouria.*

ELAPHEIBOLIA: (March-April) A celebration of "(Artemis) far-shooter": Artemis was celebrated as Divine Huntress at this festival, and was offered stag-shaped cakes by her worshippers.[24] This brings to mind the myth of Actaeon, the mythic hunter who accidentally happened upon Artemis and her maidens in their hidden grove. To enter this grove was forbidden, and in retribution for Actaeon's trespass, Artemis turned the young man into a stag, and set his own hounds upon him. *Elapheibolia* may have been a propitiation festival of the goddess who, like Dionysos, was not only the fierce and merciless protector of that which merits mercy, but also retained an aspect of "Hunter (of Men)."[25]

ELEUSINIA: "The greater Mysteries." See pages 101-131.

EPIBDA: "The Following (Day)." See *Apatouria.*

GAMELIA: (December-February) "Sacred marriage (of Zeus and Hera)." It is unknown whether or not this ceremony was similar to the Dionysian *Limnaia* performed during the festival of *Anthesteria. Gamelia* took place at the same time as human marriage ceremonies and the *Lenaia.*[26] See pages 70-73 for details regarding the *Limnaia* ceremony.

GENESIA: (September-Oct) According to modern sources, this ceremony, held in Boedromion prior to the rites of *Eleusinia*, was a commemoration of the dead. I theorize that it may have been a form of pre-Eleusinic "summoning" of the ancestors to the greater Mystery rites, since the Eleusinic visions themselves promised a form of reunion with the ancestors.[27]

GEPHYRISMOI: "Scurrilous jests" (literally: *bridge jests*), part of the second day of the *Thesmophoria* ceremony. Such jesting was also part of the gauntlet new initiates were forced to pass when crossing the Rhiti bridge into Eleusinian territory prior to the greater Mystery rites. The modern Greek word for bridge remains *gephyra*. See *Eleusinia* and *Thesmophoria*.

HALOA: (December-February) A festival name which reflects the Hellene love of words with multiple meanings, *Haloa* was a celebration of Demeter and Dionysos, or grapes and grain,[28] hailing from αλοσ (hal-ose), or *(grain)-threshing floor*, and αλοαι (al-oh-eye), or *vine-shoots. Haloa* also celebrated the cutting-back of the vine stocks after the harvesting of their fruit at the *Oschophoria*.[29]

At this time, threshing-floors were cleaned of their summertime detritus, then blessed and danced upon, the circle and spiral dances representing the labyrinthine movement of life toward death and back to life again. Blessings of the threshing-floors were most likely performed using sacra from *liknoi*, since those were known to have been carried at this festival, perhaps in some form of *liknophoria* similar to that performed at the greater and lesser Mysteries.[30]

All sacrificial offerings of Haloa were bloodless and wineless (*nephalia*), performed solely by Thyiades and priestesses of Demeter.[31] No animal sacrifice was allowed during the Haloa, as it was considered a cthonic ceremony, possibly in memory of the hero Ikarios, mythically the first cultivator of vines and worshipper of the cthonic Dionysos in Attica. Dances, blessings, and offerings were followed by a vegetarian banquet in which only women could participate; the banquet included phallic and vulvar cakes similar to those made for the *Skiraphoria, Thesmophoria,* and *Eleusinia* ceremonies. Also in common with the preceding festivals was the prevalence of rude jesting during the rites of *Haloa*. Harrison (146) theorized that the Hellene feast of Demeter and Dionysos was a primitive prototype of the Eleusinia itself, but there is no evidence that entheogens of any kind were used during the *Haloa* ceremonial.

HECATOMBIA: (July-August) Burkert implies that this festival, held on the 12th Hecatombion, was some sort of festival in honor of Apollo.[32] However, the roots of the festival's name are *heca-* and *-tom(e)*, "one hundred segments" followed by *-bia* or "violence" — "one hundred violent segments." I suspect that the *Hecatombia* was, in fact, a festival mentioned by Kerenyi in which followers of Dionysos rent the raw bodies of flayed bulls into segments by hand, a sacrifice reminiscent of the death of Dionysos at the hands of the Titans; such an act would satisfy the requirements of a festival named "one hundred violent segments," which may have originated from non-Athenian sacrificial rituals that ended a Dionysian trieteric (three-year) period.[33] A fragmentary Homeric Hymn to Dionysos (number one in Athanassakis' *...Hymns*) also bestows the hecatomb upon Dionysos as well as the resurrected Semele, after a lacunae of lost verse:

> "...And for her they will set up many statues in temples.
> As he cut you into three pieces, in triennial feasts
> men shall always sacrifice to you unblemished hecatombs."
> So said Kronion and nodded with his dark brows,
> and the lord's ambrosial mane streamed down
> from his immortal head and great Olympos was shaken.
> Thus spoke Zeus the counselor and gave orders with nodding head.
> Eiraphiotes, woman-maddener, be propitious to us singers
> who start and finish our song with you; there is no way
> for the one who forgets you to remember his song.
> So hail, Dionysos Eiraphiotes,
> and your mother, Semele, whom they call Thyone.

KALLIGENIA: "Good birth." The root word for "good" in Greek implies *cultivation* and, ultimately, eating. This ceremony consisted of a nighttime torch dance reminiscent of those held at Callichorus at Eleusis,[34] which was a spiral, circle, or "labyrinth" dance symbolic of Demeter's long search for her daughter Kore, lost to the underworld but, ultimately, granted the right of continuous rebirth as Persephone, a savior-figure who accorded her initiates at the lesser and greater Mysteries the same advantage; see *Thesmophoria.*

KALLYNTERIA: This "festival of ornamentation" was the second day of a ceremonial known to the Romans as *Vestalia*; see *Vestalia.*

KATAGOGIA: (March-April) *Katagogia*, from a word meaning "ancestry (or tribe)," was the rite that is commonly known as the greater (or urban)

Dionysia, a festival devised during the Periclean age of Athens. There was no ancient *Katagogia*; the greater Dionysia, instituted at approximately 500 BCE, was the most short-lived of all Dionysian festivals in Attica.[35] The greater Dionysia was not at all what a vast majority of individuals assume it to have been; though the *Katagogia* did include phallic processions, dithyrambs, and theatrical performances, there was none of the illicit sexual atmosphere, unrestrained revelry, or drinking which marked the Choës night of *Anthesteria*.[36]

The *Katagogia*, which was formulated just after the first Sacred War and immediately prior to the Peloponnesian conflicts was, at its base, a "panoplying party" for new *ephebes* (military cadets),[37] but its status as such may have had a relatively short life span, possibly ending with the Reforms of Lycurgus the Tyrant in the years after Philip of Macedon and his son, Alexander the Great, fought to unify all of Greece under their rule.[38] However, the practice of theatrical festivals as sacred institutions continued with the burgeoning of the *Lenaia* or lesser Dionysia, as well as with the later Christian adoption of theatrical festivities to mark Shrovetide. Theater as edification and entertainment ultimately spread throughout the world.

According to some scholars, the creation of democracy roughly coincided with the development of the *Katagogia* and the concept of the "soldier for the sake of society," as opposed to the older, Homeric ideal of a soldier fighting for personal honor and fame.[39] Forty-nine new ephebes were chosen annually from among the ten *phratrae* (tribes) which formed Athenian society to provide the city-state with approximately five hundred new cadets each year.[40]

At the commencement of the theatrical portion of each *Katagogia*, citizens arranged themselves within a given theater according to tribal ties; this seating arrangement was the duplicate of that found in the political Assembly of Athens.[41] Tribute sent from city-states politically united to Athens were arranged onstage,[42] as were those young men whose mother's spouses had died in war and who had reached the age of their ephebate. This portion of the *Katagogia* ceremony was known as the "procession of the orphans."[43] Most young Athenian men of this age were expected to provide their own panoply (sword, shield, armor, helmet, and other accoutrements of warfare) in expectation of the time when they would be called to serve, but Athens itself provided for the education and panoply of these orphans: Without a panoply, and ultimately marriage to a woman of Athenian heritage, no man could attain Athenian citizenship.[44] It is this portion of the *Katagogia* to which Isocrates refers in *De Pace* (82) when he says: "(At the festival of Dionysos)...they led in upon the stage the sons of those who had lost their lives in war, seeking thus to display to our allies...the multitude of the fatherless." Such orphans may have been considered "sons of the god (Dionysos)." [45]

The goatlike satyrs, as well as the chorus in Attic *Katagogia* tragic performances, were made up of the year's entire new ephebate, orphans and non-orphans alike.[46] Choral dances done upon theatrical stages during the Katagogia festival were performed in a formation which would come to be known in later ages as the "military square,"[47] and the five-day-long theatrical festival was a test of stamina for the cadets, as Athenaeus noted in his *Deisnosophists* 14: 268 E-F: "For the form of dancing in choruses then was well-ordered and impressive and as it were imitative of movements in full armor; whence Sokrates says in his poems that the finest choral dancers are the best in war; I quote, 'those who most beautifully honor the gods in choruses are best in war.' For choral dancing was practically like a troop review and a display not only of precision marching in general but more particularly of physical preparedness."

The *Katagogia* was prefaced by several preliminary rituals, including an *agon*, or ceremony of sacrificial games, and a bull sacrifice that included an oath-taking to Artemis Agrotera by the new ephebes at the sanctuary of Aglauros,[48] followed by a procession to the theaters themselves, where offerings would be given to the gods by the generals who led Athenian men into battle.[49] This was succeeded by the procession of the orphans and the display of allied wealth on the stages where, for the next five days, post-pubescent boys would engage in comedy and tragedy, while boys too young and men too old to take part in military service performed dithyrambs to Dionysos, "god of the Deme."[50]

The urban Dionysia was one of three festivals which celebrated the literal presence of Dionysos; the others were the *Anthesteria* and the *Lenaia*.[51] Dionysos was "introduced," or called forth, at all of these festivals with the use of a double-throated trumpet known as a *salpinx*. During the urban Dionysia, this activity occurred during the *pompe*, or procession of ephebes from the Acropolis to the theaters:

> A phallus
> A vine stock
> A goat
> A basket of figs...[52]

This is the formulary which describes the basic necessities required from a citizen taking part in the Classical Katagogian pompe — the most widely-discussed part of the urban Dionysia, yet one of the most transient — in which only male citizens participated.[53] This pompe was, in part, a phallic processional, but it also included segments led by padded dancers, and a ship-car procession.[54]

The padded dancers and ship-car (a fabricated ship carrying either a statue of Dionysos or a man representing him) are often depicted together in Classical artworks.[55] Burkert has theorized that the padded dancers symbolize people in the act of submission to a greater power, in that "padded dancers" may have been equated with women and effeminate men in the Classical Greek psyche.[56] My theory regarding the role of the padded dancers in the pompe of the greater Dionysia is similar, but more determinate: The padded dancers in the urban Dionysia comically represented enemies defeated in open warfare. In this context, the ship-car carrying Dionysos may have been symbolic of the military prowess of Athens over its enemies at sea, with Dionysos as "triumphator" (*thriambos*).[57] Ancient authors, such as Euripides in *The Bacchae*, have noted that Dionysos "has some part of Ares," god of war.[58]

At any given theater during the five days of the *Katagogia*, three tragedies and one satyr play, or five satyr plays and twenty dithyrambs — large circular formations of men or boys singing and chanting hymns — were performed daily.[59] The staggering number of Hellenic theatrical works that have been lost over time becomes apparent once it is realized that plays were almost never performed more than once, since part of the intent of their writers was to give them as an offering to the god Dionysos.[60] Satyr plays put on by new ephebes, which were taken from preexisting works, were apparently the only exception to this rule.[61]

The satyr play was an interesting phenomenon of Classical Greek theater which has been misconstrued by some scholars as a comedic genre. Although satyr plays often gave new twists to their material and ended happily, the satyr play was part of the tragic stage. Satyr players followed no strict rites or script: Innovation and invention (physical or psychological) were a key feature of satyr plays, in which satyrs appeared in unlikely places in order to express social commentary in indirect ways linked to their bemusing, unlikely presence in tragic drama.[62]

Winkler and Zeitlin infer that theater, an institution as multifaceted and paradoxical as the needs and desires of a Democratic society itself, acted as a form of "psychological growth medium" on behalf of the youth for whom the *Katagogia* was designed as a manhood ceremony, as well as for Attic society in general.[63] I concur with this hypothesis, and would expound upon it to say that, in most human societies, it is considered to be the role of youth to question existing social structure. Since such an antithetical role could be expected to be particularly substantial within the relatively open structure of a Democracy or Republic, theater may have functioned for the Periclean Hellenes as a safe haven for such experimentation to occur. The presence of satyrs at the urban Dionysia bears this out, as does the prevalence of transvestism.[64]

In many societies, the sacred time marked out by role reversal — human as satyr, citizen as "padded dancer" and defeated foreign enemy, male as female — is not specifically a time of personal license; it is, rather, one of psychological exploration of social identity prior to the recrystalization of non-festival, daily life and its accepted norms and values.[65] Sacred periods of inversion mark out boundaries and transitions: After the festival, all is as it was and yet, irrevocably, things have changed, as in the *Katagogia* the role of the new ephebe shifts from that of a youth cherished and protected by society to a man who is protector and cherisher of society.[66]

Both the goats and the vines carried in the pre-theatrical pompe were prizes and sacrificial offerings.[67] Varro, a second-century BCE poet, made a mythic image from such a ceremony in his *de re Rustica*: "Very well, eat my fruit-bearing vines; the root will still bear enough wine to pour on you when you are sacrificed."[68] I theorize that goat sacrifices were performed by — or at least on behalf of — new ephebes, those men between the age of adolescence and adulthood, or 17-20 years of age, for whom the *Katagogia* ceremony was founded as a manhood rite sometime between the fifth and fourth centuries BCE. In this context, a goat sacrifice would represent the new ephebes' sacrifice of their adolescence, adolescent desires, and adolescent traits, in order for them to become defenders of Athens and its interests and, thus, men.[69] The *Katagogia* served as a dividing line between the relative carelessness of adolescence and the responsibilities of manhood — a tenuous thing in modern society and, many feel, something sorely missed.

Most modern Democratic societies have no ceremony equivalent to the *Katagogia*, though privates, seamen, marines, and airmen entering the American military institution cut their hair prior to enlistment, a ceremony that was followed by the Attic ephebate as well (*aparkhesthai*).[70] American Veteran's Day parades and equivalent parades in other free nations might be considered to be a ghostly remembrance of the Katagogian pompe, in which veterans were highly praised.[71] However, highly tactical, technical, paid modern defensive forces, which many involved in them consider to be temporary careers, can hardly be compared to the Classical Greek military which was a non-paid, nearly lifelong, relatively non-tactical service, performed at time of need and the only road to full citizenship status for men in Periclean Greece.[72]

In *Homo Necans* (182-183), Burkert relates a ceremony purported by some ancient writers to have been part of the Katagogia, and by others to have followed it: the *Pandaia*. Very little specific information has been recorded regarding this rite, but it is known that during the sacrifice (probably of birds) which accompanied it, gravel rather than barley was used to sanctify the altar — a symbolic stoning ceremony, perhaps of the birds themselves. Erectheus was honored during the *Pandaia*, and symbolized by a specific bird, the hoopoe, whose tall crest laterally spans the whole of its head when erect.

I theorize that if birds were sacrificed in the ceremony of *Pandaia*, they represented the new warriors setting out to guard their city-state. The hoopoe is native to both Mediterranean and Aegean regions of Europe, and Greco-Roman warriors often wore helmets whose crests mimicked the rufous crest of the hoopoe: It may be inferred from this that the "warrior-crested" birds were either meant to incur death on the warriors' behalf, or that the hoopoe represented the belief that warriors killed in battle would be reborn as birds.

The Greek people apprehend the hole-nesting hoopoe's call as "Pou? Pou?," and give to this the expanded meaning of "Where, where (has my beloved gone)?" Such an apprehension links the call of the hoopoe to the myth of Eurydice; Orpheus descended into the underworld to bring her back. The kingfisher has a similar role in Greek myth, as a cthonic bird which is constantly reborn, entering and leaving the underworld through the ground holes which, in fact, it nests in.[73]

KATHODOS: "Ascent"; see *Thesmophoria*.

KHALKEIA: (October-November) This was a religious celebration in honor of a particular *deme* — that of craftsmen — in which all of Athens participated, most likely because the loom upon which Athena's yearly peplos would be woven was ceremonially erected during this festival. Both Athena Ergane (goddess of workers) and Hephaestos were honored in the rites of *Khalkeia*.[74]

KOUREOTIS: "Youth's Day"; see *Apatouria*.

KRONOIA: (July-August) This festival in honor of the deposed god Kronos was a celebration of the end of the old year; even in modern times, Western countries depict the end of one year and the beginning of the next as an elder being deposed by a toddler, a direct recollection of the mythos of the infant Kronos forcibly taking the place of his terrible father Ouranos, or, in cyclic fashion, of infant Zeus supplanting Kronos. Kronos himself was known as *Saturn* in Rome, where New Year's celebrations, known as *kalends*, were held in midwinter, rather than as midsummer as they were in ancient Greece.

Aside from the fact that a span of six months separated both festivals, the week-long celebration of *Kronoia* — which may loosely be translated as "rite of the raven" — was similar in many respects to the Roman Saturnalia festival. Both consisted of customs which survive almost unaltered to the present day in our "Christmas" and "New Year" celebrations.[75] Such festivities included the adornment of homes and persons with purifying greenery, "guising" or masking in the form of transvestism or animal impersonation, role-exchange and inversion games (e.g.: "fool" as "king"), a suspension of all labor in connection with an air of revelry and freedom which has ever marked the contrast between the dissolution of the old year and the coming of the new one in Western societies,[76] and the giving of gifts "in memory of ancient times."

LENAIA: "(Rites of) the pressing-vats," also known as the *lesser* or *rural Dionysia.* See pages 55-68.

LIMNAIA: "(Nuptial rites of Dionysos) of the Marsh," a sacred marriage ceremony held on the eve of the second day of *Anthesteria*, whose title lives on in the modern Greek words for both lake and libido; see *Anthesteria.*

MAIMAKTERIA: (November-December) No details are known of this celebration, and the meaning of the word itself is obscure, though it may be an ancient offshoot of a word meaning "maddened by wine" (*mainomenos*), from which the word "maenad" was derived. Kerenyi notes that, at some period in the winter, female adherents of Dionysos danced along the snowy ledges of Parnassos just above the temple of Apollo at Delphi, perhaps as a ritual prelude to — or as a part of, depending upon when the nearest full moon to the winter solstice occurred — the *Lenaia*.[77] If this is an accurate rendering of *Maimakteria* (and I believe it is: See pages 55-68 for information regarding the complex rituals held in mainland Greece during the *Lenean* period) then such a festival might be considered part of the ceremonies of *Lenaia*.

METAGEITNIA: (August-September) "Changing neighbors."[78] I suspect that this festival is, in fact, the "Metoecia" or *Feast of Migration* mentioned in Plutarch's *Lives...* (29), a sacrificial ceremony purportedly instituted by the mythic hero Theseus. No further information regarding this festival is given by Plutarch.

MUNYCHIA: (April-May) A celebration in honor of "Artemis of the Hill": The famous mount of Munychia near the important Athenian port of Piraeus was dedicated to Artemis. The festival itself appears to have been one of symbolic human sacrifice, recalling dramatic scenes such as those found in Euripides' *Iphigeneia*. Mythically, the Athenians were commanded by Artemis on this day to sacrifice a goat in return for a bear slain within one of her temples, but the basis of the myth which recalls the ritual itself is more convoluted than that. At the ancient temple of Artemis in Brauron, which was deserted before 500 BCE due to massive flooding, girls sent to live in the precincts and become priestesses of Artemis were known as "little bears." The ritual and mythos of the Artemis of Munychia appear to have recalled a time when the "bear" was not animal but human, a thanks-offering to the Mistress of Animals (*Potnia Theron*) herself, which was the epithet by which Artemis was known at the ceremonies held in Munychia.[79]

Concurrently, Artemis was hailed as moon goddess during the celebrations held near the port; though most of the details of the *Munychia* have been lost to history, it is known that offerings of "moon cakes" (*amphiphontes*, an ancient Greek word with no direct modern descendants) studded with candles — perhaps the precursors of the traditional Western birthday cake — were presented to Artemis at this festival.[80]

NESTEIA: "To fast"; see *Thesmophoria*.

OSCHOPHORIA: (October-November) The meaning of this festival is generally translated by scholars to mean "feast of boughs"[81] but it may also be loosely translated as "(the price of...?) wearing a dress." The *Oschophoria* included grape harvest and crushing and triumphal processions to the sea, in which worshippers carried vine branches laden with grapes.[82] All sacrificers and feast-bearers taking part in the *Oschophoria* were believed to be female,[83] but transvestism played a role in this ceremony, in memory of boys disguising themselves as girls in order to escape the labyrinth of the flesh-eating minotaur of Knossos. As the myth relates, King Minos, father of both Ariadne and the minotaur, demanded and received a yearly tribute of youths from all other Greek city-states, with which he stocked the terrible labyrinthine home of the minotaur, whom Theseus slew: It is in celebration of this slaying, or so Plutarch claims, that the *Oschophoria* was instituted — a celebration of spiritual escape from the labyrinth of death into the eternal realm of rebirth.[84]

Because of the mythic transvestism in the tale, and its probable recreation in ritual, it is difficult to know whether the "feast carriers" *were* all female, or if they just all *looked* female. Another gender-changing custom at this festival was that of a boy in "birth travail" as Ariadne,[85] a custom which linked the terrible labyrinth of the minotaur, who was death, to the labyrinth of the womb, which is life — and they are the same labyrinth, which is the Mystery teaching that many ancient Greek spiral dances symbolize.

I theorize that the *Oschophoria* festival may have been a remnant of some ancient mythopoeic thanks-feast, instituted in gratitude at that point when a shaman or priest announced that there would no longer be any need for human sacrifice.

PANATHENAIA: (June-July) "Festival of all Attica" (in modern Greek, *panethnikos* means "nationwide"). This celebration consisted of a month of rites and festivities, its most well-known portion consisting of a contest or *agon* known as *Dipolia*; the modern *agon* which we call "The Olympics" is named after the Great Games once held in Olympia in honor of Zeus and Hera.

The *Dipolia* of the *Panathenaia* was preceded by the ceremonies of *Skiraphoria* and *Arrhephoria* earlier in the month, and directly preceded by the *Bouphonia* and an all-night festivity (*pannychis*); at sunrise, freshly-made fire would be fetched and carried in a race to the Acropolis, where a great Olympic sacrifice would take place.[86] Such contests as the *Dipolia* were usually held to commemorate the death of any notary in the Greco-Roman world; I theorize that the *Dipolia* equated to the funeral games of the "Animal Master" symbolically sacrificed at the *Bouphonia*,[87] represented in later Hellenic antiquity by the bull. Once the *Dipolia* was concluded, the sacrifices made during the *Bouphonia* were consumed at a great citywide feast, the *Diomedia*.

PITHOGIA: "Festival of Crocks"; see *Anthesteria*.

PLYNTERIA: "Festival of washing"; a Greco-Roman festival of cleaning and renewal, held in honor of the Goddess of the Hearth. In Attica, Athena was also honored during the two days which marked this festival. See *Vestalia*.

POSEIDEA: (December-February) Little is known of this festival, but Parke (97) hypothesizes that it — as well as Poseidon himself — is a holdover from the pre-Ionic period, when the sea and its wealth, rather than the sky and its weather, was held to be a manifestation of the power of the greatest of the gods. Mythographers note that Zeus and Poseidon hold many symbols in common, the most ancient and weighty being that of the bull, and that both gods are modified renditions of the great gods of sea-harvesting and land-husbanding peoples come together to form a culture whose whole would be greater than the sum of its parts.[88]

PYANEPSIA: (October-November) "Festival of bean-cooking." The name of this rite harkens to the Roman *Lemuria* festival, in which the male head of a household spat out beans, with each bean intoning: "With these beans I redeem me and mine." *Pyanepsia* was held nine months after the illicit erotic festivities of Anthesteria had concluded: It is not unreasonable to theorize that this "redemption" consisted in an acceptance of any children conceived at that time, and that the beans represented a tacit acknowledgment that new arrivals born in the month of *Pyanepsion* were reincarnate ancestors.

Pyanepsia included a joyous competition among the community's children, to see who could best decorate and display their own wool-bound olive branch, or *Eiresione*; fruits, nuts, and other dainties were also hung from these branches, the number and type of items displayed on an *Eiresione* being limited only by the wealth of a child's parents, the child's own imagination, and the size of the branch. Matthews (82) notes that the custom of decorating *Eiresione* branches was revived in parts of Greece in the seventeenth century as part of the celebration of Christmas.

The myth of *Eiresione* is, on the surface, a grim tale of a young girl hanging herself and of fruit growing where her body was found.[89] The underlying role of joy found in the *Eiresione*, however — which was, apparently, not entirely unlike the joy felt by modern children when looking at a Christmas tree — links the festival with other ceremonies in honor of Demeter and Kore, whose mythos is one of life springing forth irrepressibly from death; indeed, the roots of the word *Pyanepsia* infer decay, and the eating of beans was allowed in the ancient Hellenic world only during festivals honoring the two goddesses.

To a child, such a complex spiritual concept would bring more confusion than joy. Apparently, Hellenic children were simply told that the Eleusinic goddesses turned all bad things into good things, and brought gifts and treasures — again, not unlike the implicit promise of the Christmas tree in a modern child's mind. Harrison (80) quotes from an ancient author the song of a child to the *Eiresione*:

> Eiresione brings
> All good things,
> Figs and fat cakes to eat,
> Soft oil and honey sweet,
> and brimming wine-cup deep
> that she may drink and sleep.

SKIRAPHORIA: (June-July) "Festival of the (umbrella's?) shade." This may have been the time when Eleusinic implements were made by new *mystai*: It is known that the *Skiraphoria* was a celebration in which votive offerings in the shape of human genitals, humans beings, and animals fashioned of grain, clay, and chalk were taken to a certain *megara* in Athens, which may have acted as a cthonic "storehouse" of sorts for Dionysian and Eleusinic sacra, the implements possibly left there until the Eleusinia proper.[90] This is particularly likely if the *megara* in question was located within the Athenian Eleusinion at the Pnyx of the Acropolis, but available sources do not specify. According to Aristophanes,[91] processions which carried the *sacra* were led by priests carrying parasols whitened with chalk, the bedaubed umbrella alluding to the white earth with which initiates of Dionysos and Persephone were marked prior to their being named *mystai* at the lesser Mysteries of *Agrai*.

STENIA: "Fasting"; see *Thesmophoria*.

SYNOIKIA: (July-August) The Athenian *Kronoia* festival was immediately followed by the rites of *Synoikia* — a "restoration of order," from which the modern Greek *synoche*, "continuity" and *synoikismos*, "settlement," are derived. This was yet another celebration mythically instituted by Theseus, in which offerings were made to *Eirene* ("peace," possibly a derivation of *Eiresione*, a mythical figure whose sad demise paradoxically brought, at the festival of *Pyanepsia* in the late autumn, "all good things") at the Acropolis itself. The festivals of *Synoikia* and *Panathenaia* marked the beginning of the Attic year, in which the daily order of roles and rules, labor and law were reestablished after the topsy-turvy festivities of *Kronoia* had ended.[92]

THARGELIA: (May-June) This ceremony, and not *Haloa* as some scholars mistakenly assume, was the "harvest home" of ancient and Classical Greece.[93] *Thargelos* meant "first loaf of the harvest." In modern Greek, *theros* means "summertime," that period during which the ancient *Thargelia* was celebrated. In this festival, door lintels were decorated with newly-cut stalks of grain, which were kept up until the following *Thargelia* for luck. Altar, temple, and hearth-offerings of first fruits were made, as were scapegoat offerings, to keep off famine and pestilence.

The symbolic *Thargelia* scapegoat, which for this festival could be a human being or merely a statue, was scourged with leeks, but not killed — in good years. In times of famine, pestilence, or invasion, criminals were still sacrificed in Classical Greece, as scapegoats whose fleeing souls would carry away whatever it was within the *polis* that had angered the gods. Similar ceremonies were common in many places in the world until at least the nineteenth century.[94] A comparable symbolic sacrifice may have added dramatic overtones to the festivals of *Metageitnia* and *Kronoia* as well.[95]

THESMOPHORIA: (October-November) *Thesmophoria* means "bearing the ordinance." *Bearing*, in the context of the *Thesmophoria*, refers to both the carrying of votive offerings and to the carrying out of purifications; acts of purification and offering constituted a worshipper's acquiescence to a "law laid down" — an *ordinance*: See page 98, regarding Demeter's *thesmos* to humankind. The votive offerings were also "laid down," either thrown or lowered into a deep sacred pit, a *megaron*. In ancient Athens, these were most likely the natural clefts of the Acropolian Pnyx itself.[96] This festival is commonly believed to have been the purification and appeasement ceremony which preceded the sowing of grain in the Classical Attic world, and it was fully paid for by the men of the community.[97]

The rituals undertaken at the *Thesmophoria* can be divided into three main parts; *Anodos* and *Kathodos* on the 11th Pyanepsion, *Stenia* and *Nesteia* on the 12th, and *Kalligenia* on the 13th: [98]

• Ascent and Lowering: On the first day of the festival, women would ascend to the temple of Demeter Thesmophoros, which adjoined the Eleusinion on the Athenian Acropolis, to lower newborn piglets, pine cones, and votive objects[99] into the *megaron* at the heart of the temple. These actions were symbolic of Kore's yearly return to cthonic Hades, during which time of year the planting of grain occurred. Ancient authors also record baskets of flowers being carried by the women and strewn upon the path as they climbed the hill; undoubtedly, this was symbolic of the flowery meadow where Kore was abducted, according to the Homeric *Hymn to Demeter*.[100] Lucian notes that the baskets which the women carried into the Temple of Demeter on the Acropolis also held "sacred things that may not be named and that are made of cereal paste...images of snakes and the forms of men..."[101]

• Jesting and Fasting: *Gephyrismoi* and other purificatory acts were performed on the μεδη or "middle day" of the *Thesmophoria*. Between all days of the *Thesmophoria*, women attending the festival fasted in improvised huts,[102] which most scholars agree were made of *Angus castus* (Chaste Tree) branches, while resting on crude couches made out of the same sort of branches; the presence of branches and greenery was symbolic of purification in ancient Greece, and the branches upon which the women rested at the Thesmophoria were further believed to repel snakes.[103] Burkert, however, notes that the herb used for these purposes was πεγανον (*peganon*), that mythic and possibly entheogenic herb which links the rites of *Thesmophoria* with the Mysteries that were experienced within the Telesterion at Eleusis, just as the jests and fasting do:[104] Indeed, the *Thesmophoria* appears to be a summary reenactment of the greater Mysteries, much as the *myesis* ritual (see pages 110-111) is a summary reenactment of the lesser Mysteries.

• The (re)Birth of the Fair Kore: The last day's ceremony consisted of a nighttime torch dance reminiscent of those held at Callichorus during the Eleusinia, which enacted the myth of the Goddess Demeter's worldwide search for her lost daughter.[105]

Plerosia and Kalamaia: All that is recorded of these ceremonies is that they were women's festivals, noted in conjunction with the *Arrhephoria* and *Thesmophoria*.[106] *Plerosia* appears to mean "festival of completion," while *Kalamaia* means "reaped field" or "grain stalk" — again, words which are evocative of some reenactment of the Mysteries of Eleusis, but ancient authors are silent regarding the festivals of *Plerosia* and *Kalamaia*.

VESTALIA: (May-June) The first day of this ceremony, known in Rome as "Vestalia," was *Plynteria*; as the Greek translation implies, this festival centered around the washing and repainting of temple images (*xoanoi*), and of the interior and exterior of the temples proper. On the following day of the festival — *Kallynteria*, or "festival of ornamentation" — the xoanoi were clothed in fresh garments, replaced on their pedestals, and hung with figs, a symbol of purification.[107]

At the conclusion of the *Plynteria*, ceremonial human images (*argeioi*) were woven out of straw and tossed into rivers or streams. Such images were believed to be sacred to Hades Plouton: [108] Perhaps these images embodied some "uncleanness of soul" — an impurity — which the ceremonies of cleansing and ornamentation were believed to remove. Tossing images which represented such a spiritual state into rivers or streams would have symbolically equated to sending them down the underworld river Styx, into the realm of the judge of souls in exchange for the worshipper's own, previously soiled, spirit. It may be from the Roman *Vestalia* and the related Attic rituals of *Kallynteria* and *Plynteria* that the modern concept of "spring cleaning" is derived.

CHAPTER THREE: THE LENAIA

Lenaia, also known as the "lesser," "rural," or "more ancient" Dionysia, consisted of a complex of rituals carried out at several places on the Greek mainland, a fact which has caused some scholars erroneously to assume that Lenean ceremonies consisted of little more than a movable feast.[1]

The Lesser Dionysia was held on the first full moon after winter solstice, 12th *Gamelion* by the ancient and Classical Attic lunar calendar, or anytime between the solstice on December 22 and mid-January, according to modern solar calculations.[2] "Unspeakable" (*Arrheton*) Lenaia ceremonies were conducted by Gerairai beside the rocky, freshwater swamps near Classical Athens at the sealed temple of Dionysos,[3] by Thiades at the *Korykion Antron* on the mountain of Parnassos, and by Hosioi at the temple of Delphi, which is at the foot of Parnassos.[4] During the Lenean period, the populace of Athens attended plays and dithyrambic events held in honor of what was, in essence, the "birthday" of the god, performed by bands of amateur actors, singers, and playwrights which may have wandered from village to village performing on behalf of the Dionysian nativity since the solstice itself.[5]

Similar Dionysian rites were held at roughly the same time of year throughout the Greek-speaking world, not just at Athens and Delphi.[6] Portions of the rites included the initiation of young women into their sphere of society, a celebration of woman's innate connection to the mysterious forces of life and death, part of the "awakening of Liknites" by the Thyiades at the Korykion Antron and concurrent to the consecration of Delphi by the elite Hosioi.[7]

The month of Gamelion — known as *Dadophoros* in Delphi — began a period of the Attic year sacred to the Lord of Souls, which would end in the month of Anthesterion with rites that connected the beginning and end of this, the "Dionysian Season," together in one eternal round.[8] It is important to remember that the performance of comedic plays and of dithyrambs were *not* of first importance (or even primarily found) in the ritual ceremonies of Lenaia until Classical times.[9] Dithyrambic melodies performed for the Lenaia differed from those performed for the Katagogia: They were not hymns to Dionysos the triumphator, appropriate to the male sphere; they were songs of forthcoming — of birth, which was in ancient times the purview of women alone. Plato noted in *Laws*, "Another form of song, the Birth of Dionysos (is) called, I think, the Dithyramb."[10] Lenaia was first and foremost the celebration of the nativity of the Lord of Souls, who entered and would leave the world of men through the cthonic swamps, bringing with him a mystic horde of departed spirits avid for the new life implied by the yearly rebirth of a Child of Wonder.[11]

The earliest preserved dithyramb of this type was ritually performed during the winter solstice at Elis — by women, rather than by men as was traditional with dithyrambs elsewhere:

> Hero Dionysos, come
> To thy Temple-home
> Here at Elis, worshipful
> We implore thee,
> With thy Charites adore thee,
> Rushing with thy bull-foot, come!
> Noble Bull, noble Bull.[12]

Humans noted early in Paleolithic times that the year could be divided evenly into two halves, the "dark" half and the "light" half; paradoxically, the dark half begins at the summer solstice, that point when the days begin to shorten toward autumn, whereas the light half begins at the winter solstice, that point when the days begin to lengthen toward spring. It was widely believed well into the Middle Ages that souls came to and left the earthly plane through the "solstice gates" or, as they are still referred to in Greece, the *halcyon* (kingfisher) *days*.[13] Dionysos, who would be celebrated in the festival of Anthesteria specifically as "Lord of Souls," was the bull-horned infant of the Lenaia, whose coming would ultimately bring springtime, as the iambic Delphic Paean to Dionysos as Dithyrambos ("the twice-born") notes:[14]

Come, O Dithyrambos, Bacchos, come,
Euios, Thyrsos-Lord, Braites, come,
Bromios, come, and coming with thee bring
Holy hours of thine own holy spring.
Evoe, Bacchos, hail, Paean, hail,
Whom in sacred Thebes the mother fair,
She Thyone, once to Zeus did bear.
All the stars danced for joy. Mirth
Of mortals hailed thee, Bacchos, at thy birth.[15]

Ceremonies held inside the sealed Temple sanctuary of Dionysos near what were once rocky wetlands just outside of Athens were *arrheton*, and largely hidden from non-clerics.[16] Though pious worshippers were gathered outside the temple enjoying plays and dithyrambs, like those above, performed by old men and boys and dedicated to the lord of life in death, what action the Gerairai performed within the temple proper was a mystery.[17] It is known, however, that this was the only day of the year when Dionysos' sacred Lenean mask was on public display. Scholars have long debated which ceremonies — those of midwinter and Lenaia or those of spring and the Anthesteria — are represented on ancient Greek vases which show Dionysian worshippers and singers of dithyrambs gathered near or around a mask of Dionysos. Since ancient writings themselves assert that the mask was shown *only during the festival of Lenaia*, the general term "Lenaia vases" is surely accurate.[18]

There are two main theories regarding the meaning of the Dionysian mask. I subscribe to both of them, because they combine into a premise which gives deep meaning to the rituals of both Lenaia and Anthesteria, as well as to theatrical performance in general, which began with the mask. The combined premise states that the mask's direct and unblinking stare is a form of primal confrontation, capable of driving civilized impulses and the world of everyday living to the back of one's mind and calling forth the reflexive matrix of the autonomic nervous system, from which novel emotions and impulses may arise — including but not limited to that of spiritual awe. A modern rendition of this can be seen among moviegoers, who willingly surrender everyday reality in order to immerse themselves in the emotional world of actors playing roles which are anything but a mirror of the actors' own routine existence. To the modern audience, the two-dimensional screen causes an actor to appear to be more than human — the very effect theoretically caused by the ritual mask.[19] It is my personal theory that effective acting is not a matter of emotive movement or the enunciation of flawlessly crafted lines: It is the autonomic nervous response an actor is capable of evoking, using solely his or her eyes.

Marsh Rites of the Venerable Women

Anciently, in areas of Greece outside of Attica, certain secluded Dionysian rites were held *trieterically* — over a two-to three-year period — or even *pentaterically*, over a five-year period. Within this ceremonial pattern, Dionysos would assume one or more of his alternating forms each year (divine child, bridegroom, lord of souls, lord of wine, dying and reborn god).[20] However, in Attic Greece (that portion of the mainland ruled over by Athens), all Mystery rites, including those of Dionysos, were celebrated yearly, so that rather than a procession of alternating years which held a certain significance — e.g., the year of the return-of-souls followed by the year of the divine bridegroom — all of these meanings would be condensed into the rites and ceremonies of the changing seasons of one year.[21] The period between *Poseidon* and *Anthesterion* (our mid-December to mid-March) was considered the "Dionysian season" in Attica: This season was symbolized by the dual nature of the huge, half-buried earthen vessels known as *pithoi*, used by the ancient Attic population as both primary fermentation vessels for wine, and as burial urns.[22]

It has been suggested that individuals brought their own home-brewed new wine to the Lenaia ceremony to drink.[23] This observation is not wholly accurate. At the Athenian Lenaia, a miraculous wine ceremony took place during which vats of water sealed into the temple of Dionysos turned into wine, and an unrooted, leafless vine shoot placed in among the water vats (*stamnoi*) grew into a vine ready for harvest overnight. If, indeed, worshippers brought offerings of new wine from their homes to Dionysos Limnaios, then this wine was carefully collected to refill the *stamnoi*.[24] It is more likely, however, that wine, both new and aged, was kept at the temple *en limnais* itself, since both the Anthesteric *symposion* of Choës Day and the ritual of maidens swinging over huge, half-buried pythoi both took place at the temple in the marshes.[25]

To siphon or ladle (*kythos*) partially-fermented wine off the lees of old yeast and fruit which settle to the bottom of a primary fermentation vat (*lenos*) one to three months after beginning a ferment is called *racking*.[26] During modern racking operations, the transferred wine is generally tested for flavor, color, sugar content, and further fermentation potential, prior to being transferred into secondary fermentation vessels. [27] It was this necessity around which the lesser Dionysia evolved.

Kerenyi[28] bounces back and forth between certain rites of Lenaia and those of Anthesteria as though they were one seamless ceremony. In reality, the ritual during which finished wine was placed into sealed amphorae for aging was part of the *Anthesteria* ceremony. Confusingly, certain rites held on the Anthesteric day devoted to the transfer and storage of wine were collectively known as *Limnaia*, so close in both pronunciation and function to the midwinter *Lenaia* festival that the commingling of the two rites is an understandable modern misconstruction. A deeper look at the two words reveals this: *Lenai* means "winepress," whereas *Limnos* means "marsh" or "swampland" — two very different objects, even if the winepress (or wine-vats) were located within the marsh (or marsh-temple) itself.

It was at the Anthesteric Limnaia ceremony, *not at the Lenaia*, that the Basilinna of Athens bestowed upon the Venerable Women the honor of mixing the spring wine — *gleukos*, by then a considerably more potent vintage[29] — with water for the male worshippers who gathered at the Dionysian temple in the marsh to make offerings to the cthonic gods. Only a relatively small amount of wine would actually have been drunk at this all-male ceremonial, since the wine was ladled into worshippers' *choai*, as opposed to any form of drinking cup, and the chous was primarily used in Pagan Greek ritual as a libation vessel.[30]

Several scholars theorize that something else was done within the sealed marshland temple of Dionysos during the midwinter Lenaia — something to do with that year's new wine, which had been fermenting since sometime between our October and November.[31] The midwinter procession to the Temple sanctuary *en Limnais* was led by the Athenian *Basileus*, or ceremonial priest-king, and the Eleusinian *Dadouchos*, linking the ceremony to both the divine marriage of the Anthesteria and the Mysteries of Eleusis; these clues suggest that the sacred "marsh wine" was entheogenic in nature.[32] However, I surmise that the wine imbibed at the Lenaia itself was solely new wine, and that one reason for the almost perpetual "sealing" of the Dionysian temple in the marsh was to protect amphorae of older, entheogen-laced wines kept there from falling into inquisitive hands outside the purview of ritual or symposium.

At least some Greek wine appears to have possessed a potency unknown in modern vintages, such that it was mixed heavily with water and imbibed only in very small cups, to minimize potentially hazardous effects.[33] The most likely explanation for the potency of Greek wine in ancient and Classical times is the addition to it of entheogens. Distillation of alcoholic beverages (such as wine, from which brandy is distilled) was not known to the Greeks until after the first century CE, and until the twelfth century distillation was used primarily for extracting liquid substances from non-liquid ones, such as rosewater from rose petals.[34]

By contrast, inclusion of additives to wine is an ancient process which continues in modern vintnery. Such inclusions occur throughout the process of winemaking, an act known to vintners as *amelioration*.[35] In modern parlance, primary amelioration is the process of adding sugar or honey-water, herbs, other fruits, spices, oak chips, dark grape skins devoid of juice, or other items to the must — new, still actively-fermenting wine — in order to alter or improve the final product. This is often done at the beginning of the secondary fermentation stage, when the wine is carefully removed from its primary fermenter.[36] It is at the festival of Lenaia that ancient Greek wines would have been removed from their primary fermenters and racked into secondary ones, which means that the festival of Lenaia would have been the appropriate time for performing primary amelioration as well.

Secondary amelioration includes adding fruit brandy, glycerine, oak chips, or other items to the wine, and is usually done at the end of the secondary fermentation stage, just prior to bottling; some modern wines undergo three to four amelioration steps, while others remain in their primary fermenters until they are ready to be bottled. Secondary amelioration of ancient Hellenic wine would have occurred during the festival of Anthesteria, one to two months later. Amelioration, both primary and secondary, is often performed for the purpose of enhancing both the flavor and the texture, or "body," of a wine.[37] Body is the mouth-feel of a wine. Too much body can be corrected by the addition of water or sugar-water (the Greeks were also fond of adding seawater to their wine[38]); or, it can be increased by the addition of mucillaginous herbal compounds, such as glycerine, or honey.

Another process which calls for the addition of substances to wine just after racking it off its lees and into secondary fermentation vessels is clarification, or fining. Depending upon its composition, almost any wine left untouched in its secondary fermentation vessel clarifies by itself, given enough time: Forty days, which was the most common timeframe between the Lenaia and Anthesteria ceremonies, is usual.[39] However, if the wine is jostled, is fermented in a very cold place, or simply refuses to come clear of microscopic detritus within that time, small amounts of certain inclusions — such as white fuller's clay, oak chips, or eggwhite — are added to modern vintages and allowed time to settle before the fined wine is racked.[40]

Many herbs modernly used in winemaking, and not merely the vine's fruits themselves, were mythically linked to Dionysos. There are tales of maenadic oaks, Dionysian myrtle (which is still used to fragrance some wines), the sacred strawberry tree of Dionysos, many references to the fig (which may be used to flavor wine), and the ubiquitous Dionysian fennel, as well as to herbs which have medicinal or even poisonous attributes, such as willow, asphodel, pimpernel, and ivy. Any or all of these may have provided amelioration to Hellenic wine. Some Dionysian herbs, such as the Alep pine, its pitch, and its cones, still do[41]

Likely entheogenic agents may have included absinthe, belladonna berries, cannabis, datura flowers, mandrake root, poppy sap or straw, and other substances including more innocuous flavoring or sweetening herbs still used modernly, such as woodruff.[42] Such substances were used in ancient times, as they still are in some modern cultures, to "bring forth the gods and ancestral spirits,"[43] and the Lenaia was specifically geared toward summoning the Lord of Souls and his shadow-hosts forth from the newly-filled pithoi into the world of humans, where they would remain until the Anthesteria.[44]

I theorize that the "unspeakable" rites of Lenaia *en limnais* were rites of Dionysian women as the god's "nurses," who would tear herbs and psychotropic plants for addition to the still-fermenting wine in the stamnoi in reenactment of the mythic maenads' rending of Dionysos in the form of a human baby or young animal.[45]

As noted by Classicist Carl Ruck in *Road To Eleusis...*: "The maenads apparently attempted to pacify and control their god through role impersonation as his mothers, nurses, and ultimately...when ingested, the child would have grown to manhood and the former nurses would become the god's brides..."[46] At the end of the wintertime "Dionysian period" — marked by the festivals of Anthesteria and Agrai, followed in Periclean times by the Katagogia and Apollonian advent in the Delphic month of Bysios[47] — pithoi, stamnoi, or amphorae used as secondary fermentation vessels would be drained, with much of the wine given in libation, some imbibed, and the rest stored for future ceremonial use. The rites of Anthesteria fulfilled part of a cycle, allowing the full-grown Lord of Souls to return to the underworld with his ghostly hosts, after his wintertime "nurses" had fulfilled a new duty as bridesmaids.[48]

The Lenaia wine ceremony was a mystical duty performed by the Gerairai of Athens on behalf of Dionysos, the overlord of inebriants.[49] The mystical nature of the ritual is verified by the presence at the Lenaia of the Eleusinian Dadouchos, who aided in the salpinx-summons of the god by leading the cry, "Summon the god: Son of Semele, Iacchos, bestower of wealth!"[50] The promise of rebirth from death was inherent in these ceremonies, which were conducted at the only time in the Greek year during which marriages were performed — foreshadowing the conception of new bodies for the summoned spirits.[51] The dual rituals of Lenaia and Limnaia forged a link between the realm of the living and that of the dead, one which clasped the beginning and end of the Dionysian season together elegantly: Both ceremonials intimately connected the shapeshifting mythos of Dionysos with the life-cycles of his mortal worshippers.

Lenaia represented the beginning of the Dionysian period of the year, when the wine clarifying within underground pithoi was still weak and milky — appropriate for a newborn. Spirits were believed to rise from the underworld through the newly-breached fermentation vats, following the infant Lord of Souls upward from their cthonic abodes, in hope of reincarnation. With luck, this would be provided by the newlyweds whose marriages were customarily held in the "lucky time" between mid-December and mid-February in Greece. The practice of wintertide marriages remains the norm in Greece as well as within Greek diaspora communities.[52] I theorize that the immigration and emigration of ancestral souls to and from the world of the living through wine pithoi is the reason that alcoholic beverages are modernly referred to as "spirits" or "waters of life" in most European languages.

Dionysos himself was simultaneously sacrificed and reborn at the myriad ceremonies held during the ancient Hellenic midwinter period.[53] The Gerairai were the wise elders solemnly sworn in as "mystic attendants" who would oversee the divine apotheosis from beginning to end: Anthesteric rites — when the newly-potent wine was transferred to men's choai for libation and to amphorae for aging — were also overseen by the Gerairai. The god of wine, like the wine itself, was a potent force at the Anthesteria festival which hailed the end of the Dionysian period: As bridegroom of the Athenian Basilinna[54] — the only woman with the sacerdotal power to bestow the title of Geraira and all that it entailed[55] — Dionysos would consummate a symbolic marriage which was also emblematic of a sacrifice, performed to placate any remaining spirits summoned to earth through the half-buried Lenaian wine vats, but ultimately denied rebirth.

Other rituals occurred during the Lenaian season, celebrating subsequent segments of the life cycles of Dionysos' female worshippers. Whereas the Gerairai represented a crone archetype, in Delphi a group of ecstatic, nurturant women — *Thyiades*, archetypal mothers — performed a ceremony which may have served to initiate maidens into the fundamental and mysteriously interconnected facets of life and death.

When the Thyiades Wake Liknites

The mountain of Parnassos towers over the remains of the Apollonian temple at Delphi. Though the ostensible "gravesite" of Dionysos is still pointed out to tourists within the temple, his nearby birthplace, the natal cave of Bacchos — or *Korykion Antron*, which overlooks the temple from the crags of the mountain itself — is visited by archaeologists rather more often than it is by tourists. Archaeological findings indicate that the ancient rites of the Thyiades, who processed up the mountain (*oreibasis*) to the Korykion Antron during midwinter, almost certainly consisted of a sanctification ceremony utilizing Dionysian sacra piously hidden within worshippers' *liknoi*.[56]

The liknon's primary use was that of a consecratory tool. Evolved at least in part from the winnowing-corb designed to separate wheat from chaff, the sacred cradle of Dionysos was believed to have the spiritual capacity of separating the good from the bad within an individual, and of removing the bad.[57] The Dionysian sacred basket is among the world's most novel ritual items. Comparable objects include only the cornucopia — which itself is a direct mythic offshoot of the Dionysian liknon — and the Native American power bundle.[58]

There was an arcane sense of "spiritual toy box" about the liknon, particularly after the Classical Orphic movement began to heavily influence Hellenic Mystery rites. Most extant descriptions or portrayals of liknoi indicate that they held certain fundamental items; usually lined with dried leaves or flowers, they contained dice, tops, balls, bells, mirrors — all the mythic toys with which the cannibalistic Titans beguiled the Sacred Infant which, according to Orphic myth, they were intent to destroy.[59]

No winnowing-basket could be rightly be called a liknon unless it held a carved wooden phallus, reminiscent of the Sacred Child's "heart," a symbol of indestructible life rescued from the awful Titanic feast and the wrathful fires of

Zeus by Athena.[60] Athena, as previously noted, also has her sacred basket: Dionysian items are reported to have been concealed within both the forbidden basket of Athena — carried by maidens to underground grottoes within the city during the ceremony of Skiraphoria in midsummer — and the Eleusinian *kalathoi*. According to pre-Orphic mythology, a potion or *kykeon* was prepared from Dionysos' "heart" and given by Zeus to Persephone to drink, that she might rebirth him.

Other items that were held sacred and are known to have been in the liknon were a wreath (of dried flowers, or one fashioned of gold),[61] a snake (most likely a golden amulet),[62] and golden apples (either real ones, or yet another example of the goldsmith's handiwork).[63] Masks are occasionally represented within liknoi in Classical Hellenic art, as are infants. [64] It may be that ritual masks worked as a covering for the liknon, either in place of or along with a cloth in certain ceremonials, such as the rite held by the Gerairai at the Dionysian marsh-temple during the Lenean period. Tucking infants into winnowing-corbs to sleep was a commonplace occurrence in ancient Greece;[65] though it may well be that the winnowing basket was the venerable forerunner of the modern bassinet (*liknon* remains in modern Greek usage for only one term; *liknizo*, to rock a baby), it is certain that iconographic instances of liknon-borne infants represent Dionysos as a sacred child — *Liknites, Plouton, Iacchos, Brimos, Eiraphiotes, Bougenes*, et al. Syncretic myths include that of the marsh basket of Moses and the manger-cradle of Christ.

The immanent presence of Dionysos as divine child — consecrated within the baskets in the Korykion Antron — and as Unspeakable Sacrifice, within the Pythic tripod at Delphi, is the noetic drama underlying both rites: He is reborn at *exactly* the same instant that he is sacrificed.[66] The "awakening"/coming forth of the Divine Child at the cave above Delphi complements the rites performed by the Gerairai on the outskirts of Athens; both rituals recall the older, possibly paleolithic, myth of life beginning to stir in a leather sack where a sacred vintage was hidden. As Kerenyi noted in *Dionysos...* (298): "In Athens the women who celebrated the Dionysos cult in its highest form...were called Gerairai, the 'venerables'; and those who went to Delphi each year, 'Thyiades'."[67] Both the Athenian and Delphic ceremonies were rituals at which female nature held sway,[68] and by which young girls were initiated into womanhood and the responsibilities of marriage and motherhood,[69] similar to the rites held at the precincts of Artemis in Brauron centuries earlier.[70] It is thought that Artemis may have been presiding goddess of the Parnassos liknon rites as well.[71]

Votive objects which may or may not have been included in the liknon were a Dionysian worshipper's ritual attire — which may also have acted as part of the cloth covering of the liknon[72] — woolen fillets, real or imitation pomegranates, dried grapes and figs, fir cones, dried beans, real or imitation eggs, and nuts: All of the preceding items, possibly including portions of the ritual attire, would have been acceptable as votive offerings to the cthonic gods. The symbolism of these items is multifold, and closely linked to Mystery rites.

Apples and pomegranates are symbolic of the interdependent nature of life and death. The pomegranate is the fruit of death's bloody aspect, which holds the seeds of life; while the apple is the fruit of life's abundance — which holds the seeds of death. The first of these fruits is dedicated to Kore, the second to Kore's male alter-ego, Dionysos, as *Phloios*.[73] This implied symbology is certainly pertinent: Inedible apple seeds contain cyanide, and all parts of a pomegranate except the seeds contain potentially toxic levels of alum. The fact that two seemingly mutually-exclusive states of being — life and death — are embodied in these fruits is suggestive of the ultimately eternal nature of all which lives. Anciently, pomegranate seeds were used in ritual contexts but never actually eaten; they were considered cthonic, taboo foods, as were apples, beans, lobsters, red mullet, raspberries, chickens, eggs, root vegetables, and okra.[74]

The reason given for the taboo nature of beans in the Hellenic world in general was that they were symbolic of the unborn child, and were therefore carriers of the spirits of the ancestral dead: The eating of beans, particularly by men, was believed to deny rebirth to the ancestors, except when performed under very strict circumstances within the purview of the Mystery rites themselves.[75]

Eggs were noted by ancient philosophers to be descended from "that which gives birth to all things and contains all things." Their sanctity rendered them taboo: In Orphic creation myths, the Universe sprang from an egg.[76]

Figs, though not a taboo food, were symbolic of the testes of the god when whole, and the vulva of the goddess when cut. As such, they were considered capable of purifying whatever they touched.[77] Nuts and cones were not taboo, either, but were considered symbolic of the god of indestructible life: Indeed, all evergreen plants held this distinction, and still do. Nuts were also a symbol of wisdom to the Pagan Greeks.[78]

Plutarch noted in *Isis and Osiris* (XXXV): [79]

The affair about the Titans and the Night of Accomplishment accords with what are called in the rites of Osiris "tearings to pieces"; resurrections, regenerations. The same is true about rites of burying. The Egyptians show in many places burial chests of Osiris, and the Delphians also hold that the remains of Dionysos are deposited with them near to the place of the oracle, and the Consecrated ones perform a secret sacrifice in the sanctuary of Apollo what time the Thyiades wake Liknites.[79]

It is unknown exactly how the liknon or the items in the liknon were consecrated, though it is possible that they were anointed with the same liquid mixture poured upon grave *eskhara* as an oblation to the dead in ancient Greece: Wine, water, milk, honey, and oil were mixed together and poured on the grave of a deceased hero.[80] Whether the process of consecrating the items within the liknon after climbing Parnassos and gaining admission to the Korykion Antron was considered the main initiatory step from maidenhood to young adulthood for girls, or whether further steps were undertaken, is equally unknown to modern scholars.

The Unspeakable Sacrifice

In *Dionysos: Archetypal Image of Indestructible Life* (233) Kerenyi notes that the "unspeakable sacrifice" performed yearly at Delphi must have taken place *before* the advent of Apollo to this shrine on the 7th of Bysios (roughly April 21st), and that aspects of this sacrifice included concurrent ritual activity by women concerned with Dionysian sacra.[81] Plutarch noted in the first century CE that "The people of Delphi believe that the remains of Dionysos rest with them beside the oracle, and the Hosioi offer a secret sacrifice in Apollo's shrine whenever the Thyiades wake Liknites."[82] It is most likely that the men's Delphic sacrifice and the concurrent awakening of Liknites by the women was an analogue of the veiled Athenian Lenaia ceremony, which was held between our mid-December and mid-January and considered the high point in the "rural" or "lesser" Dionysia.[83]

The "unspeakable sacrifice" appears in Classical literature as a form of reincarnation, rejuvenation, or apotheosis, hailing from the dismemberment of a sheep or goat into seven parts which are boiled in a tripod-kettle: At Delphi, this presumably occurred within the (usually covered) tripod upon which the Delphic oracle sat when making her pronouncements.[84] This yearly ritual enactment of life from death suggests the mythic dismemberment and ultimate rebirth of Dionysos, which is exactly what the "unspeakable sacrifice" performed in winter by the Hosioi symbolizes.[85] Burkert notes that the myth of Orpheus is emblematic of just such an "unspeakable sacrifice," in which the sacrifice was not an animal killed by the Hosioi, but a human Hosios-figure — which is what Orpheus represents.[86]

Burkert and others[87] also note that there were probably two groups of men who performed the Delphic tripod sacrifice and concurrent replacement of the net of interknotted fillets (*tainai*) which draped the Delphic *omphalos* ("navel").[88] One group — presumably the Pythia-consecrated Hosioi[89] — is thought to have portrayed the forces of peaceful civilization, while the second group (perhaps young men just come to adulthood, representative of the mythic Kouretes) is thought to have embodied wild, untamed, and uncivilized forces.[90] Together, both groups would have enacted the sanctifying world-rebirth scenario of Dionysos' descent into the underworld through the tripod and a re-ascent through the omphalos.

Modern scholars theorize that the tripod represented the Olympic realm while the *bathron*, or steps leading up to the tripod, represented the cthonic depths. The bathron was also considered to be the tomb or gravestone of Dionysos at Delphi, linking Dionysos to the mythical python slain by Apollo when he took over the Delphic precincts. (According to relevant myth, the "bones" of the python were stored in the Delphic tripod itself — hence the name of the woman who received mantic information via the power ostensibly contained within the tripod: *Pythia*.) This infers one of two things: That Delphi and its prophetic oracle were, originally, the purview of Dionysos, or that Apollo and Dionysos are diurnal and nocturnal aspects of a single god.[91]

A reunion of Dionysos with Semele was also implied in the ritual, since the sacred ram was seethed in the cauldron, perhaps in its mother's milk, again linking the unspeakable sacrifice of the *Hosioi* ("devoted ones") to the Lenean rites performed by the nurses of the Sacred Infant at the Dionysian temple bordering the marshes. [92] The cry given by the Daudouchos during the breaching of the miraculous stamnoi at the temple *en Limnais*, in which water was changed into wine at the behest of Dionysos, is "Iacchos, son of Semele, bestower of wealth!" *Ploutodota* is the Katharevousa translation of *Iacchos, son of Semele, bestower of wealth*. Modern students of Greek myth know this aspect of Dionysos as Plouton, who mythically offers the cornucopia — previously noted to be an equivalent of the liknon — to his worshippers.[93] Symbolically, then, Dionysos was ceremonially killed in the guise of a young animal, ultimately to be reborn through the Queen of the Dead as Lord of Souls.[94] As Burkert notes in *Homo Necans* (91-92, 125):

> Whereas the men gathered for sacrifice, for the "act" of killing, the women attended to newborn life. Thus, the polarity of the sexes bound together the course of life and assured perpetuity in the face of death...the Hosioi were the most distinguished social group at Delphi...by undergoing a special, seemingly ancient Initiation-sacrifice, they attained the status of "the purified" and were hence able to deal with "the unspeakable" on a regular basis. This probably entailed a sacrificial dismemberment. Euripides combines a similar "consecration" with omophagy in Crete.

CHAPTER FOUR: THE ANTHESTERIA

Anthesteria, a three-day-long festival held during the month of *Anthesterion*, was also known as the "more ancient Dionysia."[1] These three days of ritual centered on the racking of wine, propitiation of the dead, and issues of metempsychosis, including ceremonies alluding to transitional kingship.

Some scholars note that the ceremonies of Anthesteria were not always strictly divided between all three days. Harrison (34) observes that there were times when the ceremonies of Chytrogia and Limnaia were performed on the same day. However, the festival itself always fell in the middle of the month of Anthesterion, usually the 11th through the 13th, though some ancient writers claimed that the whole month was sacred to Dionysos, probably because the Anthesteria was closely followed by the Dionysian rites of Agrai.[2] The time of year when the Anthesteria was held equates to mid-February on modern calendars, a month-name which English speakers inherited with little alteration from the ancient Romans.[3]

During the second day of the Anthesteria, alone of all the Hellene year, the temple of Dionysos *en Limnais* was thrown open in order to accommodate the men of Athens as they took part in the Choës Day *symposion* — contests of drinking, libation, poetry, philosophizing, and dithyramb-making. As Thucydides notes (II.15): "The more ancient Dionysia was celebrated on the twelfth day of the month Anthesterion in the temple of Dionysos in the Marshes (*en Limnais*)."[4]

Anthesteria, an all-souls festival,[5] would appear to have things in common with Celtic Beltane and Samhain rites. Indeed, the worshippers' invitation to the dead to join in the ceremonies, combined with the air of consecration, eroticism, and topsy-turvy liberation, makes the Anthesteria seem like a fascinating combination of these two Celtic festivals. Also in common with the Celtic ceremony of Beltane was the use of hawthorn (*rhamnos*) in Anthesteric rites. However, instead of wearing garlands of it as the Celts did, the Greeks would wreathe freshly-pitched door posts with its flowers, and for protection from any vengeful spirits — probably portrayed by masked mummers — they would chew its leaves.[6] Ceremonies similar to those performed for the Anthesteria have also been noted among Sclavonic and Indic peoples, and the Anthesteric *symposion* shares both linguistic and ceremonial roots with the Norse *symbel*.[7]

Day of the Crocks

The portion of the festival commonly begun on the 11th day of the month *Anthesterion* centered on the reopening of the huge, half-buried *pithoi* (earthenware crocks) in which the wine had overwintered in Athenian precincts, or the transport of smaller crocks from the countryside to Athens for use in the Athenian symposion.[8] Libations were made directly from the newly-opened crocks onto the ground in memory of the ancestors and cthonic gods prior to any drinking or storage of the wine, as Plutarch noted in *Questiones Symposia* III: 7.1: "It was an ancient custom to offer some of it as a libation before they drank it, praying at the same time that the use of the drug might be rendered harmless and beneficial to them."[9] Masked ceremonials accompanied the racking of wine from underground pithoi into storage amphorae on this "day of the crocks," *Pithogia*.

It is believed that the Pithogia ceremony originated from a more ancient yearly journey of townsfolk to the graves of their ancestors, which may have featured half-buried *pithoi* as cremation urns, hence the Anthesteric preoccupation with ancestral spirits and Dionysos as "Lord of Souls."[10]

A Day of Pollution

The word *chous* (singular of choë) refers to the ceremonial pitcher from which wine was customarily poured in libation to dead ancestors or cthonic Deities, and it is this word which was used to describe the second day of the

Anthesteria proper.[11] Considered by the ancients to be a "day of pollution," Choës Day was the only day of the year when the Temple to Dionysos of the Swamps (*Limnaios*) was officially open to the public.[12] Poetry, songs, and plays were performed in honor of Dionysos as Divine Bridegroom. A great deal of playacting and mummery went on during the entire Anthesteria festival; scholars note that wine lees were often used as face-paint by mummers.[13]

Concurrent with other Choës Day rituals was the *Apatouria*, a ceremony observing the induction of boy children into their phratrae. A youngster's induction Apatouria was held on the Anthesteria after a child reached the age of three, and included the child's first taste of wine from his own miniature chous, a "children's procession" in which the little ones were hailed as heroes, and the bestowal of many presents by members of a child's clan.[14] According to some sources, a second Apatouria (or Apatouria-like) ceremony was held in Pyanepsion, on behalf of young men preparing to enter military service:[15] See *Katagogia* in Chapter Two for more information regarding military festivals.

A feast followed Choës Day proper, but it was an idiosyncratic feast in which everyone strove to maintain personal isolation and absolute silence, while the feasters meditated on the "crime of eating" (that Titanic great crime) or, as has otherwise been noted: "Human food consists of a collection of souls."[16] The myth that relates the reason for the atmosphere of gloom and grief during a feast is the tale of the pious Neoptolemos who, while taking part in the apportioning of sacrificial meat, was accidentally cut up and apportioned himself.[17]

A ritual procession took place on the eve of Choës Day, originating from the Temple of Dionysos *Limnaios* and led by chanting, hymn-singing female worshippers, after the Neoptolemic meal of each individual had ended. This processional was made in anticipation of the "sacred marriage" of Dionysos with the Athenian Basilinna (ceremonial priestess-queen chosen to rule with her husband, a ceremonial king or *Archon Basileus*, for a year), and the processional led from the Dionysian Temple sanctuary to the *Boukoleon* ("bull's stable"), located in the central *agora* ("marketplace") of Athens.[18]

The Sacred Marriage of the Athenian Basilinna with Dionysos is considered by many researchers to be a foreshadowing of the *hieros gamos*, which would take place at the ceremonies of Eleusis seven months later. The consummation of the Sacred Marriage itself may have been either real or symbolic; a statue or herm of the god may have been incorporated, or a priest of Dionysos, or the figwood phallus hidden in the liknon, or all three together; modern scholars are not sure of the exact methodology used.[19]

During the all-night *hieros gamos* ritual between the Basilinna and the god, a symposion was held by the men, who remained at the Temple *en Limnais*.[20] Each round of wine was ladled out by Gerairai, and announced by the trumpeting of *salpinges*. Salpinges were also used to "call forth" the god at the Lenaia and the Dionysia. Of all Dionysian-directed Attic festivals, these three presupposed the literal presence of the Lord of Souls, god of the winnowing fan, bull's stable, and bridegroom's chamber, master of the liberating dithyramb of the triumphator at the Katagogia, as well as the child to whom the cradle-song was sung at the Lenaia.[21] It is certain that the literal, symbolic, and ceremonial actions performed during the Anthesteric rites at Athenian Bokouleion were complements of those performed by the Gerairai during the midwinter Lenaia, or lesser Dionysia; it was during the Limnaia that Dionysos was perceived as Lord of Souls and Bridegroom — the adult version of the Sacred Child.

The Classical Limnaia recalled ancient times, when the king of a tribe — or a "replacement" king — would be sacrificed at a certain period of his reign.[22] Also referred to as a "year-king," such a replacement or transitional king was reputedly given emblematic rule of a tribe, treated like a king for a prescribed amount of time, and ultimately sacrificed in order to either symbolically or literally fructify the landholdings of the tribe, in place of that tribe's actual ruler. A transitional king's death was usually overseen or performed by the following year's transitional king, the *tanist*. Tanism was practiced at the Nemi Grove in Rome yearly, by wandering priests, until approximately 50 CE.[23]

A practice such as the ritual marriage of Limnaia between a queen and a god such as Dionysos — making the god, in effect, both *king* and *sacrifice* — would make human sacrifice obsolete, since Dionysos himself is inherently both sacrificer and sacrifice.[24] It is from the rites of Limnaia that Dionysos receives his appellation *Sosipolis*, or "city's savior." While the act of human sacrifice was not isolated to ancient Greece, the Limnaia was practiced solely in the Greek sphere: Outside this geographical area, human sacrificial rituals continued in their ancient and literal form well into the sixth century CE and, in some places, continue to this day.[25] The Anthesteric title "Sosipolis" is almost certainly where the Christians derived the appellation for (not to mention the underpinning concept of) of their own Savior, King of Kings.[26]

Two distinct and seemingly mutually-exclusive myths of Dionysos and Ariadne hail from this same king-sacrifice motif. In one version of the myth, Ariadne is killed by Dionysos, while in the second version, she is rescued by and wed to Dionysos.[27] When one realizes that whenever king sacrifice was practiced, his queen and entire household were often sacrificed simultaneously,[28] the apparent disparity between the Ariadne myths disappears and again it can be seen that the practice of human sacrifice (this time of the queen and household) becomes obsolete when a godform such as Dionysos becomes the symbolic transitional king. In such a religious system, the queen is wed to a continuously dying and reborn god, and is thereby rescued from death in the same way that a mortal king who accepts that sort of spiritual complex among his people is spared a sacrificial death by having his queen ceremonially taken to wife by Deity, who becomes, in essence, both transitional king and tanist.[29]

Furthermore, by performing the act of consummation with the god, the queen symbolically saves *everyone in the tribe or city* from death. A theatrical re-enactment of the transitional king/scapegoat (*pharmakos*) sacrificial observance may be found in Euripides' *Bacchae*, in which Dionysos tells Pentheus the king: *You and you alone shall suffer for this city*, leading him as a scapegoat through the streets of Thebes. Many scholars, such as Zeitlin, feel that the archetypal enemies of Dionysos in fact represent alternate versions of the god himself.[30]

While the women of the city took part in the erotic events of Choës night within Athens, all men of Athens were required to take part in the night-long symposion in the Temple *en Limnais* on the outskirts of the city.[31] Burkert, in *Homo Necans* (228), theorizes that the chant, "Out, out, you Keres! The Anthesteria is over!" was not in reference to the shades which lingered on, in hope of rebirth, after the offering made to them on the 13th day of Anthesterion, but in reference to non-Athenian men — perhaps those who had brought wine casks in from the country for the transfer of the beverage into amphorae — who had been allowed access to the women of Athens on Choës, the Anthesteric day of pollution.

The Day of the Potholes

A ritual offering anciently known as *Chytroi*, made to the spirits who rose into the living world when the wine pithoi were breached, was traditionally performed on the 13th day of Anthesterion. Classically, the offering ceremony was overseen by the priests of Hermes Cthonios (a Dionysian-syncretistic godform).[32] The Chytroi ritual marked a "return to normal" after the topsy-turvy, ghost-and erotica-filled days of the 11th and 12th.[33]

A customary offering of cooked grains and seeds — dedicated to the cthonic Deities and ancestors by being placed into naturally-occurring fissures in the earth[34] — took place near the Temple of Dionysos *en Limnais*, outside the city proper. Swings were set up over the half-buried pithoi outside the Temple of Dionysos Limnaios, and maidens would play on the swings (*aiora*), a symbolic enactment of life following death following life in rhythmic and apparently endless progression.[35]

Following the Chytroi offering and ritual swinging, specially-chosen young men (*Kouretes*: Roman, *Lupercai*)[36] would bless and purify the multitudes by scourging anyone they could catch with rawhide thongs soaked in water,[37] after which the scourgers and any lingering ancestral spirits would be symbolically chased away and banished from the city by the newly-purified worshippers.[38] Anciently, the practice of scourging in order to purify, bless, or consecrate was also done to the earth.[39] The Chytrogia portion of the Anthesteria was not unlike — and was probably directly related to — the Roman festival of Lupercalia, held in the Roman month of *Februa*, a name descriptive of the strips of hide used by the young men chosen to perform the act of scourging.[40]

The seed-and-grain offering of the ancient Hellenic Chytrogia festival is still served in modern times, an observance-related food called *kolyva*, a term derived from the ancient Greek word for the marsh-pits into which the Chytroi offering was made, *kolymbœthra*. Kolyva, prepared by members of the Greek Orthodox Church in observance of the end of the Lenten period, is also served at wakes and to mark the anniversary of a death. A similar recipe, known as *kutia*, is made and served at all important religious functions among the members of the Eastern Orthodox church in Russia. For the Russian recipe, see page 532 of *Please to the Table*, by Anya von Bremzen and John Welchman.[41]

The offering of old was prepared from numerous types of seeds and grains mixed with honey. The modern one includes a mixture of grains such as wheat, barley, rice and oats, as well as seeds such as buckwheat, sesame, and poppy, cooked together and mixed with honey, fruits, and herbs — raisins, figs, dates, pomegranates, parsley, and mint. Nuts are also sometimes added.

All Athenians, including children, assembled at dawn in an area near the Dionysian Temple in the Marsh. A priest would have sung or recited ceremonial liturgies to accompany the mixed-seed offering, which anciently was never eaten by the worshippers or priests themselves. It was felt that the Chytrogia offering was the food of the dead, and to partake of it would warrant the eater a sacrificial fate. Prior to the offering of mixed seeds and honey, a specially-chosen girl or unmarried woman poured out an offering of pure water (*hydrophoria*) on the ground as a bloodless libation to the ancestors and cthonic Deities.[42]

The offering of the kolyva and "chasing away" of the Kouretes was, at least in part, a propitiation of malign or "hungry" spirits, who would ostensibly attach themselves to the Kouretes (those who had already "given away" their blessings) and go with them, leaving the rest of the people, and their habitations, in peace. The Hellenic chant, "Out, you Keres, the Anthesteria is over!" may have been in reference to the "wild spirits" of the murderous Kouretes,[43] in reference to "bad ghosts" — to which the ancients attributed illness, poor harvests, infertility of animals or the land, and sometimes war — or both.[44]

In very ancient times, and perhaps in other parts of Greece, any person chosen to be chased away may actually have been ritually killed and offered up to the spirits or Deities as a dual scapegoat and intercession offering (*pharmakos*),[45] as was done in the Roman Groves of Nemi and as humans have performed worldwide from time immemorial.[46] Human sacrifice tended to be particularly likely when times were bad, and it appears to be a persistent force among human cultures. Modern sacrificial ceremonies have been revealed, for instance, among semi-Christian *brujos* of South America.[47] Even among cultures which no longer perform such sacrifice, its practice and potential spiritual ramifications still hold an honored place in both myth and society — the tale of Isaac and the ram among practitioners of Judaism, for example, or the Christian belief in Jesus as the supreme sacrifice, whose flesh and blood figure as the consecratory meal on a weekly basis.

Oulochytai

The Anthesteric chytrogia is a form of bloodless pit-offering undertaken for appeasement of those ancestral spirits to whom the sexual excesses of the Anthesteria did not grant a reincarnate status.[48] This time-honored rite gave rise to the practice of *oulochytai* — "(that which is done) in memory of ancient times" — which was the custom of sprinkling grain upon the hearth where the daily food would be prepared.[49] This was the first act of the day for any individual in ancient or Classical Greece, and the observance was dedicated to "Hestia, first and last."[50]

All altars (Olympian, ancestral, or cthonic) and hearths were sanctified by oulochytai prior to any offering or sacrifice (*iereia*). Olympian altars were also circled three times by all attendants in procession prior to any sacrificial rite.[51] Salt was occasionally mixed with the grain used for oulochytai, but this was almost certainly an Imperial innovation.[52] In any case, the sprinkling of grain or salt acts to sanctify the surface upon which they have been sprinkled, just as certainly as blood would do.[53] *Chernips* (ritual hand-washing) basins were found at the entrance of every temple. The water in them may have been purified by "firing" — thrusting hot torches or coals into the water — or it may have been purified by the addition of salt.[54]

The Making of Cthonic Sacrifices, Offerings, and Prayers

Cthonic sacrifices, offerings, and prayers differed from Olympian sacrifices, offerings, and prayers in many important ways;[55] for one thing, pits, urns, or flat areas (such as graves or stones flush with the ground) were utilized instead of standing altars. The Olympic altar was a raised platform or *bomoi*, whereas altars to the ancestors and cthonic Deities were ground-level *eskharai* or pit-*bothroi*.[56] Cthonic offerings (other than those of *enagismoi*) were usually bloodless, and depending upon circumstance, they may have also been fireless, wineless, or any mixture of these three things.[57]

A cthonic animal offering might also have been a holocaust, in which every part of the sacrifice would be consumed by fire,[58] as opposed to the customary Olympian fire-offering in which the meat is simply cooked and the gods are invited to a communal feast, of which worshippers and clerics also partake.[59] Cthonic offerings — votive or other — were usually considered arrheton (taboo, untouchable, unmentionable, the profanation of which carried dire consequences) once they had been offered up and, unlike Olympian* ritual votive gifts, cthonic offerings could not be touched, consumed, or even looked upon by either worshipper or cleric — hence the tendency to place such offerings into natural or man-made chasms, such as kolymbæthra or bothroi. [60] As can be seen, the word for the man-made bothros trench is derived from

---

* For a complete rendition of *Olympian*-style sacrificial ritual, which is outside the scope of this book, see: *http://www.cs.utk.edu/~mclennan/BA/NS.html* Another good source regarding the many different forms of sacrificial ritual is: *http://www.student.ipfw.edu/~gingkw01/SACRIFICESOURCES.htm*

bœthra, the natural marsh or karst pit. Many cultures have been known to cast precious objects into swamps, lakes, wells or pits in offering; it is likely that this evolved into the practice of casting coins into fountains.

Cthonic prayers and litanies were usually whispered or altogether silent, and ad-lib as opposed to rote, particularly when specific blessings were requested from the cthonic Deities — even if the prayer was requested of a cleric on behalf of a worshipper.[61] Another differentiation between the Olympian and cthonic rites is that the former were usually diurnal, while the latter were almost always nocturnal or, occasionally, crepuscular.[62] Sacrifices made to the winds were also cthonic in nature.[63]

Animal sacrifice was viewed in a vastly different light in the ancient world than it is in the modern American, cellophane-wrapped-meat culture, where it is largely considered to be barbaric and cruel (even while the steak is searing on the grill). In fact, the use of any animal for food in all segments of the ancient and Classical world had to be, by law (as it still is for followers of the Orthodox Jewish faith, in order for the food to be Kosher and acceptable for consumption), an act of sacrifice — an act which invited the Divine to the table, to witness a life taken on behalf of the living.

The words "sacred" and "sacrifice" come from a single root word, "sang-," from which the meaning of sacrifice is literally derived: "Sanctify," or *to sprinkle with blood*.[64] The modern world has generally forgotten the ancient originations of the words which, to its collective consciousness, say "most holy"; and few non-scholars realize that animal sacrifice in the ancient world — which refers to both the large-scale city-wide festival sacrifices and a country peasant's weekly pot of rabbit stew — amounted to the only flesh all lower and most middle-class city-dwellers ever ate. The thrice-daily meal with meat as a main course is a relatively modern extravagance.[65]

In a culture which performs ritual sacrifice, blood from the sacrifice serves particular purposes. It may be spilled upon the ground to propitiate or honor ancestral spirits, or as a medium for luring such spirits away from one area and into another.[66] To the ancient Hellenes, blood spilled around the perimeter of an area would sanctify the area in this manner, keeping vengeful spirits occupied with the blood (the ancients regarded blood as the force of life itself) and therefore outside the sanctified area. It was also believed that sacrificial blood had the capacity to bless, unite, rectify, or rebuild,[67] as shown by the old-Norse word "bløt," from which English and related Germanic languages derive such words as "bless," "build," and "blood."[68] Such was probably the use of the

Eleusinic piglets sacrificed during *myesis*, their blood used in some form of aspersion blessing rather than — or in unison with — water.[69]

The Cthonic Rites of Enagismoi, Sphagia, and Nephalia

The sacrificial ceremony of *enagismoi* was a form of spiritual rectification — a cleansing and forgiveness ceremony which brought the worshipper's immediate needs to the attention of the gods by, in effect, bringing the individual nearer the cthonic Deities (all enagismoi and related *sphagia* rituals were cthonic in nature).

One of the Initiatory rites in the cult of Cybele was a form of enagismoi: An initiate stood in a pit overlaid by a strong wooden lattice upon which a bull was sacrificed. The person in the pit would be immersed in the bull's blood, then removed from the pit and very thoroughly scrubbed with water and clay, sand, soap, or any admixture of the three.[70] It is from such a practice that Christians derived the sacred concept of "being washed in the Blood of the Lamb" for remission of sin. The word *sphagia* refers to the "offscourings" left behind after the enagismoi ritual had concluded. As is noted elsewhere in this book, *what is done* by a Pagan person is an acknowledgment of what is believed, so Pagan offscouring and rectification were not figurative allusions, but literally-performed acts. It was the offscourings themselves which were given to the cthonic gods, as the "bad" which, it was hoped, the Deities would work transformation upon.

In the enagismoi ceremony proper, a small bothros was dug and an animal slaughtered over it. Occasionally, the animal would also be made to bleed around the perimeter of a place in order to sanctify the entire area where the ritual would be performed; but the bulk of its blood would be caught in a bowl above the bothros.[71] The individuals seeking rectification would immerse part of themselves — most commonly one or both hands — in the bowl of blood. As in all cthonic rites which allowed animal sacrifice — and enagismos was most emphatically directed toward divine absolution with the aid of underworld Deities — the head of the sacrificial animal was held downward at the time of sacrifice rather than up, as opposed to the general Olympian sacrifice in which the head of the animal was held toward the sky, the Olympian realm.[72]

The blood in this sense was a sacred object to which sins, illness, bad habits et al. "stuck." Enagismos is the only sacrificial ceremony in which blood was offered to an underworld Deity. The bloodied individuals would scrub away every last trace of blood from their skin, after which specially-consecrated individuals — *engytristrai* — poured the remainder of the blood and the offscourings into the bothros. Enagismos was also practiced by warriors just prior to conflict — as was holocaust, suggesting the method by which the bodies of animals used in enagismoi rituals were offered up.[73]

The ceremony of nephalia was always a bloodless and wineless one; *nephalia* means "bloodless and wineless offering." A bothros would be dug longwise from east to west, and offerings were given while the worshipper faced toward the west. A mixture of water, oil, milk, and honey was the most common offering, but eggs, wool tufts, cakes, figs, or other fruits might also be given. As the worshipper made the offerings, prayers and requests were whispered to the cthonic gods. The temporary bothros dug for nephalia was covered with nine sprays of olive leaves (other evergreens may also have been acceptable) when a petitioner's offerings and prayers were finished.[73] The bothros into which sphagia was poured was likewise covered.

CHAPTER FIVE: AGRAI

The place classically known as *Agrai* was located on the banks of the Ilissus River on the Greek peninsula near Athens.[1] The word "Agrai" actually pertains to both the place-name and the Dionysian ritual held there. The rites of Agrai themselves are also known as the "lesser Mysteries"; similar forms of "lesser" or primary initiation were also held elsewhere in the Greek-speaking world — Macedonia and the Pontus, Magna Graeca, the islands of the Aegean, even Pompeii and central Italy.[2] The Agrai ceremony was held late in the month of Anthesterion,[3] as the initiatory experience that set the stage for over half a year of Mystery teachings which would culminate in the rites of *Eleusinia*, the "greater Mysteries." The seven months between lesser and greater Mystery ceremonies mythically represented both Kore's period of sojourn in the House of Hades, and the seven months that Dionysos was nurtured in Semele's womb.[4] Though the lesser Mysteries are often referred to solely as rites of Dionysos, they were equally rites of Persephone, as inscriptions of vows taken by ancient dedicants confirm.[5]

According to Diodorus Siculus (IV: 14), the rites of Agrai were developed as a form of divine restitution which would cleanse Heracles of his murderer's taint, since his desire was to be received at Eleusis, and no person guilty of unabsolved murder could receive the visionary blessings bestowed at the Eleusinia: "Demeter instituted the Lesser Mysteries in honor of Heracles, that she might purify him of the guilt he had incurred in the slaughter of the centaurs." Since *all* individuals were required to undergo the purificatory rites of the lesser Mysteries before seeking admission to the greater, it may be inferred that "murder," in the sense meant by the Mysteries, included the killing of animals for food. Such a conception is part and parcel of human consciousness, and ritual forms are created by all societies in order to attempt to assuage the guilt inherent in killing to eat, as well as the fear of our own deaths — a knowledge eternally intertwined with eating-guilt.[6] Such awareness was displayed by the Pagan Greeks in their New Year's rite of *Bouphonia*, but it reached a spiritual *sin qua non* within the lesser and greater Mystery ceremonies.

Adults of all professions, both sexes, and every class, from all lands known to have established trade with ancient Greece, sought out the Hellenic Mystery initiations — the first, because it offered spiritual rectification and absolution, and the second because it claimed to bring individuals face to face with the gods and with their own ancestors, as well as to offer a glimpse of what lay beyond life, a glimpse which initiates of Eleusis claimed could utterly remove the fear of death from a person's heart.[7] As in any other initiatory rite performed within any religion — from aboriginal ceremonies to the sevenfold rites of Mithras or the baptismal initiation of the Christian Church[8] — the Agrai ritual took new dedicants through a series of actions meant to symbolize the cycles of death and rebirth.

Both the Agrai initiation and the Eleusinian *myesis* ritual apparently include a fascinating recreation of this death and rebirth motif by treating the initiate as a seed[9] which is buried in the earth (the initiate was covered with chalk, white clay, or a mixture of both), thereby "hidden away" for a period of time while it is growing (ancient Dionysian initiates underwent a period of isolation within a cave or special "mystery house," an *oikos*),[10] comes unbound from the seed-coat and emerges into the air (the initiate underwent a secondary rite after the isolation period), overcomes the trials of new life (depending upon the intent of the initiate, scourging and scarification rituals took place; this may also be considered to represent the *reaping* of a plant for consumption), and is watered (the initiate performed a ritual bath or *loutrophoria*, which may also be considered to represent washing away the soil from a plant prior to consumption). If the "trial" and "ablution" rites are seen as *consumptive* rather than *growth* re-enactments, then the act of primary initiation into the Hellenic Mysteries was, in fact, a paradox, wherein the initiates came to their "new life" through the enactment of a rite which symbolized an eventual death.

Such an underlying symbolism in the lesser Mystery gives a more immediate, intimate meaning to the ear of barley shown to the *mystai* by the Hierophant during the Eleusinia ceremony: Indeed, it could be inferred that the initiate was *equated with* the ear of corn in the greater Mysteries, in much the same way he was equated with Dionysos in the lesser Mysteries.[11]

The initiation steps found in the lesser Mysteries of Agrai also appear to reflect stages of primordial burial rituals;[12] anointing the body with clay ochre and burying it, dessicating it through fire or, in the case of cremation, releasing the spirit of the deceased through the smoke given off by fire, and propitiating the deceased afterwards with liquid offerings poured on the grave, which might be symbolized either by the ritual bath or by the libation the dedicant was given.[13] As may be inferred from these comparative metaphors, the act of spiritual initiation is ancient, indeed.

These passages were meant to be representative of the mythic births, deaths, and rebirths of Dionysos himself. As Stephen of Byzantium explained in the second century CE: "The lesser mysteries performed at Agra or Agrae were an imitation of what happened about Dionysos."[14] Dionysos, as previously noted, is god of indestructible life, continuously regenerated from death. The doctrines of rebirth and reincarnation or metempsychosis (transmigration of the soul) were Orphic — one sect of the Dionysian mystery religion — as were a number of Hellenic Mystery rites by the Classical period,[15] and the pervasiveness of these beliefs among initiates was noted by both Diogenes and Empedocles: "Once on a time a youth was I, and I was a maiden, a bush, a bird, and a fish with scales that gleam in the ocean." Such afterlife ideologies were taken up in early Byzantine times by the Stoics.[16]

Inscribed gold sheets found in the tombs of certain initiates known as *Bacchoi* or *Iobacchoi*, as well as the writings of ancient authors regarding initiatory rites similar to those of Agrai, give some clue as to the nature and sequence of the rites performed during the lesser Mystery ceremony.[17] Harrison's summary of several of these tablets, found in multiple graves in Compagno, Italy, is as follows (the lacunae are intentional):

> Out of the Pure I come, Pure queen of them below, Eukles and Euboleus, and other gods and daemons: For I also avow me that I am of your blessed race. And I have paid the penalty for deeds unrighteous, whether it be that fate laid me low or the gods immortal, or...*...with star-flung thunderbolt...I have flown out of the sorrowful weary wheel; I have passed with eager feet to the circle desired; a kid, I have fallen into milk; I have sunk beneath the bosom of Despoina, queen of the underworld; I have passed with eager feet from the circle desired: And now I come suppliant to holy Phersephoneia, that of her grace she receive me to the seats of the hallowed. Happy and blessed one, thou shalt be god instead of mortal.[18]

The above summary has an undertone of myth to it. Within the mythological sphere, there appear to be three distinct tiers: metaphorical mythology, moralistic mythology, and ritualistic mythology. Metaphorical mythology deals with first and final causes, and with psychological issues: Birth, death, reproduction, creation, and personal growth are subjects commonly found in the metaphorical myth structure. Moralistic myths deal with the proper place of the individual in society. The tales of Icarus, who spurned advice and flew too high, and Narcissus, whose self-love earned him a vegetative fate, are examples of moralistic myths.

Ritual-based myths often appear to be amalgamations of metaphorical and moralistic myths, but the message of the ritualistic myth tends toward ambiguity or outright incomprehensibility, as opposed to the insightful intent of the metaphorical myth or the clear-cut value of the moralistic myth. Ritualistic mythos also compounds over time into lengthy saga form, since rituals with similar contents or purpose tend to overlap as a culture's ritualistic patterns continuously evolve and devolve: Ritualistic myth preserves lines of ritual overlap as well as pre-existing ritual pattern. The Homeric *Hymn to Demeter* is a ritualistic myth, as is the myth of Dionysos and the Titans.[19] Stephen of Byzantium's comment on the rites of the lesser Mysteries might have been more accurately stated thusly: *The tale of what happened to Dionysos is symbolic of the rites of Agrai.*[20] Euripides incorporated elements of the ritualistic mythos of Agrai into segments of his play *The Bacchae*:

> Acheloüs' roaming daughter,
> Holy Dirce, virgin water,
> Bathed he not of old in thee
> The Babe of God, the Mystery?
> When from out the fire immortal
> To himself his God did take him,
> To his own flesh, and bespake him:
> "Enter now life's second portal,
> Motherless mystery; lo I break
> Mine own body for thy sake,
> Thou of the Two-fold Door, and seal thee
> Mine, O Bromios" — thus he spake —
> "and to this thy land reveal thee."[21]

Numerous artifacts obtained from ancient gravesites, and the wonderfully preserved walls of the *Villa de Mysteri* oikos in Pompeii, provide additional information on how the rites of Agrai were performed. It is from these several sources, as well as from the work of modern scholars, that I have formulated the particulars of the Agrai ritual. All other rituals in this book are devised in a similar manner.

The Strengthening Dust

> Out of the Pure I come, Pure queen of them below, and Eukles and Euboleus, and other gods and daemons: For I also avow me that I am of your blessed race. And I have paid the penalty for deeds unrighteous...

Several elements of the lesser Mysteries might be considered "paying the penalty": Fasting, scourging, and scarification are all acknowledged components of the rites of Dionysos and Persephone.[22] However, there is more to the first portion of the tablet than the redress of a penalty; some kinship has been acknowledged, for which the dedicant expects recognition, and it is likely that the kinship alluded to is implicit in the "penalty" itself.[23] As Orphic Hymn 37 states:

> Titans, glorious children of Ouranos and Gaia,
> forebears of our fathers, who dwell down below
> in Tartarean homes, in the earth's bowels.
> From you stem all toiling mortals,
> the creatures of the sea and of the land, the birds,
> and all generations of this world come from you,
> and upon you I call to banish harsh anger,
> if some earthly ancestor of mine stormed your homes.[24]

I believe that at least part of the "penalty" alluded to in the gold burial tablet would be to reenact the role played by the ravenous Titans, who composed part of the mythic ancestry of humankind. According to Orphic generative myth, humans were considered to be dual-natured: Titanic — or unrighteous and doomed to "dwell in Tartarus" — and Dionysian, godly and pure heirs to the eternal life which that presumes, once they had "paid the penalty for deeds unrighteous" by being properly purified at the initiatory rites of Agrai and Eleusis.[25] According to modern scholarly and ancient empirical accounts, at the beginning of the Agrai ritual the initiates would anoint themselves with chalk, limestone dust, or white clay.[26] According to Harpocration:

> ...They used to besmear those who were being purified for initiation with clay and pitch. In this ceremony they were mimetically enacting the myth told by some persons, in which the Titans, when they mutilated Dionysos, wore a coating of gypsum in order not to be identified. The custom fell into disuse, but in later days they were plastered with gypsum out of convention.[27]

The substance initiates daubed themselves with in order to symbolize their "unrighteous" natures was undoubtedly a whitish clay ochre (*pælós*, which appears to hail from an ancient root that means "dust (or dirt) of strength"),[28] formed from the decomposition of acidic stone, with chalk or powdered limestone (called *titanos* in Katharevousan Greek) added for additional whitening. What has been translated in the writings of Harpocration as *gypsum* is a mistake. Gypsum ($CaSo_4 + 2H_2O$) is a hard, water-soluble mineral accretion that resembles ice shards; but ancient sources speak of heavily whitened faces and bodies.[29] Gypsum is primarily found in clay deposits, which may explain the confusion in terms.

Molecular alteration of igneous rock into clay takes eons, and is most common in areas which have been subjected to long inundation by brackish water — swampland, estuary, or alluvial deposition areas. Dionysos was known both anciently and Classically as "god of the marshes": Thousands of years after the swamplands of Athens had drained away, the one and only temple of Dionysos was called *en Limnais* — "of the Marshes." Altars to Dionysos and other cthonic deities were not built over the ground, but dug deeply into the "Tartarean realm," where soils such as clay — as well as deposits of gypsum, limestone and chalk — might be found.[30]

The gypsum-as-stucco conflation also occurs in a later portion of the Titan myth, in which Athena (or, in some versions, Artemis) encases that portion of Dionysos' body which the Titans could not consume — his heart, a Mystery euphemism for the phallus — in gypsum and hides it in a basket, out of which *Liknites* ("god of the winnowing basket") would be reborn.[31] Why encase the Divine Child's member in gypsum? The phalloi "hearts" (*kardia*) hidden in the Dionysian liknon were composed of figwood (*krade*), not gypsum.[32] However, the mysterious votive objects of the *Skiraphoria* ceremony, held in Athens at midsummer, were said to be made partially of gypsum, and they were carried concealed in a basket — an indissoluble link between the Mystery ceremonies of Dionysos and the patron goddess of Athens.[33] It may well be that *gypsum* is a misinterpretation in this context as well, and that what is being referred to in this portion of the Titanic myth cycle is the substance from which stucco derives its modern Greek name — a mysterious mineral which can be woven into a soft cloth that would be a more logical item under which to hide the sacred phallus nestled within the liknon, a mineral which, like the embryonic Dionysos, is wholly resistant to the fires of Zeus: *asbestos.*

Campbell, in *...Primitive Mythology* (101), notes that pale soils, resembling the Hellenic *pælós*, are often used to smear the bodies of aboriginal hunters, a practice dating from some unknowable time in the Paleolithic, allowing the hunters to mask the smell of their own bodies and to blend into dun grasslands or taupe sands and thereby ambush and kill their prey — an image not unlike the ravenous Titans plotting to kill and eat Dionysos, that infant god who is so often linked to the animal epiphany in Greek myth.[34] Prior to the rites of Agrai, as with all Mystery rites in the ancient Greek world, pre-purification had to be undergone. According to both Campbell and Young, the same held true for our ancient forebears prior to the hunt.[35]

Abstinence and Sacred Dreaming

> ...Whether it be that fate laid me low or the gods immortal, or...*...with star-flung thunderbolt...

At least two scholars have observed that the lacunae in the middle of this statement is purposeful, not caused by wear to the surface of the thin gold leaf upon which it was written; to paraphrase Harrison, it is like a song or hymn which is so well known that only the first and last lines of it need to be reiterated for its full meaning to come clear — a *synthema* not unlike the arcane utterance of Eleusis: "I fasted, I drank the kykeon, I took from the chest, I worked, then put back into the basket, and from the basket into the chest."[36] I theorize that in the *synthema* on the gold tablets, as much as in the *synthema* of Eleusis, full iteration of the subject to which the dedicant refers is *arrheton*, forbidden to describe except through myth and symbol. Therefore, it is to the minutiae of myth and the symbols given by the dedicant that we must look to find the unspoken meaning of the purposeful lacunae.

As noted previously, Euripides utilized many initiatory symbols in his play *The Bacchae*. C. K. Williams, in the opening lines of his translation of this play (3), has the god Dionysos utter nearly the same words translated from the initiatory scrap of gold: "Her midwife was the lightning bolt that killed her." As the ancient natal myth of Dionysos relates, it was the fiery lightning of Zeus which released the god prematurely from his mother's womb.[37] The great god of the Greeks took up his undeveloped son and sewed him into his own thigh as a surrogate womb. As noted in Chapter One, I theorize that this is an allegory for the making of wine. It has been suggested that Greek wine was ameliorated with mind-altering herbs during its brewing.[38] In a similar vein, the nascence of mushrooms, particularly mind-altering ones, was connected in ancient Hellenic belief with lightning storms.[39] Since it was common knowledge anciently that wines were recognized to be carriers of potent herbs, and that mushrooms — a Dionysian symbol — were believed to be scattered over the surface of the earth by lightning, the phrase "or...with star-flung thunderbolt" would have been capable of suggesting entheogenic agents to the Hellene mind without further exposition.[40]

The works of ancient authors regarding the lesser and greater Mystery ceremonies reveal that there were mandatory, purificatory fasting strictures imposed upon initiates prior to both the Agrai and the Eleusinia. These strictures involved particular types of food, including animal flesh, eggs, and legumes; proscriptions from later Classical times may also have included abstinence from foods considered to be the purview of cthonic deities, such as turnips, fish and crayfish, berries, okra, and apples.[41] Pythagorean Orphic sects extended these strictures into a constant act of piety, as related by this Euripidean fragment preserved by Porphyry:

> My days have run, the servant I,
> Initiate, of Idaean Jove;
> Where midnight Zagreus roves, I rove;
> I have endured his thunder-cry;
>
> Fulfilled his red and bleeding feasts;
> Held the Great Mother's mountain flame;
> I am Set Free and named by name
> A Bacchos of the Mailed Priests.
>
> Robed in pure white, I have borne me clean
> From man's vile birth and coffined clay,

and exiled from my lips alway
Touch of all meat where Life hath been.[42]

It is recorded that the lesser Mystery initiation included a sacrament of raw meat, a very emphatic ending to an ascetic period during which meat was forbidden — a ritual extreme, which served to mark out a space of sacred time.[43]

Abstinence prior to the Hellenic Mystery initiations extended to include forgoing sexual intercourse as well as the imbibing of alcoholic beverages.[44] I theorize that such abstentions derive from fairly universal and probably very ancient traditions surrounding the use of mind-altering drugs in a ritual setting.[45]

As noted in the first chapter, Hades and Dionysos were considered by the Pagan Hellenes to be alternate aspects of the same multifaceted, paradoxical godform. In the regions surrounding ancient Phrygia — the putative birthplace of Orphism — the shape-changing Dionysian archetype of death and rebirth was known as *Sabazios*.[46] According to Aristophanes, the nocturnal, initiatory "rites of Sabazios bring sleep."[47] It has long been surmised that some form or forms of drug were utilized by worshippers of the epiphanic god Dionysos; speculations range from belladonna to Amanita muscaria and opium, to more dubious contenders such as ivy or the bulbs of the wild crocus (derivatives of which are used in modern medicine to cure gout),[48] one of the many flowers mentioned in the Orphic *Hymn to Demeter* that recounts the abduction of Persephone by Hades:

> ...She was playing far from Demeter
> lady of the harvest who reaps with a golden sickle,
> gathering flowers with the daughters of Ocean,
> roses and crocus and beautiful violets,
> iris, hyacinths, and the narcissus.
> Earth brought forth the narcissus as a wonderful lure for the blossoming girl
> according to Zeus' plan to please Hades, who receives all.
> And from its root grew a hundred heads, smelling a smell so sweet
> that the whole broad sky above and all the earth laughed and the salty swell of the sea.
> The girl was amazed and stretched out both her hands to take the marvelous bauble.
> But as she did, the earth gaped open and Lord Hades, whom we will all meet,
> burst forth with his immortal horses...[49]

I theorize that it was, in fact, a flower that brought the cthonic deities of Agrai to initiates isolated for a period within a sanctified cave or oikos. As Proculus noted, regarding Hellenic Mystery rites: "In *all* the rites of initiation and mysteries the gods exhibit their shapes as many, and they appear changing often from one form to another, and now they are made manifest in the emission of formless light, now taking human shape, now again in other and different form,"[50] (italics my own). Harrison, in her detailed treatise on religious beliefs and actions pertaining to Mystery rites, *Prologomena to the Study of Greek Religion* (515), explains that literal epiphanic visitation by Deity to a number of people was the ultimate goal of all Mystery initiations.

Such an epiphany can occur in one of two ways: via human impersonation and intervention, or by the attainment of ecstatic states. The theatrically savvy Greeks would have been unlikely to experience a state of epiphany and transformation because of the appearance of a costumed mortal; furthermore, as noted in the chapter detailing the rites of Eleusinia, there are no extant written or artistic records which recount the participatory role of such an individual or individuals in either the lesser or greater Mystery rites. For the latter reason alone, such a method of epiphanic appearance in the Hellenic Mysteries can be judged, at the very least, unlikely. Also, as Juvenal noted when commenting on a Mystery cult: "Nothing there will be imitated as in play, everything will be done in earnest."[51]

Individuals may attain internal ecstatic states which alter their perception of external environmental stimuli through two avenues: by utilizing prolonged physical exertion past the point of exhaustion (often accompanied by rigorous fasting and occasionally by the infliction of physical pain, as in the Plains Indian Sundance ritual held each midsummer), or by imbibing entheogenic agents. The primary drawback of the first method is that the visionary results gained are usually haphazard and inconsistent — both among large groups of people and over time — since the method is dependent upon individual stamina, fortitude, and metabolism, as well as a willingness and outright ability to undergo such a ceremony all the way to its conclusion. The second method, which in many cultures which utilize entheogens is melded to the first method to some extent (by requiring individuals to fast and maintain days-long vigils, for example[52]), is dependent upon a consistent setting, which the ritual itself provides, and upon the dependable chemical reactions of an entheogen upon the human nervous system; thus, the second method of visionary induction is many times more reliable among groups of people over time.

It is the opinion of the author that the sleepy yet ecstatic, epiphanous portion of the rites of Agrai were conducted with the aid of poppy resin — opium — either mixed into a beverage and taken as a libation, or combined with honey and oily crushed seeds, such as sesame, and formed into cakes.[53]

There are mythic connections between the pomegranate of Persephone's eternal *palingesia* and the poppy capsule; both of these fruits were considered *symbolon mysterion*, wherein the pomegranate brings Persephone, Queen of the Underworld, to the house of Hades via a divine death that unites her to Hades in a sacred marriage. It is death, or an abduction by Dionysos (who is also Hades, Sabazios and Zagreus), that is the meaning behind the primary initiation rites.[54] The poppy capsule not only resembles the sacred pomegranate fruit that mysteriously symbolizes a death that ultimately results in rebirth, but poppy gum, like Sabazios, brings both sleep and ecstatic visions. Graves, in his *Greek Myths*, gives direct ancient epigraphic rendering of Hellenic mythology and notes that Sabazios is a barley god, annually cut down (7.1). I theorize that, in fact, Sabazios was the god of the poppies which, to this day, grow among and ripen in unison with cereal crops, and which from time immemorial were prized for their milky sap, obtained through the careful scarifying of their immature seed heads, which resemble the pomegranate of Hellenic underworld mythology.

Harrison suggests that the Agrai libation was not wine but honeyed milk, and notes that sacramentalism was part of the rites of Agrai, since iconographic evidence reveals the ritual of *kernophoria* — sacramental food and drink presented to the dedicant in a vessel consisting of many tiny cups — as part of the lesser Mysteries as well as the greater.[55] During the Eleusinia, the libation consisted of a sacred roasted-barley drink called *kykeon*; however, this sacrament is not known to have been part of the ceremonies of Agrai. Several scholars note that early Christian rites appear to have been borrowed directly from Pagan ones, which leads me, too — in the absence of a more compelling argument — to note that until very recently, both Roman Catholic and Greek Orthodox churches welcomed their newly-baptized members into the sacrament service with a drink of milk and honey, and that such a sacramental drink would have made an excellent vehicle for poppy resin.[56] Also in common with Christian rites, as noted in a previous chapter, are allusions to ritual bathing or asperging in the sacred gold plates preserved in the tombs of Dionysian initiates: [57] Just such purifying ritual actions make up the central portion of all tablets found in the Compagno area.

Kernophoria, Loutrophoria, Liknophoria: Deeds Which Purify and Set Apart

...I have flown out of the sorrowful weary wheel;

To the Orphics, life, death, and rebirth were a "wheel" whose hub was the attainment of godhood itself, and the aspiration of all Bacchic initiates.[58] Undoubtedly, this is the literal meaning of the above statement. However, such a philosophy may have been embodied by any of several ritual acts or accoutrements recorded for the lesser Mystery ceremony at Agrai.

Isolating initiates within a space meant to symbolize either womb or tomb prior to rebirth is common to most Pagan spiritual initiations:[59] Hellenes used specially-prepared houses or even caves, the latter known to the ancients as "temples of the cthonic gods."[60] Any area given such great religious importance could easily have represented a "sorrowful, weary wheel" to an initiate. The dedicant was further isolated from his surroundings by the use of a long, opaque veil, often held on the head of the dedicant by a wreath.[61]

To the ancient Hellenes, the head-wreath symbolized union with the divine. Apart from its function in the Mysteries, it was used by only three other classes of people in Pagan Greek society: The highest clerics (*Hierophantes*), the honored dead, and couples being married.[62] The use of both veil and wreath in the Mysteries was, therefore, symbolic of the new status of a dedicant, who would be "married" to the god, as Persephone was married to Hades — a more detailed "marriage" of this kind took place during the Eleusinia ceremony — and who, by making particular statements which have been shown by archaeological science to have been part of the lesser Mysteries, was considered to be coeval with Dionysos, lord of death and rebirth.[63]

The general area in which the lesser Mysteries were held was considered to be a *temenos*, or consecrated boundary. Although *temenoi* usually marked out the space directly around a temple or altar,[64] there was no temple proper at Agrai, only the aforementioned oikos or cave, and no type of altar at all. Young, in *Origins...* (213, 222), notes that the bullroarer believed to have been used for certain Dionysian rites[65] invokes the god in the lesser Mysteries, just as the gong used in the greater Mysteries invokes the goddess,[66] and that it was probably the bullroarer which was used at Agrai to consecrate the sacred *temenos*, its sound forming a sort of "virtual temple": Indeed, Dionysos, an exceedingly difficult archetype to constrain or even describe thoroughly, had only one known temple in all of Greece — the Athenian temple *en Limnais*, which was open to worshippers only on Choës day of the *Anthesteria.*

Surviving texts of lesser Mystery initiation speak of stepping into, and out of, "the circle desired." The *temenos* of Agrai may have been this "circle." However, Harrison (590-596) observes that a marriage bath or *loutrophoria*, which most likely took place in a large round bronze tub, took place during the lesser Mysteries — the forerunner of the Christian baptism for the washing away of sins.[67] It is a documented fact that both *liknophoria* (sanctification of an individual via proximity to the *liknon*, or divine cradle-basket of Dionysos) and *loutrophoria* (ritual laving, bathing, or asperging) were performed at unspecified points during both greater and lesser Mystery ceremonials:[68] These acts, too, tell us that the Mysteries were forms of Divine marriage, since liknophoria and loutrophoria were commonplace rites of Pagan Greek marriage ceremonies.[69] A ritual bath within just such a tub in the center of the temenos of Agrai, which would also serve to wash away the physical evidence of Titanic guilt from the new initiate and leave him or her both symbolically and literally cleansed, might in fact be what the Compagno tablets refer to in the following stanza:

> I have passed with eager feet to the circle desired; a kid, I have fallen into milk;[70]

Phrases regarding "falling into milk," which may be found on nearly every gold-leaf tablet excavated from gravesites of Bacchic worshippers, have often been puzzled over by scholars, who admit that no record of a bath with milk added has ever been found among ancient or Classical Greco-Roman writings or artifacts.[71] I conjecture that the loutrophoria was not a *milk* bath, but a *milky* bath — an attestation not of the literal contents of the water, but of its symbolic appearance once the dedicant's skin had been washed free of the white, chalky clay which represented that portion of human nature which was Titanic and unclean. Through the ritual within "the circle desired," whether this was in reference to the loutrophoria tub or to the temenos of Agrai, an emblematic pollution symbolic of death and destruction was thus transmuted into something resembling the pure, nourishing liquid which gives life to the newly-born.

Scholars have long noted that a ceremony of enthronement was the first part of the ritual of Dionysian initiation.[72] This implies that the presentation of the *thyrsos* (the symbolic royal scepter of Dionysos) to the dedicant also occurs at the beginning, rather than at the end, of the ceremony. If, as I theorize, acts of scarification served to separate out specific Dionysian adherents from those undertaking the Agrai initiation only as a portal to the ceremonies of Eleusis,[73] then scarification and scourging rituals would also have occurred during the *thronosis* ceremony, in mimesis of the Titans cutting and flaying the sacred Child into pieces.

Following these rituals with the oblations and libations of the kernophoria would thus symbolically transform the dedicant — who up to that point represented the newly-born Dionysos — into the Titan.[74] If this progression is accurate, then the daubing with clay and chalk would have occurred at some point between thronosis and kernophoria. In the case of the scarified initiate, perhaps the mud was smeared over any pigment applied to the cuts, to seal in color and keep the wound from bleeding. The kernophoria itself, then, would have contained the sacramental "red and bleeding feast" of which the now-Titanic Dionysian dedicant was said to have partaken.

Honeyed milk containing an entheogenic "thunderbolt," given as libation during the kernophoria either before or after an oblation of raw meat, would fulfill the "meat cooked in milk" mythos of the Titans.[75] Poppy resin used in this way may also have been a late, Orphic ritualization of opium given anciently, perhaps in wine, to moderate pain — not of simple tattooing and scourging, but of complex, seemingly universal rituals of human sacrifice, when such an initiation was a real death and not just a mythologized, ritualistic one.[76] It would be at this point that the dedicant was veiled like a corpse and led into the oikos, symbolic of a tomb of rebirth.[77] The later removal of the Titanic clay by loutrophoria, the reciting of Orphic vows, and the liknophoria, including the ceremony of "the serpent in the bosom" — all performed after the new initiate re-emerged from the oikos — would then be symbolic of an initiate's journey through the House of Hades to the river of Memory, and a subsequent rebirth into (or marriage with) Dionysian godhood, as the mask-mirroring ceremony — almost certainly the final portion of the Agrai ritual — implies. If Agrai was, as Stephen of Byzantium noted, a mimesis of "what happened to Dionysos," then from several sarcophagus friezes relating the mythic life of Dionysos, the rites of thronosis with thyrsos, scourging, bathing, and liknophoria may be verified iconographically.[78]

That Which Thou Hadst Never Suffered Before

I have sunk beneath the bosom of despoina, queen of the underworld.

In the paintings found on the walls of the Villa de Mysteri in Pompeii, a female dedicant kneels upon the ground, her head and arms resting in the lap of a seated matron, as she is being scourged. The dedicant's head is quite literally beneath the bosom of the older lady, who in the mythic ritual context of the Agrai may very well represent *Despoina*, an appellation for Persephone, goddess of the lesser Mysteries wherever they happened to take place.[79] A slightly later admission on the Compagno tablets — "I have come to the seats of the hallowed" — may describe the literal seat of this initiator and its symbolic meaning; alternatively, the admission is speaking of the act of enthronement, performed for the new initiate at the outset of both the lesser and greater Mysteries.[80]

After the rites of kernophoria, loutrophoria, and liknophoria, the most notable of purification rituals among surviving artworks which detail the lesser Mysteries is ritual scourging.[81] Scourging is an ancient form of purification; simply put, to scourge is to "drive the evil out." In the parlance of the planting motif, to scourge is to *thresh*.[82] This implies that scourging was meant to be a painful ordeal, one that bad spirits — which might be causing an individual to behave less than ideally — would not want to stay and experience. However, documentation reveals that at certain festivals, such as the *Thargelia*, the act of scourging was painless and wholly symbolic. It seems that the ancients expected the spirits to flee *simply at the thought of* scourging, a spiritual practice which modern psychotherapists might call negative behavior modification. It is possible that the scourging rite performed at Agrai was equally symbolic.

As previously noted, the ceremony of Agrai was mythologically instituted by Demeter as a purification ceremony that would expiate the commission of both physical and spiritual crimes and allow a person to be "reborn" in spirit or, as portions of gold-leaf initiatory texts attest: "Bad have I fled, better I have found."

The ancients had an incomplete understanding of cause and effect; this led them to regard "(the) bad" — bad harvests, bad health, bad behavior — as the work of maleficent spirits, rather than the outcome of exhausted soil or bad seed, microorganisms or poor sanitation, and personal choice or mental instability.[83] What modern people call mulching the soil, following hygienic principles, and behavior modification therapy, our ancestors of the not-so-distant past would have called *performing acts of purification.*

Use of scourging by the Pagan Greeks to drive away evil *keres* is attested by the fact that the Hellenes regarded the unseen spirits which brought both pestilence and blessing, as well as the madness of love, to be winged figures; such creatures appear constantly on artwork depicting the lesser Mysteries.[84] Late Classical Hellenism used these ambivalent creatures as the template for Eros, god of romantic love. Christianity borrowed from the same mythology of unseen winged creatures of fate to develop the prototype of the modern angel.

It is known that some *mystai* were cut or tattooed with the mark of the ivy leaf, trellis, snake, goat, or similar Dionysian symbology, usually on the right arm or hand: a memento of the "new life" bestowed by the Mysteries in particular, or of the latent indestructibility of life in general.[85] It is thought by some scholars that the tattoo as religious symbol is a defining mark of the Thracian origin of Dionysos, since in Greco-Roman society at large, the tattoo was primarily the mark of the slave or the criminal, whereas in Thrace it was a mark signifying sanctity.[86]

Harrison notes a common saying of Classical Hellenism: Πολλοι μεν ναρθηκοφυροι, παγροι δε τε βακχοι, or: *Many hold the thyrsos, but few (of these) are Bacchoi.*[87] This statement may be grounded in the act of scarification as well as in ethical ideology; it is likely, considering the general meaning of the tattoo in Greco-Roman society, that only adherents of Dionysos, who at some point in their lives planned to be ministers of his rites, received the tattoo. However, all initiates held the *thyrsos* during their enthronement at the lesser Mystery ceremonial, when specially-chosen priests would dance around them and howl, in imitation of the Kouretes at the birth of Dionysos.[88]

Iobacchoi tablets found in other locations also relate the idea of *suffering* pertaining to the dedicants, as well as the ultimate outcome of that suffering:

> Welcome, thou who hast endured such suffering as thou hast never before suffered! Human, thou hast become a god; a kid, thou hast fallen into milk![89]

> ...[textual lacunae caused by wear or irremediable difficulties in translation]...but so soon as the spirit hath left the light of the sun, to the right...of Ennoia, then must man...being right wary in all things. Hail, thou who hast suffered the suffering. This thou hadst never suffered before. Thou art become God from Man. A kid thou art fallen into milk. Hail, hail to thee journeying on the right...Holy meadows and groves of Phersephoneia"[90]

The Serpent of Knowledge

> I have passed with eager feet from the circle desired: and now I come suppliant to holy Phersephoneia, that of her grace she receive me to the seats of the hallowed.

There were at least two aspects of the Classical lesser Mysteries which appear to be "borrowings" from Greece's northern neighbors of Thrace and Thessally. The first of these is a ritual involving a real or symbolic serpent.

Ancient authors speak of a "gold snake sliding through the bosom" of the initiate at some point during the Classical Agrai ceremony.[91] It is widely assumed that this pertains to a live or symbolic snake kept in the liknon; that this "snake blessing" represented a rebirth from the symbolic initiatory death, as well as oneness with the gods; and that it probably took place immediately after the liknophoria, when the sacred basket of Dionysos was opened and its contents revealed.[92]

The snake, which represents the ancestral soul to Hellenes both ancient and modern, was specifically associated with Dionysian Orphic rites. The Greek word for serpent remains *ophis*, while serpent is *phidai*: The nearest words having the same root are *euphia*, which means intelligence, and *sophia*, or wisdom. These roots are not associated with words relating to cunning, cleverness, knowledge, or skill. It was the quality of *wisdom* with which the serpent was identified — and continues to be identified — in the Greek mind. In other words, the etymology of the word "orphic" itself is probably derived from the same Katharevousan sources as "serpent" (*ophis/phidai*) and "wisdom" (*sophia*); assuming that the *or-* derives from a root which has to do with vision (as does the *or-* in "oracle"), it means "serpent-wise vision(ary)." It was *wisdom* the Orphic hoped to gain in this life, in preparation for the next, and the snake figured as the symbol of divine wisdom through continual rebirth, in Orphic rites and lore. Since many of the rituals that make up the Mysteries are known to be of Orphic origin or influence, particularly after about 600 BCE, I suspect that the snake ritual is specifically Orphic in derivation, an implant from northern locales.[93]

The snake, as well as the fish, has for millennia symbolized the reborn soul among populations in such far-flung locales as Polynesia, South America, Australia, and India, as well as in Greece.[94] The reasons behind this are complex and require a detailed explanation for their full meaning to come clear.

The serpent's natural ability to shed its skin, and thereby be "reborn," linked it to the moon in the minds of our ancient forebears, because it appeared to them that the moon likewise shed flakes of itself, ultimately to reappear whole once more.[95] It is generally considered that the festivals of most ancient cultures were based upon particular cycles of the moon, since the passage of time itself was counted, in large part, by the moon's phases. This popular belief may be contrary to circumstance — I theorize that the mythos of resurrective deities either subsumed or blended into earlier, Paleolithic theologies concerning the moon sometime during the early Neolithic period, when mankind learned to sow and harvest.[96]

Sowing, harvesting, and the intermediate growth of plant life is seasonal — based upon the motion of the sun around the earth, a motion which can most accurately be tallied, by both ancient and modern humans, through the awareness of which "moon" the sun is in. The modern term for *month* in all modern cultures comes from either the English, the Sanskrit, or the native word for *moon*. In most ancient societies, threshing floors were molded in a circle, like the full moon, and the tool of reaping (originally a branch into which sharpened pieces of flint were embedded), ultimately evolved a crescent shape.

Like the moon and its resurrective Deities — many of whom were female, since the female sheds blood without any visible wound just as the snake sheds its skin without wounding itself, and the human female fertility cycle often approximates that of the moon from full to new to full again — vegetation had its time of death or reaping, but rituals of planting and propitiation always caused it to return.[97] It is quite possible that the first purposeful burying of seed corn in the soil was a form of pit-offering ritualistically covered over by leaves or dirt, a propitiation ceremony to an underworld Deity of regeneration, a god or goddess of rebirth.

It is likely that the mythic serpent which tempted the Judeo-Christian first couple and caused their expulsion from an idyllic Eden was equally linked to the moon and its cycles — knowledge of which is imperative in order to plant and harvest, or in the terms of Genesis: "gain sustenance by the sweat of your brow...," which is a command given by Deities of many cultures, e.g., the *thesmos* of Demeter to the Greeks.

Moon phase continues to be a factor whenever major festivals of resurrective Deities are planned. Classically, the Hellenic Lenaia rites were begun at the nearest full moon to the winter solstice, and the modern Roman Catholic celebration of Easter is always held on the Sunday nearest the first full moon after the vernal equinox. The Greek Orthodox Easter is held on the first dark moon — that time when the moon ceases waning and begins to wax toward full once more — after the vernal equinox. According to Burkert in *Greek Religion* (225), that period when the dark moon began to grow once more was considered auspicious by the ancients, and the dark of the moon signified movement from one month into the next.

The ancient Attic calendar was based solely upon the phases of the moon that went to make up one solar year, hence the undefined period of time which followed midwinter: There are generally thirteen full moons (and, occasionally, as many as fourteen) in any solar year. To the Pagan Greeks and Romans, the full moon was generally considered inauspicious, hence the Greco-Roman practice of bestowing unfavorable attributes upon the *ides* — that time when the moon appeared completely full, marking the middle of the month. At that time, by custom, Greco-Roman people performed no work or other transactions, since the three days during mid-month were *nefas* (from which English gets the word *nefarious*).[98] Since work could not be performed at this time of the month, this was the most common time to celebrate the festivals of the deities of resurrection, who until the time of Christ were also the cthonic Deities of death, associated in the minds of the ancients with the full moon and the serpent.[99] The rites of Agrai were always celebrated during the time of the month when the full moon had begun to wane — the end of the month of Anthesterion, after the festival of Anthesteria, held in honor of the spirits of the dead, had concluded.

Golden Memory

It is the opinion of some scholars, including myself, that the "golden snake" enclosed within the sacred basket was not a real snake at all, but a symbolic one. Such a symbolic serpent of gold was commonplace in Hellene society; one was given to each child that was born — it was accepted into a household as a protective amulet. I conjecture that it was this amulet, a symbol of divine protection, which was carefully formed into the small, thin golden tablet upon which a *synthema* of initiatory rebirth was inscribed by pious initiates as a "memento of memory."[100]

The Mysteries, both lesser and greater, were considered *anamimneskomai*. This may be translated into English as "Re-enaction (or *mimesis*) of something which helps one recover memories." *Anaktoron*, the altar-room of the Eleusinian

Hierophant within the Temple of Demeter at Eleusis, is a word with similar connotations. Unlike *Anaktoron*, however, *anamimneskomai* has a double meaning: "a memento."[101]

It was as a "memento" that a recollection of the revelations of lesser and greater Mystery rites was meant to be carried in the psyches of the initiates — not only throughout the remainder of their initiated lifetimes, but into the afterlife realm, and possibly even into succeeding lifetimes, as the following gold-leaf texts demonstrate:

> Thou shalt find on the left of the House of Hades a Well-spring,
> And by the side thereof standing a white cypress.
> To this Well-spring approach not near.
> But thou shalt find another by the lake of Memory,
> Cold water flowing forth, and there are Guardians before it.
> Say: "I am a child of Earth and of Starry Heaven;
> But my race is of Heaven (alone). This ye know yourselves.
> And lo, I am parched with thirst and I perish. Give me quickly
> The cold water flowing forth from the lake of Memory."
> And of themselves they will give thee to drink from the holy Well-spring,
> And thereafter among the other Heroes thou shalt have lordship...[102]

> In the house of Hades there is a spring to the right, by it stands a white cypress; here the souls, descending, are cooled. Do not approach this spring! Further you will find cool water flowing from the lake of recollection. Guardians stand over it who will ask you in their sensible mind why you are wandering through the darkness of corruptible Hades. Answer: I am a son of the earth and of the starry sky; but I am desiccated with thirst and am perishing: Therefore give me quickly cool water flowing from the lake of recollection. And then the subjects of the Cthonian King will have pity and will give you to drink from the lake of recollection...and indeed you are going a long, sacred way which also other *mystai* and *bacchoi* gloriously walk.[103]

In the following tablet, the initiate and the well of memory appear to converse:

> I am parched with thirst and I perish...Nay, drink of Me, the well-spring flowing forever on the right, where the cypress is. Who art thou?...whence art thou?...I am son of Earth and of starry heaven.[104]

Harrison (578-580) recounts that, in the rites of the oracle of Trophionos, drinking of separate wells of forgetfulness and memory was a physical act; the ritual preceding the oracular pronouncements contains other literal elements of the lesser Mysteries, including ritual fasting, purifications, isolation within a mystery house, washings and anointings, the donning of new clothes, and the eating of sacrificial flesh. Although, as the beginning of this chapter notes, the rites of Agrai took place beside the river Ilissus ("silt-filled"), it is not recorded whether literal libations from — or ritual immersions in — the Ilissus also occurred at Agrai.

Oneness with Deity

Happy and blessed one, thou shalt be god instead of mortal.

At a certain point in the lesser Mystery, a mask was held up over the new initiate's shoulder in such a way that the initiate would see the mask mirrored within a bowl of water rather than their own face.[105] As noted upon the tablets previously mentioned, the initiate was to pronounce themselves "a child of earth and of the starry heaven."[106] Hesiod uses the same description when describing the parentage of gods: "Sing the holy race of Immortals ever existing, who from Earth were born and born from Starry Heaven."[107] The implications of the act of mirroring the mask, as well as the ritual of thronosis, is one of identification between Dionysos — who, mythically, was son of the earthbound, mortal Semele and of the sky-god Zeus — and the new initiate: *Thou shalt be god instead of mortal.*[108]

In *Arcana Mundi* (17), Luck notes that many of the terms and practices used by Classical Greco-Roman practitioners of magic were borrowed from the Hellenic Mystery rites: A number of such "borrowings" appear to have been part of the rites of Agrai. The most notable of these was a rite in which a dedicant gazed into a water-filled bowl in order to catch a glimpse of their new oneness with the Mystery deities — a gift implicit in the worship of Dionysos, in whose cult a worshipper was considered to be able to take upon themselves the very aspect and faculties of their god.[109] According to all existing information, the dedicant received their vision of oneness within the torchlit, water-filled bowl in the most prosaic and non-visionary of ways as a mask was held up over their shoulder and mirrored in the bowl, which was tilted at a slight angle. Such a "vision" might not be quite so prosaic, however, if, as I surmise, the initiate was just recovering from the dream-inducing influence of a heavy dose of opiates. Clear and detailed representations of the rites of mask-mirroring — as well as those of scourging, kernophoria, and the memorization or recital of initiatory segments — may be found perfectly preserved on the walls of the Villa de Mysteri.

Chapter Six: The Sacred Mystery Rites of Eleusis

For almost two thousand years, the Eleusinian (advent") Mysteries, held in honor of Demeter and Persephone, were the most famous and influential religious cult in the ancient Greek world. The Roman historian Cicero spoke highly of the impact of Eleusis on Greco-Roman culture: "Though Athens brought forth numerous divine things, yet she never created anything nobler than those sublime Mysteries through which we became gentler and have advanced from a barbarous and rustic life to a more civilized one, so that we not only live more joyfully but also die with a better hope."[1] Death held no fear for the *epoptai* — those who had seen visions at Eleusis and who returned to guide new dedicants (*mystai*) through the rites. The Greek dramatist Sophocles stated: "Thrice happy are those mortals, who having seen those rites depart for Hades; for to them alone is granted to have a true life there."[2]

Although it was forbidden for initiates to reveal and enact what they saw and heard inside the *Telesterion* (the place of *telete*, or ceremonial function), initiates were free to testify to the emotional impact of the mystery experience — and many did. By all accounts, the ancient Greeks experienced transformative mystical visions during the eighth night at Eleusis.[3] In the first century BCE, Diodorus Siculus (V: 48-49) commented on the efficacy of the mysteries: "Now the details of the initiatory rite are guarded among the matters not to be divulged and are communicated to the initiates alone; but the fame has traveled wide of how these gods appear to mankind and bring unexpected aid to those initiates of theirs who call upon them in the midst of perils. The claim is also made that men who have taken part in the Mysteries become both more pious and more just and better in every respect than they were before."

Historical Background

Much is known about the more public aspects of the nine-day ceremonies, but a curtain of secrecy has always obscured what transpired once the initiates entered the walled sanctuary at Eleusis for the final day of the ceremonies. Those mysteries were revealed only to individuals who vowed — under threat of imprisonment or death — to never reveal or re-enact the ceremony's holy secrets. Considering that a few thousand initiates attended the Mysteries each year, it is truly miraculous that the veil of secrecy at Eleusis was maintained intact for roughly two thousand years.[4] Indeed, the great Mystery ceremonies of Eleusis were held so sacred throughout Greece that, during the ongoing wars and hostilities between the city-states of Athens and Sparta, a 55-day-long "holy peace" was declared each year in order to allow the Greeks on both sides to celebrate the Eleusinia.[5]

Unfortunately, the Mysteries of Eleusis did not fare so well under the Christianized Roman Empire, probably because they posed a competitive threat to the growth of Christianity. Once the Roman emperors (who needed a stable bureaucratic structure to shore up the tottering empire) officially adopted Christianity as the state religion, the Church patriarchs set out to get rid of competitive mysteries. When the Roman Emperor Valentinian mandated an end to the Mysteries in 364 CE, the Greek proconsul bravely refused to comply, declaring that the banishment of the Eleusinia and its associated rites would make life unlivable for the Greeks because the Mysteries "hold the whole human race together." In direct defiance of the Western emperor of the Roman Empire, the Eleusinian hierophant ordered that the Eleusinia be celebrated as always.[6]

Due to the veil of secrecy surrounding the Mysteries, efforts to reconstruct what transpired during the final night within the Telesterion have forced me to piece together fragmentary bits of evidence, culled from many, sometimes contradictory, sources. The Eleusinian initiates themselves, sworn to maintain secrecy, tended to record general comments often couched in carefully-worded symbolic language. In the last several centuries, archaeologists have uncovered considerable iconographic evidence recorded on funerary urns, bas-reliefs, and sculptures connected to the Mysteries, but such evidence is subject to speculation, leaving room for conflicting interpretations.

One recorded feature that set the Eleusinian Mysteries apart from most other ancient mystery rites of the Mediterranean world was that first-time dedicants underwent a two-part initiation with an extended educational process provided between the two rites.[7] Any person wanting to attend the greater Mystery rites at Eleusis had to first undergo a preliminary initiation known as the *Agrai*, or "lesser Mystery," that was held in a precinct of Athens during the month of *Anthesterion* (approximately February 14-March 12 on the modern calendar), a full seven months prior to the greater Mystery rite itself, which was held in the month of *Boedromeon* (our mid-September to mid-October).

It is generally assumed that the Mysteries — due to their strong association with the agricultural goddesses Demeter and Persephone — derived from prehellenic agricultural rites. However, it is important to understand that the ceremonies at Eleusis were not a "harvest festival," as some authors in the Northern hemisphere have misconstrued; the Greek harvest actually took place in spring, the time of year when Persephone was abducted by Hades. The ancient Greeks recognized two seasons, combining fall with winter (the wet months) and spring with summer (the dry months). The legend of Persephone's abduction by Hades, and Demeter's subsequent refusal to let plants grow, certainly provided apt mythic ground for the barren, rainless Greek summers. The "seven months" that Persephone spent with Hades was the dry summer — the "time when nothing grows" in Greece; it was during these months that new initiates underwent lengthy and pious training in preparation for the greater Mysteries.

Although held in the fall, the Eleusinia and subsequent Thesmophoria festival were, respectively, celebrations of the storage and planting of grain,[8] honoring that which goes into the ground to be reborn. In the same way that Persephone was swallowed by the depths of Hades' realm and hidden from her Mother, the grain must be hidden away beneath the earth in order for it to return and be reborn. For this reason, the regenerative aspects of the cthonic Deities were honored at both Agrai and Eleusis, and the focus of the rituals was on death and rebirth, or return. By all reports, the rites revealed to participants transforming revelations regarding the meaning behind the mysteries of life and death.[9]

Eleusinian ceremony clearly involved much more than a mere agricultural fertility celebration; these rites were a life-changing spiritual experience that started with a ritualized initiatory descent into the underworld at Agrai, culminating in a profound, ecstatic rebirth experience at Eleusis. While drawing numerous parallels between the Eleusinian Mysteries and later Christian views on the mysteries of resurrection, Classical scholar Sanderson Beck (1997) suggests that the Eleusinian rites provided participants with a direct experience of their divine immortal souls while still alive on earth. Other Classical scholars, including Joseph Wolberg and Carl Ruck, have suggested that the Mysteries may have been inspired or influenced by ancient Indo-European rites similar to the Haoma and Soma rites described in the Avesta and the Rïg Veda.[10]

Beyond speaking Greek, the only formal prerequisite for participating in the greater Mysteries was that any person who had committed murder or crimes against society had to be ritually cleansed before taking part in the greater Mysteries. Greek myths indicate that Demeter established the lesser Mysteries at Agrai specifically for the purpose of cleansing the hero Heracles of his murder of the Centaurs, in preparation for the greater Mysteries.[11] In *The Frogs* by Aristophanes, the chorus admonishes all with evil and profane thoughts to be still (*euphemete*) and purify themselves before participating in "the sacred dance of the mystic choir."[12] This restriction — requiring purification before participation — must have been considered indispensable because the historian Suetonius records that, when Nero visited Athens, his guilt kept him from participating in the Mystery rites.[13] Since most Dionysian mysteries were associated with the use of inebriating psychoactives, the ceremony at Agrai probably included the use of an entheogenic sacrament — quite possibly an opiated wine or some other psychoactive — and it is possible that the initiation at Agrai, and the following seven months of Mystery teachings, functioned as a screening and purification test, weeding out unworthy candidates before they approached the Eleusinian rites. In any case, it was said that the lesser Mysteries made *mystai* — literally, "ones with eyes closed" — out of new dedicants wanting to attend the greater Mysteries.

During the seven months between the lesser and greater Mysteries, the *mystai* were indoctrinated into the legends of Demeter and Persephone. This instruction was necessary because not everyone who took part in the Mysteries was from Greece — many came from Rome, Egypt, and other parts of the Mediterranean. Moreover, not everyone who spoke Greek knew very much about the esoterica of the Mysteries. The everyday religion of ancient Greece focused primarily on the worship of Hestia of the hearth, household deities, and the ancestral spirits of one's deme or phratrae.[14] For these reasons, the *mystai* spent seven months steeping themselves in the mythos and morés surrounding the cthonic deities involved in the Mysteries.

The Sacred Way at Eleusis

The greater Mysteries were a physically demanding, nine-day-long festival that began on the fourteenth day of Boedromeon, eight days before the Eleusinia proper, with the gathering of the Eleusinian *epheboi* — "(escorting) warriors" — and attendant priestesses at the sanctuary in Eleusis. In ritual procession, these individuals carried *kalathoi* (sacred baskets containing ritual implements and foodstuffs which would be needed by the mystai; it may be assumed that they were brought wholly or partially empty from Eleusis, and that the mystai filled them as part of the ceremonies leading up to the procession to Eleusis from Athens) along the *Via Sacre* to the Athenian Eleusinion.[15] The *Via Sacre*, or Sacred Way — which ran a distance of roughly fourteen miles between Athens and Eleusis — was dotted with shrines commemorating the story of Demeter's search for her daughter Persephone. Archeological evidence indicates that the shrines were built by *epoptai* in appreciation of the transformative power of the Mysteries.[16]

Many of the preliminary rites held during the first few days, while the mystai were still gathered in Athens, seem to have involved acts of purification designed to spiritually prepare the initiates for the final night of Mysteries.[17] For the entire nine days of the Eleusinia ceremony (*Boedromeon* 14-22), all dedicants observed abstinence-fasts as one form of purification. Some may have fasted from all food and water during the daylight hours, breaking the fast each evening, following the example of Demeter.[18]

On the third day, Boedromeon 16th, each mystai bathed ritually in the sea with a piglet. It was believed in the ancient Greek world, as among some modern indigenous cultures, that the pig had the power to absorb evil and keep it away from humans. In some cultures, the pig is later sacrificed to the gods as a surrogate for the initiates; it is known that the Eleusinic piglets were also sacrificed.[19]

On the sixth day, Boedromeon 19th, the dedicants, their associate *mystagogoi* ("those who guide the veiled"), and the epheboi all participated in another procession, now carrying the kalathoi of sacred items from Athens back to Eleusis. It is reported that a statue of the sacred youth Iacchos was carried in this procession by the *Iacchogagos*, a man specifically consecrated for this task.[20] In much the same way that the fir tree swathed in violets symbolized the resurrection god Attis of Phrygia, Eleusinian participants carried laurel and myrtle branches tied with wool, symbols of the ever-dying, ever-reborn Iacchos, a physical reminder of the promises made by this shapeshifting godform — namely, that the initiates themselves would suffer and die like the god and, like the god, be eternally reborn.[21]

After the day-long trek from Athens to Eleusis, the dedicants would reach the Bridge of Rhiti, which spanned slender saline rivers that flowed into a salt lake near the Rharian Plain of Eleusis. Records suggest that the participants danced during all or part of their procession along the Sacred Way,[22] and after a 14-mile journey, they would certainly have been exhausted.[23] Nonetheless, at the bridge itself, the dedicants had to pass a gauntlet of observers who hurled insults and risqué jokes at them, in an ancient purification practice known as *krokosis* or *gephyrismoi* ("bridge jests"), a practice intended to both humble the dedicants and to protect them from evil.[24]

Once the bridge was successfully traversed by all dedicants, they would stop to rest and light torches for the remainder of their journey into the town of Eleusis. All that night, until dawn, the *mystai* and their attendant mystagogoi would perform dances beginning at the well of Callichorus; the name of this Eleusinic well means, concurrently, "good song" and "song of cultivation"; the well was also known as *Parthenion*, or "of the Maiden." The Bacchanalian nature of this dancing ceremony, known from ancient sources as "the Night of Torches," is parodied in the chorus of Aristophanes' *Frogs*. Certain terms used by the satirist indicate that the torch dances took place shortly after the *gephyrismoi* gauntlet was passed by the mystai on the Rhiti Bridge:

> Come with wild and saucy paces, mingling in our joyous dance...
> Come, arise, from sleep waking, come the fiery torches shaking, O Iacchos!
> O Iacchos!...
> O Lord of the frolic and dance, Iacchos beside me advance!
> For fun, and for cheapness, our dress thou hast rent,
> through thee we may dance to the top of our bent,
> reviling, and jeering, and none will resent.
> O Lord of the frolic and dance, Iacchos, beside me advance![25]

The rending of clothes is a universal sign of mourning; mythically, the well of Callichorus in Eleusis is where the grieving Demeter rested, in the guise of an old woman, as she travelled the world in search of her abducted daughter Kore.[26] As noted earlier, branches were carried by the procession in memory of the cthonic sacred child, Iacchos. The Night of Torches in all likelihood consisted of a labyrinthine torch dance by branch-carrying mystai ("Iacchos beside me advance!"), beginning at the well and winding through the streets of Eleusis, to call the populace of Eleusis forth with jests and cries of *Iacc'o Iacch'e* ("Come, arise, from sleep waking, come the fiery torches shaking, O Iacchos! O Iacchos!...") to help in the search for the lost Kore, whom the *mystai* may have attempted to call forth from the underworld by beating the earth with their branches — knocking on the outer door of the House of Hades, where Persephone reigned as Queen of the Dead.[27]

Dionysos' presence at Eleusis as a form of triple-god is confirmed by numerous sources, both ancient and modern, refuting the stance of Mylonas (*Eleusis...275* and footnotes) that the Dionysian Mysteries were unrelated in any way to those of Demeter and Persephone. The most unmistakable sign of Dionysos' presence at Eleusis, and of the unity of native Hellenic Mystery rites in general, is the use of the liknon as the final purificatory tool prior to the entry of the mystai into the Telesterion. Sophocles poetically asserts the lordship of Dionysos at Eleusis in *Antigone*:

> Thou of many names, delight and wonder
> of the Theban bride, Child of the pealing Thunder,
> Thou who dost rule over Italia's pride
> and at Eleusis in Deo's bosom wide
> dwellest, Deo, she the Mother of all,
> Bacchos, Bacchos, on thee we call.[28]

After the strenuous exertions of the Night of Torches, the next day and evening were almost certainly spent resting, fasting, and visiting nearby shrines in preparation for the main events that began on Boedromeon 21st. All morning on the eighth day, dedicants attended sacrificial offerings in the *Temenos*, or outdoor sanctuary, of the Telesterion.[29] Customarily, goats, rams, and bulls were offered to Aesclepios, Dionysos, Poseidon, and Artemis at the *Temenos*. The piglets brought with the mystai were sacrificed later, just prior to the ceremony of *myesis*.[30]

Myesis and Liknophoria

Prior to being allowed into the Telesterion proper on the ninth day of the Eleusinic ceremony, the mystai were required to undergo a final rite of purification within the large *caryatid*-pillared portals leading up to the single entrance of the Eleusenic Temple of Demeter itself. Aristophanes' *Clouds* parodies these rites, known as *myesis*, which in modern Greek simply means "initiation";[31] since only an individual's experiences within the Telesterion itself were forbidden to divulge, the ceremony of myesis itself can be found vividly represented on numerous Classical artworks. The most notable act of myesis from these artworks is the enthronement of a single unclad initiate upon a chair or stool covered with a large sheep's fleece (the *dioskodion*), the initiate's head and lap covered with a long and presumably opaque veil. Such artworks also often represent the sacrifice of one or more piglets by attendant clerics, as does the Lovatelli Urn which depicts the myesis of the mythic hero Heracles; according to recent archaeological evidence, the piglets sacrificed at this ceremony were cooked and eaten, presumably once the activities within the Telesterion had ended.[32]

The myesis ceremony would have represented a time of transition between secular and wholly spiritual states of being, a cleansing capable of removing all mundane, non-Eleusinic concerns from the minds of the mystai immediately prior to their entry into the *Telesterion* — a final and irrevocable rite of passage through which the greater Mysteries would be approached.[33] The psycho-spiritual transition of myesis appears to have been accomplished by placing the dedicants into a compromising position — that of complete ritual nudity — which would work to draw their minds back to both the fundamentals of existence, and to those things they experienced during their primary initiation at Agrai. According to Plotinius, "...to those that approach the Holy Celebrations of the Mysteries, there are appointed purifications and the laying aside of the garments worn before."[34] To the ancient and Classical Hellenes, the Mysteries of Eleusis were the ultimate path to paradise — *Elysium* or the Elysian Fields. As Mircea Eliade has noted in *The Sacred and the Profane...* (135): "Paradise implies the absence of garments...all ritual nudity implies an atemporal model, a paradisal image." Another method used during myesis to increase the sense of transition from daily reality into the unknown and potentially frightening realm of the gods was a ritual performed at some point after the initiate had been enthroned on the sheepskin-covered stool: Certain individuals, armed with spears and shields according to some accounts — perhaps the epheboi escort of Eleusis — would dance around the initiate, making threatening noises. A similar dance is spoken of for the thronosis ceremony performed at the beginning of the lesser Mystery of Agrai. Such a dance was representative of the mythic actions of the Kouretes at the birth of the sacred Child; a press of dancing men meant concurrently to conceal the newborn, and to threaten potential enemies of the enthroned infant.[35]

From this point, the actions performed in the ceremony of myesis appear to be a summary re-enactment of the rites performed seven months earlier at the lesser Mysteries of Agrai — those remembrances of "what was done to Dionysos."[36] As Burkert summarizes in *Greek Religion* (78): "When other portrayals of Heracles' initiation show the use of the liknon as well, late systemization was able to speak of a purification through the elements water, fire, wind. There is also a purification by earth..." As was also true of the initiation at Agrai, all purification steps known to have been taken during myesis appear to mimic a ceremony of planting: The seed placed within the earth, compelled to grow through warmth (fire) until it sprouts into the upper air, where it is nourished and compelled to grow to maturity through applications of water. The *Liknophoria*, which was the final focus of the myesis ceremony, further ties this ritual to a planting and harvesting motif.[37]

The liknon was held over a dedicant's head during some form of anointing and blessing given after the earth, fire, air, and water purification steps of myesis had concluded. In antiquity, the *liknon* — literally a winnowing basket — had two mundane functions: as a tool to separate grain from chaff, and as an impromptu, mobile cradle for a baby.[38] Its Mystery functions and meanings were also dual, reflecting its secular functions and transmitting a similar message: a cradle in which indestructible Life lies swaddled, where death is transformed, and from which new growth proceeds.[39] Held over an initiate's head, the liknon's purifying function was to divide the good from the bad and toss away the bad, the way its mundane counterpart would treat grain and chaff.[40]

The Eleusinic anointing and blessing might have incorporated blood from the sacrificial piglets of the mystai. "Thrice blessed" is a common reference to Eleusinic initiates[41] and, though this may simply be in reference to the triad of initiatory rites the dedicant undergoes (*Agrai, myesis* and *epopteia*), there does appear to have been some form of blessing bestowed during the ancient ceremony of myesis, though exactly what it was remains as much an enigma as exactly what litany the Hierophant spoke to the dedicants after they had entered the Telesterion and begun the Mystery ceremony.[42] It may have been during myesis, when individuals were taken by their mystagogoi either separately or in groups — the men, perhaps, in the greater Propulaea and the women in the lesser, though the exact method by which individuals were grouped to undergo myesis is not known — that the mystai made the solemn vow of the Classical Hellenic Mysteries: To remember — not just on a daily basis, but throughout successive lifetimes — the sacred knowledge dispensed in the Telesterion, where the spirit world of the gods and ancestors would be brought into contact with the living world of humankind.[43]

Exactly what happened during the eighth night — what Beck calls the Holy Night of Holy Light — was part of the secret mysteries that were not supposed to be revealed (arrheton). Nonetheless, many accounts state that the eighth night of the Mysteries involved a very intense and provocative experience which altered a dedicant's perceptions of life, death, and the afterworld. Aristeides the Rhetor wrote, "Eleusis is a shrine common to the whole earth, and of all the divine things that exist among men, it is both the most awesome and the most luminous. At what place in the world have more miraculous tidings been sung, and where have the *dromena* called forth greater emotion, where has there been greater rivalry between seeing and hearing?"[44]

At the Heart of the Mysteries

Some Classics scholars, notably Paul François Foucart, have suggested that the eighth day of the Mysteries essentially involved a theatrical enactment of the story of Demeter and Persephone[45] and that the sublime spiritual experience manifested at the climax of the Mysteries probably involved a play or other dramatized performance of the reunion of Mother and Daughter. However, it is doubtful that a mere theatrical production would have impacted initiates year after year in the way that the Mysteries did. The visions were said to produce a "deepening of dimension," and a sense of self-acceptance, or life-acceptance, which lingered in the psyche of each participant, leading them to view life with more joy, and death with less fear. Furthermore, spectators in the Telesterion, the setting of the *dromena* ("things done"), were ultimately known as *epoptai* ("those who have seen" or "those whose eyes are open"), whereas spectators in both the Athenian assembly and in the theater, the setting of the *drama* ("enactment") were known as *theatai*, a title utterly unrelated to any known

Mystery rite. Theater and its concurrent dramatic productions were originally entirely political in nature, disallowing foreigners attendance and strictly separating viewers by guild, clan, and gender (see pages 40-45 for further information and sources regarding the original ceremonial purpose of Hellenic theater), whereas the Mysteries were utterly apolitical, allowing entrance to all who were willing to submit to purification strictures. These facts demonstrate that *dromena* and *drama*, while sounding superficially alike, have little or no relevance to one another as far as the activities within the Telesterion were concerned.[46]

Kerenyi has argued that staging a dramatic play capable of transforming the lives of initiates would have required professional actors,[47] and there is little evidence pointing toward the use of professional actors at the Eleusinia. In addition, the many-pillared structure of the Telesterion would have interfered with the viewing of theatrical productions. In fact, since the roof of every Telesterion built during the temple's long history was supported by numerous columns — far more columns than were actually required to hold up the roof[48] — it can be assumed that the pillars played some key role in stimulating the Eleusinian experience. Kerenyi proposed that, instead of a theatrical production, the dromena may have involved a sacred dance weaving between the pillars, similar to the labyrinthine rope-dances once performed on the island of Delos, during which the celebrants sought ecstatic union with the divine.[49]

Dancing may have played a part in the ceremony, but Kerenyi's proposal does not adequately explain some extant reports on the Mysteries. Although initiates were forbidden to reveal exactly what happened at the climax of the Mysteries, they were permitted to testify as to the impact of the experience. Proculus observes: "In the most sacred Mysteries before the scene of the mystic visions, there is terror infused over the minds of the Initiated." In a similar vein, Aristeides wrote: "Within this hall, the mystics were made to experience the most bloodcurdling sensations of horror and the most enthusiastic ecstasy of joy." Because it is doubtful that even skillfully staged dramas or dances would have "inspired terror" in the Greeks, seasoned theater-goers that they were,[50] it must be assumed that the things said, shown, and done inside the Telesterion were of an altogether different nature.

Based on comments made by the ancient epoptai themselves, it may be assumed that the participants saw mystical revelations into the nature of the afterlife. Many reports indicate that participants saw spirits moving through the room and hovering above ground; Plato called them *phantasma* or ghostly apparitions.[51] The first-century CE Pagan Proculus commented on the ephemeral nature of the things seen: "In all the Initiations and Mysteries, the gods manifest themselves in many forms, assuming a great variety of guises; sometimes they appear in formless light, again in quite a different form."[52]

Some ancient sources indicate that a fire was kept burning atop the *Anaktoron* (altar-room of the Hierophant, whose floor was composed of a single unhewn stone)[53] throughout most of the night. The interplay of lights and shadows filtering through drifting smoke and past the many pillars in the Telesterion would have created haunting, dreamlike images. In addition, it is reported that people moved through the room carrying vessels on their heads and torches in their hands.[54] It is easy to see how the mystai, primed by months of preliminary instruction and days of fasting, might see shadows of figures moving through the smoke as spirits. All accounts indicate that the Eleusinian Mysteries culminated in a communal visionary experience that transformed the initiates. The wording of some accounts suggests that at least some of the "things seen" at Eleusis were internal visions — not a theatrical performance. In the *First Ennead* VI: 7, Plotonius writes: "Each in the solitude of oneself shall see that solitary-dwelling existence, the apart, the unmingled, the pure, that from which all things depend, for which all look and live and act and know, the source of life and of intellection and of being."

Numerous modern scholars maintain that the "visionary experiences" at the heart of Eleusis were stimulated at least in part by a mind-altering entheogenic substance or substances;[55] I concur with this assessment. Ancient sources reveal that initiates drank kykeon — a potion made of several secret ingredients — and that it played a vital role in the Mysteries.[56] A two-handled metal vessel known as an *angos*, used to serve kykeon, is depicted prominently on many Eleusinian funerary vases and bas-reliefs as well as on the *kistai* (chests) atop the heads of the caryatids which supported the roof the Lesser Propulaea,[57] bearing visual testimony to kykeon's central role in the Mysteries. Next to the contents of the kykeon, the most guarded secret of the Mysteries is what transpired at the climax of the Holy Night of Holy Light, when the hierophant displayed *ta hiera* ("the sacred") to the initiates.

The materials utilized in the greater Mystery rites by the worshippers are known, having been revealed by those, such as Clement of Alexandria,[58] intent upon discrediting the Mysteries. Some scholars, such as Mylonas,[59] caution that such writings should be taken with a large grain of salt, given the prejudiced intent of their authors. However, all of the items listed by those who would reveal the Mysteries make sense and can be given a logical role in the context and format of the rites that pious Pagan authors of antiquity hint were performed within the Telesterion. What Christian refutationists would *not* have seen arranged within the great pillared hall would have been the Mystery visions themselves. If (as I and others conjecture) the Mystery of the Eleusinia was, in fact, brought about by entheogenic agents introduced ahead of time into either the liquid used to make the kykeon or into the sesame cakes molded in geometric and erotic shapes — which are among the items that Clement and others attest to as part of the Eleusinic sacra — then anyone who refused to partake of either the oblation or libation given in the Temple of Demeter would be utterly incapable of experiencing the mystery of the Mysteries at all. The night in the Telesterion would seem to such an individual to be an endless and meaningless movement of items into and out of baskets and chests: Indeed, this is, at its base, what Clement suggests the ritual within the Telesterion was. It is wholly reasonable to assume that Christians would see in the libations and oblations given in the Telesterion a sort of parody of their own sacrament, and would refuse to take part in such Pagan blasphemy; and, not imbibing either kykeon or cakes, they would mistake the sacra within the kalathoi as the easily dismissible Pagan "holy," because the visions — which the sacra were nothing more than passive vehicles to provide — were never experienced.

For this reason, I do not believe that Clement and his ilk misrepresented the sacred tools of the Holy Night of Holy Light; I tend, rather, to think that they would have attempted to be as thorough as possible in their descriptions, the better to make their dismissive mockery of "these they call their holy things!" truly sting. The Christian refutationists simply failed to differentiate a sacred tool from a sacred vision — a perfectly human confusion of metaphor with reality, a metaphor behind which the clerics of Eleusis kept their visionary secrets quite safely hidden until the wholesale destruction of the Eleusinic sacred precinct and, presumably, its clerics sometime around 400 CE.[60]

According to Christian sources, the contents of the kalathoi consisted primarily of an array of foodstuffs, including seeds of the pomegranate, sesame, and poppy; mixed grains including rice, oats, wheat, and barley; peas and lentils, honey, oil, and dried fruits such as figs and raisins — foods suspiciously reminiscent of the *chytroi* offering given to appease the spirits of the dead on the final day of the Anthesteria (see pages 69-79 for more information regarding both this festival and offerings *per se*). Herbs such as white poppies, sage, and marjoram, as well as boiled eggs, sea salt, honeycomb and tufts of raw wool were also included in the Eleusinian cista mystica: All of these were also common cthonic and ancestral offerings.[61] The beans mentioned by ancient authors may or may not have been eaten; beans were considered to be the food of the dead, taboo in ancient and Classical Greece at all times except during the celebration of the Mysteries. The Romans, too, held that the eating of beans — specifically broad beans — was to revivify the souls of the dead within oneself.[62] Such a belief gives a clue as to the implicit message underlying the Hellenic Mysteries. As Burkert notes in *Homo Necans*: "The uncanny, provocative source of reproduction is transformed into the fruit of the earth, which itself holds the power of perpetuating life...Even 'domesticated' food must reach man by way of the unspeakable sacrifice."

The tools of the mystai contained within the kalathoi included a mortar and pestle, a hair pick or comb — considered by some scholars to be symbolic of the hanging hair-fringes of the female vulva and thus a physical representation of the two goddesses of Eleusis, but I suggest a more direct explanation: That it was used as a fork or whisk, neither of which was in use until the seventeenth century, to mix the kykeon ingredients together after the liquid had been added — a knife, certainly used for cutting and eating portions of the oblation, and one of the most interesting implements of the Mysteries, a *kernos*.

A number of these fascinating objects have been found during archaeological excavations of the area directly surrounding what was ancient Eleusis. Most of those unearthed somewhat resemble large escargot dishes. In general, scholars assume that the outer cups of these elaborate ceramic ritual items were used to hold the foodstuffs of the Eleusinic oblation, with the central, larger section used to hold the mixed and filtered kykeon. However, judging by the general size and shape of the kernoi found at Eleusis, it would have been difficult, if not impossible, to actually drink the kykeon from the inner bowl; a spoon, or small ladle, would have been required to scoop the kykeon out of the kernos.[63] It is fascinating to note that Clement, in his description of the ritual items utilized for the Eleusinia, does include ladles as part of the sacra contained within the *kalathoi*. Some kernoi have been found at Eleusis, however, which appear to have been purely decorative rather than functional, because of the numerous and exquisitely tiny forms of their outer cups. Harrison (160) provides a drawing of just such a kernos, which may have been a votive offering to the deities of Eleusis rather than a utilitarian object.

It is unknown whether the libation of the Eleusinia, which was composed of roasted barley flour and pennyroyal, according to those who have recorded its known contents,[64] preceded or followed the oblation of foodstuffs which, as Callimachus noted, were passed from mystai to mystai in the *kalathoi*:

> As the basket comes, greet it, you women, saying "Demeter, greatly hail! Lady of much bounty, of many measures of corn." As the basket comes, from the ground you shall see it, you uninitiated, and gaze not from the roof or from aloft...neither then nor when we spit from parched mouths fasting...[65]

I theorize that the libation preceded the oblation. I base this very likely hypothesis upon the *synthema* ("password") of the Eleusinian Mysteries itself:

> I fasted, I drank from the kykeon, I took [*oblation materials*] out of the *kiste*, worked, placed [*oblation materials*] back in the basket (*kalathos*) and from the basket into the *kiste*.[66]

There is a widely accepted belief among those who study the phenomenon of Eleusis that "I worked" had to do with the grinding of the barley and pennyroyal in the mortar.[67] However, a problem exists with this idea as regards the synthema itself, since such a situation would have had the barley and pennyroyal of the kykeon being ground after the kykeon had been imbibed. I suspect that this mix-up lies in the syntax given the word *worked*.

J. W. Fernandez, while documenting the entheogenic *Tabernanthine iboga* vision quest rituals of the Fang people of Africa,[68] noted that they always referred to the *iboga* ceremony as "doing the work of the ancestors," wherein *work* is seen as taking upon oneself the hallucinogenic experience *so that the ancestor spirits may arrive and speak* — not terribly unlike Eleusinic beliefs of the ancient Greeks, wherein Persephone as Queen of the Dead appeared among the hosts of ancestral spirits.[69] Fernandez himself utilizes this context for the word *work* in his article: "...the mix of instrumental and expressive modes of being in any culture is dependent upon the satisfactions of the work of that culture and the ecstatic possibilities found in that work."[70] I am convinced that, in drinking the kykeon, the mystai undertook the "work of their ancestors (and cthonic gods)" and that this, rather than physical labor of any kind, is the meaning behind the Mystery utterance, "I worked." Indeed, the amount of time which would have been required for all mystai to partake of the oblation after drinking the kykeon would have given an entheogen time to begin to *work* — affect the dedicants — if that entheogen was, in fact, part of the liquid component of the kykeon.

The clerics of Eleusis, including priestesses of Demeter, the *Dadouchos* who sounded the gong,[71] the *Hierokeryx* or "herald of the Hierophant,"[72] and the chief priest of the Mysteries, the *Hierophant*, would have carefully monitored the assembled dedicants to determine when the entheogenic agent(s) had begun to effect the mystai, to know just when to begin subsequent portions of the ritual on the Holy Night of Holy Light. The word Hierophant translates as "he who shows the holy things." This has mistakenly led some scholars to believe that the entire Eleusinia was conducted in silence, and that the Hierophant did nothing more than hold up a stalk of grain for everyone's meditative viewing. The writings of Hellenic authors show that nothing could be farther from the truth. There was some form of litany or litanies sung or spoken by the Hierophant. The Homeric or Orphic hymns which allude to Eleusinic myths were probably sung during libation and oblation, but ancient sources hint that there was more. A "book of stone" is mentioned by Porphyrus, out of which the Hierophant read a litany to the assembled dedicants:

> We are led before the Hierophant. From a book of stone, he reads to us things which we must not divulge under penalty of death. Let us say only that they are in harmony with the place and circumstance. You would laugh, perhaps, if you heard them outside the temple, but you have no desire to laugh as you listen to the words...and as you look at the exposed symbols. And you are far from laughing when, by her special language and signs, by vivid sparkling of light and clouds piled upon clouds, Demeter confirms everything that we have seen and heard from her holy priest.[73]

It is, of course, possible that such a "book of stone" is a metaphor of some sort. Nevertheless, unless and until such a book is found, the exact words of any litany the Hierophant spoke to the mystai must remain unknown. Several ancient sources mention that the final object displayed by the Hierophant was a sheaf of barley. Significantly, archaeologists have found realistic-looking barley stalks made of gold.[74] Other sacred symbols which may have been revealed to the mystai could have included phallic emblems of Dionysos enclosed within the liknon.[75]

Porphyrus also offers an informative description of the final revelation, which exhibits traits typical of many entheogenic rites: "Then, finally, a light of serene wonder fills the temple; we see the pure Elysian fields; we hear the chorus of the blessed ones. Now it is not merely through an external appearance or through a philosophical interpretation, but in fact and in reality that the

Hierophant is become the creator and revelator of all things; the sun is but his torchbearer, the moon, his helper of the altar, and Hermes, his mystical messenger...The ritual has been consummated, and we are seers forever."[76]

According to Young (*Origins...* 326), Porphyrus' choice of the word "consummated" was not random: The term *legomena*, the "things spoken" during Hellenic Mystery rites, is a word with multiple meanings. Its alternate meaning may be found in the root *legein*, or "to lie with." According to ancient scholars as well, some sort of Sacred Marriage occurred during the rites of Eleusis:

> Is there not the *katabasion* and the solemn meeting of the Hierophant and the priestess, each with the other alone; are not the torches then extinguished and the vast crowd believes that its salvation depends on what these two enact in darkness?[77]

A myth exists of Demeter lying in the fields with a mortal man (Iason) in order to return fertility to the fields. Mythically, Iason is both that mighty hunter who "seizes" Demeter, and the first Hierophant who performs the Sacred Marriage with Demeter.[78] Iason is ultimately killed by the thunderbolt of Zeus for his impertinence in daring to carry off and lie with a goddess. In ancient and Classical Greek thought, *mushrooms* were considered to be the offspring of Zeus' "thunderbolts"; they were sometimes referred to as *keraunia lithos*, or "thunder stones" — a theogenic natural history which links folk beliefs in the nascence of mushrooms from lightning or thunder to the death of Iason, and thus to the Eleusinic rites themselves.[79] From her union with Iason, Demeter gives birth to *Ploutos*, or "wealth (of the fields)," yet another Eleusinic appellation for Dionysos.[80] In the Eleusinic myth cycles of Mother and Daughter, both are "carried away" and consummate the endless dance of life conceived through death *ad infinitum*. It matters little which myth cycle — Demeter's or Persephone's — is referred to in this case, for Mother and Daughter are alternate aspects of the same goddess.[81]

Most scholars still consider the union of Hierophant and Priestess during the Eleusinic rites speculative, but comments by both Christian and Pagan ancient scholars suggest that the Sacred Marriage, performed within the Anaktoron just after the Hierophant litany that concluded the main portion of the ritual, was indeed part of the rites of Eleusis: "Why is the priestess of Demeter carried off, unless Demeter herself had suffered the same sort of thing?"[82]

Usually, sexual activity anywhere within a temple's precincts was forbidden by Hellenic law.[83] At certain rituals, however, acts forbidden on a day-to-day basis served as one form of sacred inversion of the normal order in Hellenic society, a sort of boundary marker in time.[84] Marriage itself was considered a form of initiatory rite by the Classical Greeks.[85] A Sacred Marriage ceremony, whether literal or symbolic, as part of the rites of Eleusis would have been emblematic of a whole new way of being in the minds of the initiates, thereby "marrying" the mystai themselves to "the source of life and of intellection and of being," as Plotinius said in *First Ennead* VI, 7.[86] It is likely that any Sacred Marriage performed at Eleusis was symbolic rather than literal, since the Hierophant was known to partake of hemlock as a purifying act, and that could conceivably cause at least partial impotence.[87]

As the Sacred Marriage took place, all fires were doused and the mystai were left to darkness in the crowded hall to experience the *deiknymena* ("things seen") that the active principles in the kykeon would have begun to stage for the participants.[88] Both the willingness to suspend rational judgments and the tendency to find profound meanings in simple truths are highly suggestive of entheogenic rituals. Moreover, the fact that thousands of novice worshippers entered the Telesterion each year for nearly two thousand years, and almost all experienced much the same life-altering visions, is suggestive of a programmed entheogenic experience. To be sure, the lengthy training of the mystai would have provided ample opportunity to mold the expectations of the participants and help ensure a conformity of visions. However, the consistently profound, life-transformative impact of the Eleusinian experience can best be explained by the use of an entheogenic sacrament.

A Pantheon of Entheogens

The ancient Greeks were familiar with such a broad pantheon of psychoactive plants that it has been difficult to pinpoint exactly which psychoactive plants were used in the Eleusinian kykeon. Greek artists certainly left unequivocal iconographic evidence directly linking psychoactive substances with the principal goddesses of the Mysteries. There is a magnificent Greek statue (c. 420 BCE), now in the Vatican Museum, that shows Demeter holding sheaves of barley and two unmistakable opium capsules.[89] The many-seeded poppy capsule was considered a symbol of Demeter's role as goddess of fecundity and agriculture, and brooches and pins shaped like poppy capsules were worn by childless women as charms to increase their fertility.[90] The poppy flower was also closely associated with Persephone. Poppies were not the only psychoactive linked to Demeter and Persephone — there is iconography from Eleusis that shows them holding up unmistakable mushrooms.[91]

Based on historic, literary, and archaeological evidence, various scholars have identified different substances as the "most promising" candidates for the Eleusinian kykeon. The list has included ergot (*Claviceps* species, which contains LSD-like alkaloids); opium extracts (*Papaver somniferum*); fly agaric mushrooms (*Amanita muscaria*); and several types of psilocybic mushrooms (*Gymnopilus, Psilocybe,* or other species). At this point, I would like to review the "credentials" of the candidates proposed by other authors.

As mentioned, there is ample iconographic and literary evidence linking poppy capsules not only with Demeter but also specifically with Eleusis. Three unmistakable pods of poppies are clearly depicted, together with other symbols of Demeter, on an ancient bas-relief of Pentelic marble that was probably looted from the Eleusinion in Athens and cemented into a lintel in one of the oldest churches in Athens.[92] A Boeotian plate (number 484), now found in the National Archaeological Museum in Athens, depicts an enthroned Demeter holding two ears of cereal, two poppy pods, and a torch.[93] Since both Demeter and Persephone, the goddesses of the Mysteries, are often depicted in Classical Greek art holding sheaves of barley and poppy capsules — barley being one of the alleged components of the kykeon[94] — Kerenyi and others have promoted the theory that opium was obviously used at Eleusis.[95]

There are several problems with the theory of Eleusinic opium use. First, opium was far too well known and too readily available in the ancient Greek world for its use to be considered a sacrosanct secret. Heraclites, physician to Alexander the Great's father Phillip, promoted its use as a general pain reliever.[96] Stores selling opium-laced medicines were commonplace in both Greece and Rome. Greek legends are rich with accounts of people entertaining guests using wines laced with the inebriating poppy and other psychoactive plants.[97] Clearly, the common usage of opium, as well as the prohibition against using wine during the Mysteries, argues against its use as a secret ingredient in the kykeon.

Second, opium has a decidedly soporific effect on users. It is not by chance that the Greek god of Sleep, Somnus, is often depicted holding poppy-heads, and the Greek god of dreams, Morphius, lends his name to the opium extract *morphine.* Even when consumed in moderate amounts, opium tends to make people groggy, and in excessive amounts, it can lay people prone.[98] There is evidence that opiated wines were used at the healing temples of Aesklepios, specifically in order to induce *incubatio*, or healing dreams.[99]

Using sleep-inducing drugs in the kykeon on the final night of vigiling in the Telesterion would have been counterproductive. It is reported that the mystai and epoptai were restricted to ten tiers of stairs stretching along three sides of the Telesterion;[100] considering that as many as three thousand individuals squeezed into the Telesterion each year, each participant would have had approximately one square foot of tier space — hardly enough room to sit, much less sleep, during the ceremonies. In addition, the ceremony included libations, oblations, litanies, and liturgies; it can be assumed that the participants needed to stay awake through the night to participate in these things. Using an opiated drink that tended to cause a "dreamy sleep" or physically prone condition would have been incompatible with the vigil. For these reasons, I propose that the depiction of poppy capsules and flowers in connection with Demeter, Persephone, and the Mystery rites may be best explained by their use in the Lesser Mysteries at Agrai, in which Dionysos was equated with Sabazios, a Deity whom ancient writers claimed "brings sleep."[101]

At each yearly celebration of the Eleusinia, one boy from the community of Athens was chosen as "child of the hearth," *pais*. This child symbolized Demophoön, the mythical son of Metaniera, to whom Demeter sought to grant immortal life by putting him to sleep in the fire of the family's hearth each night. Concurrently, the pais vicariously represented all individuals physically unable to attend the Mysteries. Through the young *pais*, all those not at the greater Mystery rites would nonetheless obtain the blessings of the rites. Another application for opium at the Eleusinia may have been to soothe the "child of the hearth" to sleep.[102]

The Flaw in "St. Anthony's Fire"

Based on the numerous portraits showing Demeter and Persephone holding sheaves of barley or other grains and the fact that barley is mentioned in the *Hymn to Demeter* as one of the ingredients used in kykeon, scholars have long speculated that barley played a vital role at Eleusis. In 1978, a trio of highly respected researchers — amateur ethnomycologist R. Gordon Wasson, pharmacologist Albert Hofmann, and Classics scholar Carl Ruck — argued that the primary entheogenic agent used in the Eleusinic kykeon might have been an extract of ergot, a fungus that infects various types of grains and grasses.[103]

The first obstacle to the ergot theory is that the most common form of ergot, *Secale cornutum*, grows on rye, and rye didn't grow in ancient Greece. That problem was solved when Hofmann determined that ergot of barley, *Claviceps purpurea*, contained essentially the same psychoactive and toxic alkaloids as ergot of rye. Moreover, the barley-ergot fungus is purple — a color associated in ancient Greece with childbirth, the underworld, and Demeter's robes.[104]

The second obstacle to the ergot theory is that *C. purpurea* contains a number of toxic substances along with its psychoactive alkaloids, as does *S. cornutum*. In moderate doses, these ergot toxins can cause irreversible peripheral nerve damage, leading to gangrene and epileptic tendencies in humans, a combination of conditions known in medieval times as "St. Anthony's fire." In larger doses, these toxins can cause death.[105] Hofmann proposed — based on his knowledge that ergonovine was a water-soluble alkaloid extracted from ergot — that the Greeks might have been able to extract the psychoactive alkaloids by soaking ergot-infested flour in cold water, thereby filtering out the insoluble toxic alkaloids, and then using only the potentiated water in the kykeon.[106]

However, Hofmann never successfully established that naturally-occurring ergot alkaloids were actually capable of producing ecstatic entheogenic experiences. Hofmann's so-called "ergot experiment" was conducted with a commercially-extracted and modified form of ergonovine, and it resulted only in a mildly psychoactive state — nothing at all comparable to the dramatic visions attested to at Eleusis, or those produced by Hofmann's synthetic brain-child, LSD-25. To my knowledge, no one has actually tested a cold-water extract of *Claviceps purpurea* flour to see if it actually provides a safe, effective entheotropic experience.[107]

The American ethnomycologist R. Gordon Wasson and the English poet Robert Graves were the first scholars to seriously propose that some type of psychoactive mushroom might have been used in the ancient Eleusinic Mystery rites. Inspired by his psilocybin experiences with the Mazatecs of Mexico,[108] and intrigued by a painting on an Attic vase of two mushroom-shaped objects floating above the head of the hero Perseus,[109] Wasson theorized that the Greek Mystery rites might have involved the use of a psychedelic mushroom. In his 1958 foreword to the revised *Greek Myths*, Robert Graves casually suggested that the ambrosia of the gods mentioned in Orphic, Dionysian, and Eleusinian myths was probably *A. muscaria*, or possibly a *Paneolus* species. Graves had been intrigued by the image on an Attic vase of a mushroom-shaped object directly between the hooves of Nessus the Centaur — a serendipitous discovery, since he knew that the mythic Centaurs lived in the mountains and had a reputation for inebriation. The association with Centaurs is potentially noteworthy as *Panaeolus subbalteatus*, a mildly psychoactive mushroom, thrives on horse dung.[110] Grave's interest in a Greek mushroom connection was further inspired by an etching on an Etruscan mirror (now in the British Museum) that shows a mushroom-like object beneath the feet of the legendary Thessalian healer Ixion. If the object is indeed a mushroom, its shape, size, and edges are suggestive of *Panaeolus subbalteatus*.[111] As Graves noted, Ixion was once invited to visit Olympus and allowed to feast on the ambrosia of the gods. In light of references in the *Hymn to Demeter* that speak of the goddess feeding Metaneira's boy ambrosia (divine sustenance), it is intriguing that the Greeks sometimes referred to mushrooms as *broma theon*, "the food of the gods."[112]

Probably the most unequivocal evidence of an Eleusinic mushroom connection can be seen in a marvelous fifth-century BCE marble bas-relief, originally found at Eleusis and now in the Louvre. The bas-relief depicts Persephone and Demeter each holding a large, well-defined mushroom aloft in her right hand; each goddess seems to be looking directly at the mushroom held by the other. Based on the size and shape of the fungi, it can be assumed they are dried specimens of *A. muscaria* or fresh specimens of a *Gymnophilus* or *Panaeolus* species — only the absence of coloring prevents a more precise identification.

There are several secondary characteristics of *A. muscaria* that might support its use in the kykeon. First, its potency definitely seems to be enhanced by preliminary fasting,[113] and fasting was considered an integral element in the Mysteries. Second, *A. muscaria* dramatically increases one's visual sensitivity to light,[114] a trait that might explain the numerous reports of brilliant light in the accounts of the initiates. The primary obstacle in considering the candidacy of *A. muscaria* as an ingredient in the kykeon is that few scholars of the Classics have personally assayed this psychoactive, and even fewer have experienced the full entheogenic power of *A. muscaria* that comes with imbibing the urine of those who have eaten the mushroom. Knowing that Wasson himself identified *A. muscaria* as Soma partly on the basis of ancient Vedic references to people drinking Soma "pissed by the gods,"[115] I looked for — but could not find — any direct evidence that suggested drinking urine was part of the Eleusinian Mysteries.[116]

A more pressing problem with *A. muscaria* as a candidate for the kykeon is that its pharmacological potency seems to depend upon its host plants, and its psychoactive effects may depend upon personal differences in metabolism, psychological makeup, and expectations of a worshipper.[117] Nonetheless, based on firsthand reports from various authors, it seems clear that *A. muscaria* can produce psychoactive results that are comparable to the effects attributed to both Soma and the Eleusinian kykeon.

Communions of Divine Flesh and Blood

Expanding on Wasson's research linking *A. muscaria* with Soma, classicist Joseph Wohlberg suggested that the ancient Thracians, Phrygians, and Greeks preserved traces of Indo-European Soma rituals in their worship of Dionysos.[118] As in the Soma rites, the Dionysian rites reportedly involved "eating the god's flesh" and "drinking the god's blood" in order to become one with Deity and experience feelings of immortality.[119] While some scholars have assumed the terms referred to the flesh and blood of grapes turned into wine, Wohlberg cites an interesting passage in *The Bacchae* by Euripides which infers that, after eating the "divine flesh and blood" of Dionysos, King Pentheus experienced strange feelings and began to see double.[120] Because the passage states that the king saw Dionysos simultaneously in both his human form and his theriomorphic shape as a bull, Wohlberg theorizes that Pentheus was not drunk on wine but under the influence of an ecstatic sacrament. Based on another passage in *The Bacchae*, which states that ecstatic Dionysian Initiates wore special ritual garments of spotted fawn skin with tufts of white wool when performing rituals designed to make them feel at one with their god, Wohlberg suggests that the spotted fawn skin would have made an apt symbol for the spotted caps of *A. muscaria*.[121]

The flaw in Wohlberg's analysis is his assumption that the worshippers of Dionysos ate fresh *A. muscaria* mushrooms and also drank them in the form of a liquid hallucinogenic substance, produced by crushing them in the manner of grapes.[122] Since most cultures that use *A. muscaria* are aware that the dried mushrooms are many times more psychoactive — and less nauseating — than fresh ones, it is unlikely that *A. muscaria* were consumed raw in Greece (or elsewhere).[123]

Based on the mushroom-like images in Greek art, and the definitive mushrooms in the bas-relief of Demeter and Persephone, it must be considered whether a psilocybic mushroom of the *Gymnopilus* species, or perhaps one of the *Psilocybe, Stropharia, Panaeolus,* or *Conocybe* species could have been used in the Dionysian or Eleusinic rites, either as primary entheogenic agents or as substitutes when *A. muscaria* was not readily available. There are several mushrooms in the *Gymnopilus* family that are visually similar to the ones depicted in the bas-relief of Demeter and Persephone which might have lent themselves to being eaten as the flesh and blood of gods.

Although *Gymnopilus spectabilis* is definitely less psychoactive than *Stropharia cubensis,* it exhibits several interesting secondary traits that might link it to Wohlberg's Dionysian rites and, possibly, the Eleusinian Mysteries. The saffron-yellow *G. spectabilis* tends to stain a dark purplish-blue when cut, bruised, or juiced,[124] and mycologist Paul Stamets mentions an interesting case of a man who, after mistakenly eating a tuft of *G. spectabilis,* not only experienced hallucinations but also suffered from priapism — a most curious reaction in light of the prevalence of Dionysian phallic themes at Eleusis.[125]

There is, however, one aspect about all the mushroom candidates previously mentioned which always nagged at me. Due to substantial weather variations in ancient Greece, harvesting a large supply of mushrooms each year in time for the Mysteries would have proved challenging. In the entire history of the Eleusinia — roughly two thousand years — there was only one instance in which the Eleusinia was *not* held.[126] This fact, coupled with the large number of participants, suggests that the kykeon either contained a very abundant substance or that multiple entheogens were used. It is known that many species of psilocybic mushrooms are relatively easy to propagate on a manmade matrix and harvest when matured; the most reliably entheogenic are, furthermore, grown on cakes of *barley,* the grain held sacred in the Eleusinic rites and a specific component of kykeon. Based on the variety of hallucinogenic substances associated with Demeter, Persephone, and Dionysos, it could be that more than one psychoactive was used in the kykeon. It is also possible that different psilocybic mushrooms might have been used from year to year, with weather determining the selection of the mushroom species. However, both of these theories raise other complications, since using different entheogens can produce significantly different effects upon the worshipper, and the extant records suggest that the Eleusinian experience was fairly consistent year after year.

An interesting solution to the problem may be provided by the next kykeon candidate, *Peganum harmala.*

Peganum Harmala: Seeds of the Soul

My interest in *P. harmala* was first sparked by a brief comment in Wasson's *Soma: Divine Mushroom of Immortality* by Paul Anton Boetticher, who "...maintained that 'oμωμι (homœmi) was another word for μωλυ (mœly) or πεγανον (peganon), the mountain rue, and that it was a substitute used by the Greeks when they no longer had the *höm* itself, the original sacred plant..."[127] The reference to *peganon* sent me searching for information about "mountain rue," which I finally found listed as "Syrian rue," the common name for *Peganum harmala*.

P. harmala, a.k.a. Syrian rue,[128] grows throughout the Mediterranean, the Near East, and the Himalayas. In addition to being used to make a dye known as Turkish Red, it has a long history of being used as a medicinal and magical plant. The Greek herbalist Dioscorides suggested that *moly* — the famed yet unidentified magical plant that Hermes gave Odysseus to defend himself against the magic of Circe[129] — may have been Syrian rue, although scholarly and experiential research on *P. harmala* indicate that Syrian rue, by itself, is a decidedly mild psychoactive which produces little more than a sense of relaxation and time-expansion.[130]

However, there have been reports of other entheogenic explorers using *P. harmala* as a substitute for the harmaline-containing vine *Banisteriopsis capii*, the key potentiating agent of South American *ayahuasca* brews.[131] Although not very psychoactive in itself, the harmaline found in *B. capii* performs a vital function in the ayahuasca potion, making it possible for the intestines to absorb other psychedelic alkaloids that would otherwise be neutralized by monoamine oxidase enzymes.[132] Upon learning that harmalines were being used to increase the potency of other entheogenic mixtures, I began to wonder if *P. harmala* could have been used in the Eleusinian kykeon as a potentiating agent. Research on *P. harmala* soon led back to some of the very mushroom species previously identified as kykeon candidates.[133]

One of the most intriguing aspects of *P. harmala* used as a potentiating agent is that it seems to generate a sense of communicating with spirits. As an anonymous individual quoted by D.M. Turner verifies: "I began to feel as though my room was filled with the 'spirits' of musicians, artists, and visionaries whose genius had most strongly affected my life. And I felt as though I were amongst friends."[134]

From the surviving records of the Eleusinia, it is known that the ancient Greek-speaking world believed they came face to face at Eleusis with their cthonic divinities and ancestor spirits. Since adding harmala to other psychoactives tends to both increase their potency as well as generate visions of spirits, it could help explain how thousands of Eleusinian initiates each year experienced visions of the gods and spirits of the underworld.

The Link Between Fasting and Kykeon

As already mentioned, there are numerous ancient references which speak of participants fasting as part of the nine-day-long Eleusinic rites. Porphyry's *On Abstinence from Animal Food IV* mentions injunctions regarding fasting during the Mysteries, and the canonical *Hymn to Demeter* itself states, "Then for nine days queenly Deo wandered over the earth with flaming torches in her hands, so grieved that she never tasted ambrosia and the sweet draught of nectar, nor sprinkled her body with water" (line 50). The Greek Callimachus mentions "...fasting on the sacred days of Rharian Demeter,"[135] and he explains that the fast was modeled on Demeter's abstinence from food and drink: "Thrice did you seat yourself on the ground beside the fountain Callichorus, parched and without drinking, and did not eat nor wash."[136]

Since it would be lethal for an individual to go a full nine days with neither food nor water, and thousands of people, young and old, participated in the Eleusinian Mysteries, it may be inferred that the nine-day fast was not an absolute fast but rather some type of abstinence-fast. The tradition of fasting in conjunction with the Mysteries is compatible with the use of most entheogens, but it lends support to the candidacy of *A. muscaria* and *P. harmala*, which are both traditionally associated with fasting.[137]

Although those things "abstained from" in ancient Greece were not necessarily the same as those avoided during modern *ayahuasca* fasts, there are certain parallels. For instance, the *Hymn to Demeter* explains that the Eleusinian dedicants abstained from wine throughout the ceremonies, following the example of Demeter who refused a drink of wine from Metaneira.[137] Assuming *P. harmala* was used in the kykeon, fasting from fermented food and drink might have helped minimize gastrointestinal cramping.

Fasting from food and water is a fairly universal purification and trance-induction method used in many spiritual practices.[139] Burkert notes in *Greek Religion* (78-79) that the Mystery strictures included not only fasting and purifications, but an abstinence from sexual relations for a predetermined period of time, and Harrison cites an ancient Mystery oath: "I fast and am clean and abstinent from all things that make unclean and from intercourse with man."[140] While the specific effects of sexual abstinence on the use of harmala has not been studied, many Amazonian *vegelista* diets involving the use of harmaline-containing *ayahuasca* also insist that participants practice sexual abstinence around ceremonies.[141]

The Significance of the Mystery Rites

As Karl Kerenyi observes in *Eleusis...* (179), the content of visions — whether induced by extended fasting or by enteogenic substances — tends to be heavily influenced, if not determined, by the user's expectations and appropriate spiritual preparation as well as the overall state of mind of the person taking an enteogenic substance, and the surroundings in which the enteogen is imbibed: *Set and setting* of the visionary experience.[142] In contrast to the unstructured "trip" associated with "recreational" uses of drugs, the enteogenic experience at Eleusis would have been programmed by the primary initiation at Agrai and seven months of preliminary instruction, long before the nine days of Eleusinic rituals began. In addition, the nine-day-long Mystery rites — with preparatory purifications, fasting, mythic structure, and final ritualized ceremony — would have further enhanced a common, sacrosanct set and setting, leading the initiates toward the mystical goals of the rituals.

As Epictetus noted in *Discourses III, 21*: "These things are done both in due place and due time...when accompanied with sacrifice and prayers, when a man is first purified, and when he is disposed in his mind to the thought that he is going to approach sacred rites and ancient rites. In this way the Mysteries are useful, in this way we come to the notion that all these things were established by the ancients for the instruction and correction of life."

The well-known litany, "Brimo has brought forth Brimos (or, the Strong One has birthed the Strong One): Meditate upon these things, O people, here and when you leave this place!" was given by either the Hierophant or a priestess of Demeter, most likely near the end of the ceremonies in the Telesterion at the dawning of the tenth day.[143] After having experienced the ritual and received the visions and wisdom of the ancestors, there would be little doubt in any participant's mind that it was they who were being referred to as both *Brimo* and *Brimos* in this mystic liturgy. Some indelible transformation had occurred, something numinous had been brought to birth.[144]

Anciently, the morning of the tenth day was spent in a spiral dance on the Rharian Plain. Two tapering, wide-mouthed vessels (*plemochoai*) were carried by the Eleusinic clerics in this procession, and during the central point in the dance, their contents were flung out toward the east and toward the west while all in attendance cried: "Hye! Kye!" (*Rain! Conceive!*). It is speculated that these containers held seed corn and blood and water from myesis ablutions.[145] The ancient Hellenic method of blessing any altar prior to sacrifice or any hearth prior to using it was to strew it with either barley grains or barley meal, and it would appear that one of these rituals evolved from the other.[145]

The act which signified the end of the spiral dance, and perhaps the beginning of a feast for the mystai, was the sounding of a horn carved from a conch shell,[146] the labyrinthine spirals of which may have been, like the dance itself, evocative of the epiphanic message of eternal rebirth from death which was the underlying significance of the Mystery rites: To live one must eat, which is to kill; and to be reborn requires the sexual act. The renunciation of these things, as well as their ceremonial resumption, was the focus of the entire nine days of Eleusinic rites.

As Mircea Eliade noted in *The Sacred and the Profane...* (101-103): "The immolation of the Divine Being inaugurated not only the need to eat but also the doom of death and, in consequence, sexuality, the only way to ensure the continuity of life...the true sin is forgetting...The food plant is not *given* in nature: it is the product of a slaying...for the vegetable world to continue, man must kill and be killed: in addition, he must assume sexuality to its extreme limit..."

In summary, the psycho-spiritual message of the Mystery Rites of the Mystery Night at Eleusis was something like this:

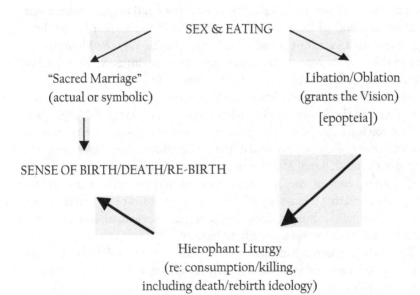

SEX & EATING

"Sacred Marriage" (actual or symbolic)

Libation/Oblation (grants the Vision) [epopteia])

SENSE OF BIRTH/DEATH/RE-BIRTH

Hierophant Liturgy (re: consumption/killing, including death/rebirth ideology)

It appears that the rationale underlying the Eleusinia was a powerful socio-spiritual modification of the most basic physical drives. The need for the modification — some might say *justification* — of animalistic impulses into a higher moral, spiritual stratum appears to hail from human conscious awareness of cause and effect. A need to modify raw animal instinct forms the basis of *all religious urge* in either positive or negative sense, e.g., killing to eat and therefore assuaging guilt via some form of repentance or restitution, or formalizing sex and birth in such a way that it can be seen as a symbol of the carnation and revivification of souls. This modification of animalistic drives through the teachings and visions of the Mysteries was certainly what Diodorus meant when he wrote: "...men who have taken part in the Mysteries become both more pious and more just and better in every respect than they were before."[148]

It was by utilizing this focus on the most basic of human drives — consumption and reproduction — that Eleusis bestowed upon its initiates the presence of their ancestors and Deities, a visionary, apotheotic revelation through which the mystai realized that life itself is found at the heart of death,[149] and through which a person's perception of the sorrows and difficulties in one's own life — as well as the perception of inevitable death — was shifted, replaced by a sublime but powerful solace.

By the modification — the "rending" — of that which is animal within humankind, the Dionysian might access that which is human. The Mysteries granted the epiphany which transformed that which was merely human into its optimum state — *ta Hiera*, or That Which Is Divine.

FOOTNOTES

CHAPTER ONE

1. Schuré, 407.

2. Athanassakis, *Orphic Hymns* 117, 120; Burkert, *Greek Religion* 13; Harrison, 263-267; Kerenyi, *Dionysos...* 111-114 & FN 220.

3. Athanassakis, *Orphic Hymns* 41-42, 57.

4. Harrison, 563, 573-596.

5. Campbell, *...Primitive...* 101; Hofmann, Ruck and Wasson, *passim.*

6. Burkert, *Greek Religion* 295; Harrison, 559; Kerenyi, *Dionysos...* 106-125.

7. Burkert, *Greek Religion* 152-156; Campbell, *...Occidental...* 13, 50; Harrison, 263-266, 286-292; Kerenyi, *Eleusis...* passim.

8. Athanassakis, *Orphic Hymns* 5-7, 115; Campbell, *...Primitive...* 184; Harrison, 290, 552; Hofmann, Ruck and Wasson, 112.

9. Burkert, *Greek Religion* 58-59, 161 / *...Necans* 255-259; Campbell, *...Occidental...* 138, 237-401; Davis, *passim*; Harrison, 452; Hofmann, Ruck and Wasson, 19, 142; Otto, 142; Robertson, *passim.*

10. Athanassakis, *Orphic Hymns* 131; Burkert, *Greek Religion* 159; Mallory, 26-27.

11. Hofmann, Ruck and Wasson, 69, lines 16.5-22.5

12. Campbell, *...Primitive...* 101, 183-188; Kerenyi, *Dionysos...* 113-114.

13. Burkert, *Greek Religion* 159; Campbell, *...Occidental...* 8-27; Harrison, 20-51; Kerenyi, *Dionysos...* 119.

14. Burkert, ...*Necans* 222; Campbell, ...*Occidental*... 264-274; Harrison, 35-40; Hofmann, Ruck and Wasson. 50, 98, 107, 119 FN 4; Kerenyi, *Dionysos*... 278 FN 21; Winkler and Zeitlin, 126-127.

15. Ferguson, see under *Christ*; Halliday, 14, 92; Robertson, 3-4.

16. Williams, C.K. 3-4.

17. Burkert, *Structure*... 29-30; Campbell, ...*Primitive*... 309-311; Gimbutas, 175-183; Graves, *White Goddess* 66-67; Kerenyi, *Gods*... 260-261; Otto 9, 110; Radin 188-191; Segal, Ch. 1 *passim*; Winkler and Zeitlin, 65; Young, 191.

18. Burkert, ...*Necans* 22, 72, 85, 296-297; Guthrie, *Orpheus*... 41, 100, 250-251 & FNs; Hofmann, Ruck and Wasson, 46, 55, 99; Kerenyi, *Dionysos*... 107-108, 300, 349-350, 373 / *Gods*... 273-274; Otto 137-142, 190; Turcan, 29-31, 79, 159-166, 187, 215-221; 319-327.

19. Burkert, ...*Necans* 222; Kerenyi, *Gods*... 273; Otto 117; Winkler and Zeitlin, 49, FN 83.

20. Burkert, *Greek Religion* 109 / ...*Necans* 243, 246; Kerenyi, *Dionysos*... 119-125; Otto 85; Winkler and Zeitlin, 138, FN 6; Young, 226-227, 244-247, 304.

21. The word *thyrsos*, the magical staff of Dionysos, is derived from a root which may be translated as "opener of the gates." See also Burkert, *Greek Religion* 198, 238-239, 284, 331 / ...*Necans* 223-226; Detienne, *Dionysos Slain* 43-47; Furst, 200; Graves, *Difficult*... 97-98, 105-106; Harrison, 146; Hofmann, Ruck and Wasson, 51-52, 99-103; Otto, chapter 12, *passim*; Turcan, 68-69, 86 FN 30.

22. Campbell, ...*Occidental*... 264; Guthrie, *Orpheus*... 111 & FNs, 114, 155, 194; Harrison, 479, 487, 586, 598; Hofmann, Ruck and Wasson, 374; Otto, 34.

23. Burkert, *Greek Religion*, 239-240; Dodds, 68-69, 86 FN 30; Harrison, 43-52, 464; Hofmann, Ruck and Wasson, 53, 101, 106-107, 112-113; Kerenyi, *Dionysos*... 225-226, 276, 289, 292, 298, 300; Otto, 80-81, 114-115, 142, 194; Turcan, 296.

24. Aoumiel, 20-24; Burkert, *Structure*... 29-30; Campbell, *Primitive*... 121-122; Danielou, 40-92; Hofmann, Ruck and Wasson, 57; Kerenyi, *Dionysos*... 387; Segal, Ch. 1, *passim*; Winkler and Zeitlin, 65; Young, 132, 303.

25. Burkert, *Greek Religion* 223-225; Guthrie, *Orpheus*... 41, 100, 250-251 & FNs; Kerenyi, *Dionysos*... 229-232; Luck 209; Otto 144; Plutarch *Isis and Osiris* 361 A-E; Turcan, 68-69, 86 FN 30, 296; Winkler and Zeitlin, 269.

26. Aoumiel, *passim*; Danielou, *passim*; Kerenyi, *Dionysos*... 120-190.

27. From Otto 195, FN 44. See also Harrison, 401, 439, 575.

28. Burkert, *Greek Religion* 31-51; Campbell, ...*Occidental*... 59; Mallory, 66-69; Otto, 52; Young, 217, 298-306.

29. Campbell, ...*Occidental*... 19, 69-72, 144-155; Kerenyi, *Dionysos*... 276-277; Legg 20-50; Luck 5-6; Mallory, 66-73, 184; Winkler and Zeitlin, 202.

30. Pinsent, 73, 76, 78, 88-89, 109; Ruck ...*Hyperboreans* 177-207; Trippett 66.

31. Bierlein, 274, 281-282, 290-295; Burkert, *Greek Religion* 163 / ...*Necans* 45 FN 43, 245, 290 FN 29; Campbell, ...*Occidental...* 138, 234, 324 / ...*Oriental...* 47 / ...*Primitive...* 324-359; Danielou, *passim*; Eliot, *passim*; Gimbutas, 182-183; Guthrie, *Orpheus...* 41, 98-102, 182, 250-251 & FNs; Harrigan, *passim*; Hofmann, Ruck and Wasson, 105 & FNs; Kerenyi, *Dionysos...* 381-387 / *Heroes...* 213-214; Otto, 195; Trippett, *passim*; Turcan, 29-31, 79, 159-166, 187, 215-221, 299, 319-327; Young, 155, 132, 205-206, 221-222 & FN.

32. Burkert, ...*Necans* 86-215; Danielou, *passim*; Harrison, 200-500; Hofmann, Ruck and Wasson, *passim*; Kerenyi, *Dionysos...* *passim*; Winkler and Zeitlin, *passim*.

33. Foulkes, 22; Kerenyi, *Dionysos...* 1-12.

34. Burkert, ...*Necans* 86-215; Danielou, *passim*; Harrison, 200-500; Hofmann, Ruck and Wasson, *passim*; Kerenyi, *Dionysos...* *passim*; Winkler and Zeitlin, *passim*.

35. Also an epithet given to *Pan*; Sutton, 70 FN 1.

36. Or pit trap; snarer; god who captures alive (Harrison, 478-481). The name's ancient roots may hail from *Zagros*, a Middle-Eastern mountain chain where archaeologists have discovered early traces of winemaking (Foulkes, 22-23); A possible linguistic descendant may be *Zagaya* (Spanish; "spear").

37. Burkert, ...*Necans* 86-215; Danielou, *passim*; Graves, *White Goddess* 173, 327-331; Harrison, 200-500, 587; Hofmann, Ruck and Wasson, *passim*; Kerenyi, *Dionysos...* *passim*; Winkler and Zeitlin, *passim*.

38. The Oriental Dionysos has wings (Guthrie, *Orpheus...* plate 12, 98, 101-102; Harrison, 655).

39. Williams, C.K. 66.

40. Burkert, *Greek Religion* 31, 149 / ...*Necans* 73-82; Harrison, 496-498, 560-564; Gimbutas, 181; Hofmann, Ruck and Wasson, 58; Kerenyi, *Dionysos...* 57-58, 79-118, 264, 275-276, 288; Young, 355 FN 29.

41. Dodds, 277; Otto, 13, 136, 151, 188; Winkler and Zeitlin, 126-127; Young, 222.

42. Burkert, *Greek Religion* 30-45, 292, 295, 323; Harrison, 474, 487, 563, 568; Kerenyi, *Dionysos...* 373-374; Otto, 34.

43. Danielou, 89; Kerenyi, *Dionysos...* 61, 295, 306; Sutton, 73 FN 13F.

44. Burkert, *Greek Religion* 109, 223 / ...*Necans* 243, 246; Campbell, ...*Occidental...* 225; Graves, *Myths...* 27.A; Kerenyi, *Dionysos...* 119-125, 241-261, 319; Otto, 85, 135; Winkler and Zeitlin, 138 FN 6.

45. Burkert, ...*Necans* 22, 72, 83, 295-297 & FNs; Eliade ...*Return* 142-164; Henrichs, 267-268; Hofmann, Ruck and Wasson, 54; Jakloski 92; Kerenyi, *Dionysos...* 107-108, 200, 349-350, 373; Otto, 137-142, 190.

46. Campbell, ...*Occidental...* 281-285.

47. Burkert, ...*Necans* 222; Harrison, 35-40; Otto, 113, 117, 136, 151, 188; Winkler and Zeitlin, 126-127.

48. Graves, *Myths...* 136.J; Otto, 182-188.

49. Ferguson, see under *Bishop*.

50. Burkert, ...*Necans* 123, 125; Harrison, 403, 502; Kerenyi, *Dionysos...* 141-142, 217-218, 228-233; Otto, 190-194; Potter and Johns 78; Turcan, 299-325, 327-333.

51. Burkert, ...*Necans* 6, 233 FN 12; Dodds, 278 FN 1; Ginzburg *passim*; Jackson 44; Kerenyi, *Dionysos...* 364; Luck 209; Otto, 134, 166; Plutarch *Isis and Osiris* 31 A-E; Turcan, 77, 315-325.

52. Burkert, ...*Cults passim*; Campbell, ...*Occidental... passim*; Dowden *passim*; Eliade ...*Return passim*; Halliday *passim*; Harrison, 420-590; Hofmann, Ruck and Wasson, *passim*; Leadbeater *passim*; Meyer *passim*; Robertson *passim*.

53. Aoumiel, *passim*; Dodds, 8-9, 64-101; Wohlberg 333, 338; Young, 219, 221.

54. Burkert, *Greek Religion* 293-295 / ...*Necans* 89 FN 29, 105, 109, 181; Graves, *White Goddess* 218-219; Harrison, 589-596, 659-673; Kerenyi, *Dionysos...* 246-256.

55. Burkert, ...*Necans* 256-259; Campbell, ...*Primitive...* 189-190 / ...*Occidental...* 312; Harrison, 152-153; Mallory, 118; Williams, Hector 37.

56. Burkert, *Greek Religion* 98.

57. Levi-Strauss, *Raw...* 336-338 / *Honey...* 413-414; Sutton, 72 FN 7F.

58. Burkert, *Greek Religion* 239-240 / ...*Necans* 41; Harrison, 43-52; Hofmann, Ruck and Wasson, 50-53, 98, 606 & FNs, 120 FN 2; Kerenyi, *Dionysos...* 225-226, 228-233; Otto, 80-81.

59. Pinsent, 52-53.

60. Harrison, 645-646; Otto, 171-188; Young, 351-352 FN 41.

61. Burkert, *Structure...* 29-30; Kerenyi, *Dionysos...* 311 / *Gods...* 259, 273; Ruspoli, 56; Segal, Ch. 1 *passim*; Winkler and Zeitlin, 63-96.

62. Campbell, ...*Primitive...* 229-242; Ripinsky-Naxon, *passim*.

63. Aoumiel, *passim*; Burkert, *Greek Religion* 10-24, 52-53; Campbell, *Historical Atlas...* Volume 1 Part II and Volume 2 Part I; Devereux, 54-76; Hofmann, Ruck and Wasson, 48-49, 91; Kerenyi, *Dionysos...* 5 -125; Mallory, 63-74; Wohlberg 334; Young, 209.

64. DeKorne, 67 & *passim*; Devereux, *passim*; Hofmann, Ruck and Wasson, *passim*; Ginzburg, *passim*; Kamrisch, Ott, Ruck and Wasson, *passim*; Pahnke, *passim*; Schultes, and Hofmann, 10-11, 86-91; Smith, *passim*.

65. Turcan, 64-101.

66. Antipater of Thessalonika. See Burkert, *Greek Religion* (332) regarding the Dionysian — *agathos daemon* — attitude toward that which is bad vs. that which

is good. For more information regarding "shamanic" and/or "psychological" theories of theater, see: Winkler and Zeitlin, 6-9, 19, 103, 126-128, 247 & FN 28, 254 & FN 44, 312-313, 324-329 & FN 4.

67. Aoumiel, 102; Burkert, *...Necans* 113-115, 183; Guthrie, *Orpheus*...116-118; Harrison, 498, 586-587; Hofmann, Ruck and Wasson, 48-50, 98; Kerenyi, *Heroes...* 282, 285; Sutton, 86.

68. Campbell, *...Primitive...* 1-21.

69. Tannahill, 154-158, 166-168.

70. Papazian, 32-49.

71. Kerenyi, *Dionysos...* 35-39; Papazian, 37-44; Tannahill, 166-167.

72. Gimbutas, 267-270; Harrison, 29; Hofmann, Ruck and Wasson, 50, 53, 128; Kerenyi, *Dionysos...* 30-60, 73-74.

73. Burkert, *...Necans* 113-115, 183; Harrison, 358, 362 FN 2, 498, 586-588; Otto, 166.

74. Danielou, 93-94; Guthrie, 146 FN 35.

75. Burkert, *...Necans* 87, 90-91; Danielou, 54-61; Kerenyi, *Dionysos...* 48.

76. Otto, 65.

77. Williams, C.K. 45.

78. Campbell, *...Primitive...* 395; Danielou, 130-150; Gimbutas, 116; Hofmann, Ruck and Wasson, 105 FN 2.

79. Campbell, *...Primitive...* 379.

80. Kerenyi, *Dionysos...* 167.

81. Ruspoli, 112.

82. Burkert, *Greek Religion* 201 / *...Necans* 113-115, 183; Gimbutas, 178-183; Guthrie, 116-118; Harrison, 356-358, 390,586-587; Kerenyi, *Dionysos...* 113-118, 123, 279-280 / *Gods...* 250-251, 255 / *Heroes...* 282, 285; Turcan, 314; Young, 303-306.

83. Campbell, *...Primitive...* 309-311; Gimbutas, 175-176; Graves, *White Goddess* 399; Ruspoli, 83.

84. Kerenyi, *Dionysos...* 113-118; Guthrie, *Orpheus*...116-118, 146 FN 35; Hofmann, Ruck and Wasson, 14; Luck, 206-207. Wohlberg (338, quoting Kuhn's work on the Vedic Sämhita texts) notes that the "sewn-in" appellation also applies to the god as *Soma*, or an ancient mushroom-derived Indo-European/Finno-Ugrian entheogen. See the *Eleusinia* chapter in this book for more information regarding this line of thought.

85. Matthews, 31.

86. Burkert, *Greek Religion* 76, 78; Eliade *...Sacred...* 130-137; Foulkes, 22; Guthrie, *Orpheus...* fig. 18A, 267-271 & FNs; Harrison, 498, 595; Hatch, *passim*; Jones and Pennick, 59; Turcan, 125-129, 221, 223.

87. Burkert, ...*Necans* 249 & FN 3; Ferguson, see under *Baptism*; Harrison, 595-598 & FNs.

88. Ferguson, see under *Diocese.*

89. Jones and Pennick, 52; Norwich, 44.

90. Cooper, *passim*; Dodds, 244, 277; Guthrie, fig. 18A, 267-271 & FNs; Leadbeater, *passim*; Matthews, 50-55.

91. Aoumiel, 98; Guthrie, *Orpheus...* fig. 18A, 267-271 & FNs.

92. Campbell, ...*Primitive...* 281; Jones and Pennick, 150.

93. Jones and Pennick, 75-76; Kerenyi, *Dionysos...* 299; Matthews, 13-15; Young, 132, 221 & FN.

94. Burkert, *Greek Religion* 167; Harrison, 498, 595; New Testament — Matthew 1:1-16, 15:21, 20:30-31, 21:9; Williams, C.K. *passim.*

95. New Testament — Matthew 16:15 / Mark 15:2, 8:27-29 / Luke 9:20 / 1 John 4:10; Williams, C.K. *passim.*

96. Kerenyi, *Dionysos...* 175-179; New Testament — Matthew 23:35-38 / Luke 13:31-35.

97. Kerenyi, *Dionysos...* 147; New Testament — Matthew 28: 6 / Luke 24:6 / John 4:7-26.

98. Burkert, *Greek Religion* 164; Hofmann, Ruck and Wasson, 145; Farnell, 612 Vol. II; Kerenyi, *Dionysos...* 113 FN 222, 349; New Testament — Matthew 9:15, 25:1-10 / Mark 2:19-20 / Luke 2:10, 5:34-35 / John 3:29, 14:16-20.

99. Burkert, *Greek Religion* 164; Guthrie, fig. 18A, 267-271 & FNs; Kerenyi, *Dionysos...* 256-259; New Testament — John 15:1-2.

100. Aoumiel, 59; Kerenyi, 299; New Testament — John 2:1-11, 4:45.

101. Burkert, ...*Necans* 8-9 & FN's, 272 FN 27; Campbell, ...*Occidental...* 184; Harrison, 452-453, 595-598 & FNs; Kerenyi, *Dionysos...* 254; New Testament — John 1:29, 36; Acts 8:32; 1 Corinthians 5:6 / Revelations 5:12-13, 6:16, 7:10-14, 12:11, 13:8; Otto, 132.

102. Aoumiel, 59; Kerenyi, ...*Dionysos* 169-170, 290 and plates 52A through 55; New Testament — Matthew 21: 5 / Mark 11:7 / Luke 19:35 / John 12:14-15; Old Testament — Zachariah 9:9 — see also the Old Testament *Apocrypha* of Ezekiel.

103. Campbell, ...*Inner Reaches...* 50 / ...*Primitive...* 388-390; Kerenyi, *Dionysos...* 248 FN 175; New Testament — John 3:15 / Old Testament — Numbers 21:5-91; Young, 220.

104. Burkert, ...*Necans* 258; Campbell, ...*Primitive...* 171, 444-451; Harrison, 312; Hofmann, Ruck and Wasson, 62-65; New Testament — Matthew 8:30-32 / Mark 5:11-13 / Luke 8:31-33.

105. Burkert, ...*Necans* 8-9 & FNs; Kakoure, 49-59; Kerenyi, *Dionysos...* 180-204; New Testament — Mark 16:19 / Luke 24:51; Young, 226-227, 244-247. See also *http://www.dhashura.com/book/diochris/dio1.htm* for further references to and correlations between these deities.

106. Fox, *passim.*

107. Jones and Pennick, 53-110.

108. Ferguson, see under Diocletian, Gnostic Sects, Monks, Stylites.

109. Durant, 727-729.

110. Ginzburg, *passim.*

111. Other titles given are either descriptive rather than cultic, or are not specifically Attic Greek (e.g., "Klodones/Mimallones," which are Macedonian descriptive terms; see Harrison, 397-398).

112. Burkert, *Greek Religion* 95-98; Garland ...*Life* 76-85.

113. Harrison, 394, 397, 401, 498; Kerenyi, *Dionysos...* 217.

114. Burkert, *Greek Religion* 65; Guthrie, 118, 147 FN 40; Harrison, 400, 402, 491, 590-593; Turcan, 77-79.

115. Harrison, 392; Kerenyi, *Dionysos...* 217.

116. Burkert, ...*Necans* 124-125; Harrison, 401, 500-507; Kerenyi, *Dionysos...* 223-225, 235-236.

117. Harrison, 479, 501-507.

118. Kerenyi, *Dionysos...* 298; Winkler and Zeitlin, 107.

119. Kerenyi, *Dionysos...* 316-348; Winkler and Zeitlin, 4 & FNs, 20-37, 58-62 & FNs, 107, 126.

120. Kerenyi, *Dionysos...* 52; Henrichs, 12.

121. Harrison, 474; Kerenyi, *Dionysos...* 351-352.

122. Burkert, ...*Necans* 69-71 & FNs; Sutton, 25; Turner, 122-124; Winkler and Zeitlin, 66-67 & FNs.

123. Winkler and Zeitlin, 24 & FNs.

CHAPTER TWO

1. An exhaustive, month-by-month list of festivals may be found at: *http://www.sites.netscape.net/heartdargent/Nov00.htm* — See also Burkert, *Greek Religion* 225-337; Harrison, 29; Hesiod's *Works and Days* II 770-828; Pickard-Cambridge, *Festivals... passim*; Winkler and Zeitlin, 287; Whitehead, 163-164.

2. Burkert, *...Necans* 35-36 & FN 4; Winkler and Zeitlin, 37-42 & FNs.

3. Parke, *passim;* Pickard-Cambridge, *Festivals...passim.*

4. See also Burkert, *Greek Religion* 226 and Harrison, 29.

5. Hecatombia on the 7th Hecatombion and Kronoia on the 12th.

6. The Heröis festival was similar to the Thesmophoria, except that it celebrated Semele's return from the Underworld as Thyone, and it was held at Delphi; see Graves, *Myths...* 27.11; Harrison, 402.

7. As noted by Burkert in *Greek Religion* 225; "...the month is in principle a genuine moon. Harmonization with the solar year is achieved through the insertion of additional months in a very arbitrary manner."

8. The *Agrionia* is a non-Athenian, trieteric festival known as either "The Boeotian Lenaia" (Burkert, *Greek Religion* 290) or "The Boeotian Anthesteria" (Otto, 103-119). This festival, probably held in spring, celebrated Dionysos as Lord of Souls, either in the sense of his "rebirth" (e.g., relative to the "unspeakable sacrifice" of the Lenaia, since the women attending the ceremony were themselves apparently pursued ritualistically by a priest bearing an ax, much as the Hosioi may have been chased at Delphi [see Lenaia for more information, as well as Burkert, *...Necans* 168, 178 and Kerenyi, *Dionysos...* 177, 182]), or in the sense of his return to the underworld (since, in Boeotian myth, Dionysos fled to the depths of the sea after the first bloody Agrionia was ended). Details of the Agrionia ritual include the use of masks (Burkert, *...Necans* 171), white/black polarity in the use of garments (*ibid.* 175), and the ritual sacrifice of a young animal by women (*ibid.* 171).

9. The Panathenaia was held *after* the Synoikia according to Burkert (*Greek Religion* 232).

10. See http://www.sites.netscape.net/heartdargent/Nov00.htm, as well as Burkert, *...Necans* 119-124 & FNs. See Anthesteria for more information regarding the ceremony of *Apatouria,* in which a child was "introduced" to his clan deity(ies).

11. The Arrhephoria ceremonial is often, incorrectly, placed at the Thesmophoria proper, under the guise of the *Kalligenia;* however, *Scholion...II, 1* clearly states that the Arrhephoria was held just prior to the time of the Panathenaia ceremonies. See also Harrison, 121-123, 131-134 for details.

12. Harrison, 122-123.

13. Parke, 144-145.

14. Burkert, *Greek Religion* 230-231 / *...Necans,* 149, 156; Campbell, *...Primitive..,* 40-100; Harrison, 110-114; Parke, *passim;* Pickard-Cambridge, *Festivals...passim.*

15. Guthrie, *Orpheus...* 196; Harrison, 110-114.

16. Burkert, *Greek Religion* 231 /...*Necans* 4, 11, 16, 42, 46 FN 46, 76, 102, 126, 140, 147, 165, 179, 130; Harrison, 111-112; Young, 232.

17. Munychion is known as *Bysios* in Delphi, and that is the more well-known month-name for the epiphany of Apollo; Kerenyi, *Dionysos...* 222, 233-235.

18. Burkert, *Greek Religion* 201; Harrison, 33-36; Kerenyi, *Gods...* 117.

19. Harrison, 30-38.

20. Parke, 168.

21. Harrison, 27-28.

22. Harrison, 23-27, 642-643.

23. Burkert, *Greek Religion* 230-231.

24. Parke, 137.

25. Burkert, *Greek Religion* 151; Harrison, 72-73.

26. Kerenyi, *Dionysos...* 297-298.

27. Garland, ...*Death* 105; Parke, 53-54.

28. Harrison, 145; *Scholion to Lucian,* Dial. Metrer. VII, 4. Both grain and wine were stored in underground pithoi, pointing to the cthonic realm of Demeter/Persephone and of Dionysos as Lord of Souls.

29. Harrison, 146.

30. Harrison, 148; Kerenyi, *Dionysos...* 218-219, 271-272.

31. Brumfield, *passim*; Harrison, 147-149.

32. Burkert, *Greek Religion* 231.

33. Kerenyi, *Dionysos...* 85-87, 203.

34. Harrison, 126, 130, 270.

35. Burkert, *Greek Religion* 227; Kerenyi, *Dionysos...* 168-173, 309-318; Otto, 83; Winkler and Zeitlin, 26-27 & FNs, 49, 125. Classical writers have called the Anthesteria "the more ancient Dionysia" e.g., before the advent of formalized theater; see Burkert, *Greek Religion* 237; Harrison, 34; Otto, 53; Winkler and Zeitlin, 48 FN 82, 374.

36. Winkler and Zeitlin, 98, 237-270 & FNs.

37. Artemidoros, 1.54; Burkert, *Greek Religion* 227, 256, 262-263 / *Structure...* 29-30; Kakoure, 212; Kerenyi, *Dionysos...* 316-317, 381; Osborne, 97-109; Peradatto & Sullivan, *passim*; Segal, 158-214; Sekunda, 57; Siewart, 102-111; V. W. Turner, *passim*; Whitehead, 97-109; Winkler and Zeitlin, 22, 24 & FN 81, 29-33, 42-43, 58-62, 66-68 & FNs, 98, 101-102, 106, 113-114, 124 & FN 80, 237-270 & FNs, 278-280.

38. Keegan, 258-259; Sekunda, 57.

39. Winkler and Zeitlin, 108-114 & FNs, 278; Xenophon, 1.2-4 - 1.2-10.

40. Winkler and Zeitlin, 22 & FNs, 38 & FN 55, 45 FN 72.

41. Thompson & Wycherley, 48-52; Pickard-Cambridge, *Attic Theater...* 337 & FNs; Vernant & Vidal-Naquet, Ch. 1 & 3 *passim*; Winkler and Zeitlin, 4, 13, 16, 39-41 & FNs, 238-239 & FNs, 336-365.

42 Isocrates, 82; Winkler and Zeitlin, 101.

43. Loraux, 26-31; Winkler and Zeitlin, 105-106. Athenian citizens (*astoi*) were conferred their citizenship through their mother's line, not their father's; Hignett, 343-347; Loraux, 36-31; Whitehead, 106-109; Winkler and Zeitlin, 195-196, 267-268 & FNs.

44. Hanson, 57, 70; Hignett, 343-347; Whitehead, 106-109; Winkler and Zeitlin, 267-268 & FNs.

45. Winkler and Zeitlin, 36 FN 48; Young, 224-226, 349 FN 14.

46. Lawler, *passim*; Winkler and Zeitlin, 6, 22, 44, 50-55 & FNs, 229.

47. Hanson, 80; Lawler, *passim*.

48. Burkert, *Greek Religion* 234, 312 / *...Necans* 54-57. 65 & FN 31; Kerenyi, *Dionysos...* plates 61 A & B; Siewart, 102-111; Winkler and Zeitlin, 16-19, 29-30, 99-114, 124 & FN 81.

49. Winkler and Zeitlin, 99-101.

50. Seaford, *...Cyclops* 53-58; Winkler and Zeitlin, 49-50, 101, 216-227 & FNs, 224, 263, 287; Young, 239.

51. Kerenyi, *Dionysos...* 199.

52. Burkert, *Greek Religion* 99-101, 163 / *...Necans* 237-238 & FNs; Kerenyi, *Dionysos...* 285-288; Otto, 164; Winkler and Zeitlin, 99.

53. Kerenyi, *Dionysos...* 296-297, 333; Winkler and Zeitlin, 37.

54. Burkert, *Greek Religion* 99-101, 163, 257, 262-263, 290 / *...Necans* 68-72, 237-238 & FNs; Kerenyi, *Dionysos...* 44-45; Otto, 80-81; Winkler and Zeitlin, 175-177, 203-205.

55. Kerenyi, *Dionysos...* 168-172, 309, & plates 17-20 and 56-59B, Winkler and Zeitlin, 99.

56. Burkert, *...Necans* 49-70.

57. Burkert, in *...Necans* 58 & FN 1, 68-69 / and *Structure...* 39-41, notes that it is a primate tendency to give phallic displays when asserting dominance and to present the rump when showing submission. Burkert also notes in *...Necans* (70) that the phallus carried in the pompe represents life triumphing over death. Some scholars (e.g., Simon Goldhill in *Nothing to do with Dionysos...* 97-129) disagree with this apotropaic theory of the symbol of the phallus and the

padded dancer. I too theorize that the padded dancer "presentation" as symbolic of simple submission is not wholly correct, since in human society, to turn one's back to another — and particularly to display the buttocks — is generally seen as an insult, not a sign of submissiveness. See also Winkler and Zeitlin, 41 FN 63, 103, 108-109 & FN 37.

58. Graves, *Myths...* 27.12, 35E; Hanson, 103; Keegan, 255; Winkler and Zeitlin, 49 FN 83.

59. Comedy, particularly the style known as new comedy, was performed at the Katagogia, but tragedy appeared to have been the main focus of that festival. See Winkler and Zeitlin, 4-5 & FNs, 265, 274-313 & FNs, 327, 330-335 & FNs. There were up to one thousand performers in any given dithyramb. See Burkert, *Greek Religion* 106, 290; Kerenyi, *Dionysos...* 330-348; Winkler and Zeitlin, 4-5 & FNs, 48-50, 287.

60. Kerenyi, *Dionysos...* 335.

61. Sutton, *passim*; Winkler and Zeitlin, 325 & plates 11-16.

62. In a sense, satyr plays may be considered the forerunner of tragicomedy. See Demetrios, *On Style* 169; Kerenyi, *Dionysos...* 333, 339-340; Lawler 88-93; Pickard-Cambridge, *...Attic Theatre* 120, 125; Sutton, 26-27, 32, 39-40, 50 & Fns, 52; Winkler and Zeitlin, 53-54, 58-62 & FNs, 129, 229, 235, 265, 274-313 & FNs, 327, 330-335 & FNs, 309.

63. Winkler and Zeitlin, 6.

64. Burkert, *...Necans* 58, 69-71 & FNs / *Structure...* 29-30; Sutton, 25; Winkler and Zeitlin, 18, 66-67 & FNs, 78, 118-129, 216, 227, 325-335 & FNs.

65. V. Turner, 122-124; Winkler and Zeitlin, 18, 60 & FN 126, 64, 69, 139, 245-249.

66. Babcock, *passim*; N. Z. Davis 97-123; Stallybrass and White, Ch. 1 *passim*; Turcan, 291-292; V. Turner, *passim*; Winkler and Zeitlin, 126 & FNs. Such "reversals" also refer to mockery as a purifying force; see Burke, 178-204; Burkert, *Greek Religion* 287; Harrigan, 26; Harrison, 28-31; Hyde, 336-338; Winkler and Zeitlin, 327-328.

67. Our "tragedy" comes from the Greek *tragodia*, or 'song on the occasion of a he-goat'; Kerenyi, *Dionysos...* 249, 318, 322 FN 154.

68. Kerenyi, *Dionysos...* 249.

69. Winkler and Zeitlin, 24-25. Some Classicists contend that the urban Dionysia may have been a 'modernization' of or borrowing from a more ancient festival; see Winkler and Zeitlin, 16, 28 FN 16, 35 FN 45. My theory is that theater arose from politics, which arose from myth, which arose from ritual; the framework of this theory may be found in Winkler and Zeitlin, *passim*, especially 245-249 & FNs. For the general "goatiness" of pubescent youth, see Hippocrates' *Epidemics* 2-51. Such a 'sacrifice for the sake of society' may be inferred in Aristophanes' *Birds*, in which a goat is sacrificed for a city foundation, which may be symbolic

of the ephebes and their fathers sacrificing for the city, though Winkler in *Nothing to do with Dionysos...* suggests that there was no actual goat sacrifice performed at the Katagogia at all, or that Aristophanes' mention of goat sacrifice "...may have been some sort of joke." (Winkler and Zeitlin, 59 FN 121).

70. Burkert, *Greek Religion* 57, 70.

71. Winkler and Zeitlin, 1-4-106 & FNs.

72. Hanson, *passim.*

73. Graves, *White Goddess* 186-187, 251, 436 & FNs.

74. Nilsson, 88; Parke, 92-93.

75. Graves, *White Goddess* 66-67, 181; Mathews, 23-26.

76. Inversion — or "topsy-turvy" — festivals are an ancient form of purification. See Burke, 178-204; Burkert, *Greek Religion* 287; Harrigan, 26; Hyde, 336-338.

77. Kerenyi, *Dionysos...* 217-221.

78. Harrison, 29, 347.

79. Harrison, 72-73.

80. Parke, 138-139.

81. Kerenyi, *Dionysos...* 144-147; Plutarch/Fuller, 27.

82. Kerenyi, *Dionysos...* 162; Plutarch/Fuller, 27.

83. Pinsent, 109-110; Plutarch/Fuller, 27

84. Graves, *White Goddess* 329; Kerenyi, *Dionysos...* 102-103, 144-146, 162; Plutarch/Fuller, 27-28.

85. Plutarch/Fuller, 25-27.

86. Burkert, *Greek Religion* 231-234.

87. Burkert, *...Necans* 46-48; Harrison, 111-114.

88. Burkert, *Greek Religion* 138; Young, 301-305, 321.

89. Harrison, 75-82; Plutarch/Fuller, 26.

90. Harrison, 134-137.

91. *Ibid.*

92. Burkert, *Greek Religion* 231-234.

93. Harrison, 75-118.

94. Edgerton, 143; Harrison, 98-114; Ross and Robins, *passim*; Tierney,robins, *passim.*

95. Harrison, 110; Matthews, 183.

96. Harrison, 38, 137-144.

97. Harrison, 121-131, 143.

98. See http://www.sites.netscape.net/heartdargent/Nov00.htm

99. Those made of flour-paste at the Skirophoria; Harrison, 122.

100. Harrison, 125; Hofmann, Ruck and Wasson, 69.

101. *Scholion to Lucian,* Dial. Metrer. VII, 1.

102. Other Eleusinic elements in the Thesmophoria include water purifications and an enforced period of chastity; Harrison, 121-122 & FN 1.

103. Brown, 370-371; Harrison, 130.

104. Burkert, ...*Necans* 193.

105. *Callichorus* is "the virgin's well," also "the good well" and "the well of cultivation"; Hofmann, Ruck and Wasson, 71.

106. Harrison, 134-136.

107. Harrison, 114-119.

108. *Ibid.*

CHAPTER THREE

1. Kerenyi, Dionysos... 296-296. Also see http://www.cs.utk.edu/-mclennan/ BA/ JO/Len.html

2. Graves, *White Goddess* 399; Kerenyi, *Dionysos...* 293-294; Pickard-Cambridge, 30; Plutarch, *Isis and Osiris* 364D, 365A.

3. Harrison, 65, 68, 620; Kerenyi, 293-294; Pickard-Cambridge, 30, 36.

4. Burkert, *Greek Religion* 291 / ...*Necans* 90-92, 16-130, 237; Harrison, 59 FN 2, 60-65 & FNs, 461 & FNs, 557; Kerenyi, *Dionysos...* 198, 217-219, 223 FN 99, 222-224, 256-261, 290-291 / *Gods...* 254-265; Otto, 80-81, 190; Winkler and Zeitlin, 210-227 & FNs; Young, 218.

5. Harrison, 402-403, 440-441; Hofmann, Ruck and Wasson, 50, 106-107; Kerenyi, *Dionysos...* 332-336; Pickard-Cambridge, 30-36; Strabo, *Iacchus* 401; Sutton, *passim*; Winkler and Zeitlin, 286.

6. Burkert, ...*Necans* 168, 173, 178; Kerenyi, *Dionysos...* 177-182, 299.

7. Burkert, *Greek Religion* 239-240; Harrison, 43-52, 402, 464, 604; Hofmann, Ruck and Wasson, 53, 101, 106-107 & FNs, 112-113; Kerenyi, *Dionysos...* 222-226, 255-261, 276, 289, 292, 298-304 & FNs, 384-385 / *Gods...* 271; Otto, 80-81, 114-115, 142, 194; Winkler and Zeitlin, 87, 107.

8. Midwinter; Guthrie, *Orpheus...* 132; Kerenyi, *Dionysos...* 335-336.

9. Burkert, *...Necans* 124-125, 222; Harrison, 147; Hofmann, Ruck and Wasson, 50, 106 FN 2, 124-125; Kerenyi, *Dionysos...* 279, 298-304, 381; Otto, 117. See Winkler and Zeitlin, (286, 394) for information regarding the originally apolitical nature of the Lenaia (see *Katagogia* re; the political use of both comedy and tragedy in Classical Athens). I theorize that if comedy was in fact used as a form of political commentary, and if comedies written only by previously-unheard-of writers or foreigners were primarily found at the Classical Lenaia festival (Sutton, *passim*; Winkler and Zeitlin, 47 FN 80, 102) which was overseen by women, then this, plus the low access of women to the political forum, functioned to allow foreign and female political influence some voice in Athens after the development of democracy, yet still keep it outside the Assembly of phratrae proper (Winkler and Zeitlin, 330 & FNs).

11. Kerenyi, *Dionysos...* 343; Matthews, 65-66.

12. Harrison, 437; Kerenyi, 180-184 & FNs, 293; Otto, 80-81.

13. Graves, *White Goddess* 186-187; Matthews, 14-15, 40.

14. Harrison, 431-441; Kerenyi, *Dionysos...* 115-115 & FNs, 245, 270, 299, 362.

15. As found in Harrison, 438.

16. Burkert, *Greek Religion* 269, 276; Kerenyi, *Dionysos...*225 FN 108, 261, 296.

17. Pickard-Cambridge, 30, 36.

18. Burkert, *...Necans* fig. 7.

19. Kerenyi, 327; Korshak, 18-25 & FNs, 43, 114; plate 48 shows an ancient Hellenic "eye cup" — the probable ancestor of modern Greek charms worn to turn away evil — bearing a full-frontal rendition of the Dionysian mask; Winkler and Zeitlin, 84-85.

20. Kerenyi, *Dionysos...* 278.

21. Burkert, *Greek Religion* 291 / *...Necans* 125 FN 49; Harrison, 46-47, 538-539; Kerenyi, *Dionysos...* 141-142, 151, 198-204, 214-222, 231-238, 295; Otto, 84-85.

22. Burkert, *...Necans* 227-241; Harrison, 43-52, 131. Edited excerpts reprinted from *Circle Network News Nature Spirituality Quarterly,* Issue 64.

23. Kerenyi, *Dionysos...* 291.

24. Otto, 98-100; Ranke-Heinmann 81-81; See also *http: //www.dhashura.com/book/diochris.diol.htm*

25. Kerenyi, 292, 303-304.

26. Foulkes, 110, 598; Garey, 257.

27. Foulkes, 109.

28. Kerenyi, *Dionysos...* 198-199, 283-300. The midwinter Lenaia, Anthesteric Limnaia (February/March by our calendar) and other ceremonies are commonly

confused and/or conflated among other scholars of the Classics — see Burkert, *Homo Necans* 235-237 and FNs 21-26; Hofmann, Ruck and Wasson, 128. Kerenyi also tended to mix up his rural and urban Dionysias (*Dionysos...* 297-299), which is understandable when the timings of, items used in, and meanings behind these celebrations are considered (see *Lenaia* and *Katagogia* for details). Harrison, in *Prologomena...*, appears to conflate the Hosios and Thyiad sacrifice/awakening rites of midwinter with the Panathenaia-related *midsummer* rites of Charila, Heröis, and Stepterion, also held at Delphi, but in honor of Semele as *Thyone*, the raving and reborn one (Harrison, 77, 106-116).

29. Kerenyi, *Dionysos...* 291.

30. Burkert, *...Necans* 233; Kerenyi, *Dionysos...*290-306; Otto, 100.

31. Kerenyi, *Dionysos...*215, 276, 279, 293-296.

32. Kerenyi, *Dionysos...*279, 332-336; Hofmann, Ruck and Wasson, 55, 119 FN 4.

33. Harrison, 446-447; Kerenyi, *Dionysos...* 59-60; Ott, *Pharmacophhilia...* 121-124.

34. Hofmann, Ruck and Wasson, 51-52, 98-107 & FNs; Kerenyi, *Dionysos...*326; Ott, *Pharmacophilia...* 122-123; Otto, 98-99; Pausanias, 6:26, 1-2; Tannahill, 293.

35. Foulkes, 114, 122, 450; Garey, 253, 256.

36. Foulkes, 109-114, 122, 450; Garey, 257.

37. Garey, 254.

38. Foulkes, 448.

39. Kerenyi, *Dionysos...* 294.

40. Foulkes, 118, 596; Garey, 182-183, 254-256, 258.

41. Brown, 316; Foulkes, 450; Graves, *White Goddess* 173-174, 183; Harrison, 158, 540, 560; Kerenyi, *Dionysos...* 260, 274, 282, 327 / *Gods...* 255-256. 259; Matthews, 90; Otto, 152-159.

42. Brown, 243, 286; Devereux, *passim*; Furst, 219; Hofmann and Schultes, *passim*; Hofmann, Ruck and Wasson, 99-107 & FNs; Pickard-Cambridge, 30.

43. Furst, 210 231, 259; Hofmann and Schultes, 112; Hofmann, Ruck and Wasson, 97-11 & FNs.

44. Burkert, *...Necans* 71; Campbell, *Primitive...* 295-296; Harrison, 61, 521, 533-534, 589; Kerenyi, *Dionysos...*160, 260, 299-300 / *Gods...* 274.

45. Burkert, *Greek Religion* 64-66 / *...Necans* 41, 224 FN 39; Harrison, 43-52, 402-403, 407, 464, 557, 604; Hofmann, Ruck and Wasson, 46, 50-53, 98-99, 106 & FNs, 119 FN 4, 120 FN2; Kerenyi, *Dionysos...*225-226, 256, 279, 273-315 & FNs, 361, 384-385 / *Gods of the Greeks* 271; McLennan, *passim*; Otto, 42, 67, 80-81, 114-115, 194. Prior to the performance of Lenean plays or Dithyrambs, the Dadouchos would cry "Euphemete!", which can be translated as "be still!" or "speak no evil!"

This command was given by the officiating priest at the beginning of any sacrificial ceremony; *it was not given at any other time* (Burkert, *Greek Religion* 73, 199, 248, 273 / *...Necans* 4). Therefore, it is not unreasonable to assume that something was sacrificed at this ceremony. There is no record of animal sacrifice being made at the Temple sanctuary *en Limnais*, though it was customary to sacrifice a bull whenever dithyrambs were to be sung (Kerenyi, *Dionysos...*318). I theorize that *Dionysos himself* was the sacrifice in the context of the Lenean ceremonies, and that the stamnoi of wine ladled out by the Gerairai was the extent of the "blood sacrifice" given to the cthonic gods honored at the Lenaia (Kerenyi, *Dionysos...*190-193; Burkert, *Greek Religion* 163-164, 238 / *...Necans* 224-226 & FNs, 238; Harrison, 436-441; Turcan, 314). It is also known that the worshippers partook of the new wine themselves, much as worshippers at a sacrifice to the Olympic gods would partake of the roasted flesh of a sacrifice. The wine given in libation at the Lenaia may have gone by the euphemism of "blood," or even "milk" or "honey" (*meli* or *gleukos*) in the same way wine offerings to the cthonic Great Mother did (Harrison, 91-93, 441-443; Hofmann, Ruck and Wasson, 52, 99-103, 104 FN 1). See Part 3 of the Anthesteria chapter, which discusses forms of sacrificial offerings to the cthonic gods, which often demand *nephalia* — wineless/bloodless/fireless offerings.

46. Hofmann, Ruck and Wasson, 106-107 & FN2.

47. Kerenyi, *Dionysos...* 233-234.

48. Kerenyi, *Dionysos...* 290-304; see the Anthesteria chapter and *Limnaia* for further details.

49. Hofmann, Ruck and Wasson, 46, 50, 91, 99; Kerenyi, *Gods...* 274; Ott *Pharmacophilia...* 122-123.

50. Hofmann, Ruck and Wasson, 96; Kerenyi, *Dionysos...*173-174, 180, 312, 323; the Eleusinian Dadouchos ("herald of the Hierophant") was always chosen from the family Kerykes; in all of ancient Greece, the secrets of entheogenic rituals were handed down only by and through the Kerykes and Eumolpidai families.

51. Kerenyi, *Dionysos...* 303-304, 307, 312-314.

52. Kerenyi, *Dionysos...* 297-298.

53. Graves, *White Goddess* 399; Kerenyi, *Dionysos...* 284; Young, 219-220.

54. Kerenyi, *Dionysos...* 293, 307-308, 312, 315. Anciently, Dionysos was considered the Basilinna's "true husband."

55. Kerenyi, *Dionysos...* 293, 307-308.

56. Burkert, *Greek Religion* 292, 295; Campbell, *...Primitive...* 186-187; Harrison, 522-523; Kerenyi, *Dionysos...* 4-45, 222-225, 354-357 / *Gods...* 253-256; Otto, 80-81; Winkler and Zeitlin, 203-205.

57. Campbell, *...Occidental...* 226.

58. Harrison, 525-526; Kerenyi, *Dionysos...* 387. See *http://www.Ioway.nativeweb.org/text/ioway/library/sbchapter3.htm* or enter "ancient Indian sacred bundles" into any web search engine to find information regarding Plains sacred bundle significance and use.

59. Graves, *Myths...* 30.A, 30.1; Kerenyi, *Dionysos...* 265-271.

60. Guthrie, *Orpheus...* 82, 98, 108, 120-123, 203; Kerenyi, *Dionysos...* 311.

61. Kerenyi, *Dionysos...* plates 84-89 and pages 289-290.

62. Bremmer 71; Dodds, 281 FN 2.

63. Graves, *Myths...* 30.1.

64. Kerenyi, *Dionysos...* plates 84-89 and pages 289-290.

65. Harrison, 522-525.

66. Burkert, *...Necans* 123, 125; Harrison, 403, 503; Kerenyi, *Dionysos...* 44-45, 141-142, 217-218, 228-233, 265-278 / *Gods...* 254-255, 263-265; Otto, 80-81, 94; Turcan, 314; Winkler and Zeitlin, 175-177, 203-205.

67. Hofmann, Ruck and Wasson, 14; Kerenyi, *Dionysos...* 44-55, 211-212, 225, 256 FN 198, 277; Otto, 147-148.

68. Kerenyi, *Dionysos...* 296-297; Winkler and Zeitlin, 85-87.

69. Hofmann, Ruck and Wasson, 105; Kakoure, 212; Winkler and Zeitlin, 87, 107. It is worth noting that items used in all Dionysian initiation rites (veil, fleece, liknon) were also used in ancient and Classical Greek marriage ceremonies; see Burkert, *...Necans* 45 FN 42, 273-274; Harrison, 62, 521, 533-534; Kerenyi, *Dionysos...* 260 / *Gods...* 254-256.

70. Burkert, *Greek Religion* 151; Hofmann, Ruck and Wasson, 105; Pinsent, 28; Kerenyi, *Dionysos...* 48-49, 150-157. Brauron was a place of initiation sacred to the goddess Artemis (Kerenyi, *Heroes...* 117); the association was not unlike the college of Vestal Virgins of Rome. See Chapter 1 for the ancient association of the bear to Dionysian-type worship.

71. Burkert, *Greek Religion* 151, 222-223, 262.

72. Kerenyi, *Dionysos...* 218; Williams, C.K. 11, 17, 20.

73. Graves, *Myths...* 27.10 / *White Goddess* 257-258, 314; Harrison, 436, 641.

74. Diogenes Laertius, VII: 77, also found in Harrison, 586-590, 673; Flavius Claudius Julianus, *Orations* Vol. III: *Letter to a Priest*; Graves, *White Goddess* 167; Harrison, 149-150; Kerenyi, *Dionysos...* 369.

75. Burkert, *...Necans* 285; Harrison, 35-36, 150, 544, 628; Kerenyi, *Dionysos...* 78-83.

76. Graves, *...Myths* 30-31; Harrison, 628; Kerenyi, *Dionysos...* 369; Plutarch, *Questiones Symposia* 3,1.

77. Harrison, 114-119.

78. Graves, ...*Myths* 30.3; Kerenyi, *Dionysos...* 336; Otto, 157; Wohlberg 340.

79. See also Burkert, ...*Necans* 123 and Harrison, 439.

80. As long as the mixture is not shaken during consecration, it is mostly oil which will come into contact with everything, and nothing will go rancid or attract insects. I theorize that this liquid mixture, equivalent to that given in libation to the ghosts of the ancestors (*spondai*; Burkert, *Greek Religion* 70-73) was used in the ancient Lenaia to consecrate the liknon and its contents — Burkert, *Greek Religion* 70-73; Harrison, 595.

81. See also Burkert, ...*Necans* 124-125.

82. Burkert, ...*Necans* 260-261.

83. Burkert, *Greek Religion* 254-256 / ...*Necans* 90-92, 116-130 & FNs; Harrison, 59 FN 2, 60-65, 403, 461 & FN 2, 502, 557; Kerenyi, *Dionysos...* 141-42, 217-218, 223 FN 99, 228-237, 259-261; Otto, 81, 190, 194; Strabo, *Iacchus* 401; Winkler and Zeitlin, 210-227 & FNs.

84. Burkert, ...*Necans* 123-130; Kerenyi, *Heroes...* 264 plate 63; Pinsent, 78-80.

85. Burkert, ...*Necans* 124-127; Kerenyi, *Dionysos...* 44-45, 110-114, 256-279 / *Gods...* 254-255, 263-265; Hofmann, Ruck and Wasson, 118-119; Otto, 81; Winkler and Zeitlin, 175-177, 203-205.

86. Burkert, ...*Necans* 232 & FN 6; Diodorus *Siculus*, 4.25; Guthrie, *Orpheus...*61; Harrison, 502-507, 512-516, 604.

87. Burkert, *Necans* 116-130.

88. Burkert, *Greek Religion* 103-104 / ...*Necans* 83-130, 67, 26, 381; Otto, 191-192; Kerenyi, *Dionysos...* 228. The Delphic Omphalos was a cone-shaped standing-stone with a hole or "navel" on top in its center, and it represented the *Axis Mundi* (or world-tree) of the Attic world, that place in which Olympos, the earth, and the House of Hades were interconnected.

89. Kerenyi, *Dionysos...* 236-237 & FNs.

90. Burkert, *Greek Religion* 103-104; Kerenyi, *Dionysos...* 266, 381.

91. Burkert, ...*Necans* 123-124 & FNs; Kerenyi, *Dionysos...* 230-237.

92. *Heröis*, the celebration of Semele's return as Thyone, was also celebrated at Delphi later in the year.

93. Hofmann, Ruck and Wasson, 55, 96 FN 6; Winkler and Zeitlin, 168-206, 203-205.

94. Kerenyi, *Dionysos...* 83, 110-114, 248-249, 265, 278-279; Hofmann, Ruck and Wasson, 18-119. For a theory of the Delphic Omphalos as cervix of the goddess of the underworld, see Gimbutas, 149. See the *Anthesteria* chapter for details regarding the practice of *sphagia*.

CHAPTER FOUR

1. Burkert, *Greek Religion* 237; Harrison, 34; Otto, 53; Winkler and Zeitlin, 16, 48 FN 2. For an excellent treatise on the *Anthesteria*, see: http: //www.cs.utk.edu/~ mclennan/BA/JO-ANT.html

2. Harrison, 34.

3. Harrison, 49-51.

4. Also found in Harrison, 34.

5. Burkert, ...*Necans* 216, 227; Harrison, 35-37, 48-55; Hofmann, Ruck and Wasson, 102; Kerenyi, *Dionysos...* 303-304, 349; Otto, 117.

6. Burkert, *Greek Religion* 226-230 / ...*Necans* 229; Harrison, 39-41.

7. Harrison, 36.

8. Burkert, *Greek Religion* 237 / ...*Necans* 216-217; Kerenyi, *Dionysos...* 302-303.

9. Harrison, 33.

10. Burkert, ...*Necans* 216, 222, 227, 241; Harrison, 35-37, 43-52, 48-55; Kerenyi, *Dionysos...* 303-304; Otto, 117.

11. Burkert, *Greek Religion* 70-73, 237 / ...*Necans* 221; Harrison, 37-38, 40-41, 221; Kerenyi, *Dionysos...* 156, 169-175, 303-315, 364).

12. Burkert, ...*Necans* 217; Harrison, 39 & FN 2.

13. Burkert, *Greek Religion* 238-240 / ...*Necans* 229, 235-238; Kerenyi, *Dionysos...* 198-199, 281-284, 315-322, 371-373; Otto, 86; Winkler and Zeitlin, 16, 28 & FN 16. The painting of faces with wine lees was also done by actors at the festival of Lenaia; see Kerenyi, *Dionysos...* 327, 333-336.

14. Burkert, *Greek Religion* 237; Kerenyi, *Dionysos...* 295, 306.

15. Burkert, *Greek Religion* 237, 254; Kerenyi, *Dionysos...* 306; Parke, 88-92; Winkler and Zeitlin, 24 & FNs.

16. Burkert, *Greek Religion* 237-239 / ...*Necans* 220, 233; Harrison, 39-41; Hofmann, Ruck and Wasson, 102; Kerenyi, *Dionysos...* 312; Tierney, 446.

17. Burkert, ...*Necans* 119-120.

18. Burkert, *Greek Religion* 95, 109, 237-240 / ...*Necans* 220-226, 232-238; Campbell, ...*Oriental...* 196; Harrison, 33, 536; Kerenyi, *Dionysos...* 119-128, 160-161, 187, 293, 299, 300-315, 350-362 and plates 76a-86b, 97a; Otto, 80-85, 100.

19. Burkert, ...*Necans* 71, 234 & FNs, 237; Harrison, 538-539; Kerenyi, *Dionysos...* 106-108, 309-311 / *Gods...* 255-256; Hofmann, Ruck and Wasson, 134; Otto, 158; Winkler and Zeitlin, 204 & FN 121. Wherever the figwood phallus is revealed

from a liknon, *entheogen use seems to concurrently appear*; see Hofmann, Ruck and Wasson, 102, & FN 6.

20. Burkert, *Greek Religion* 237, 240 / ...*Necans* 216, 219, 27, 230; Harrison, 37-55, 90-92, 540, 542; Kerenyi, *Dionysos...* 218-219, 271-272, 303-304, 312-313, 349, 355-362; Otto, 100, 117; Plutarch, *Quaestiones Symposion* III-VIII; Winkler and Zeitlin, 127.

21. Kerenyi, *Dionysos...* 199-204.

22. Burkert, ...*Necans* 149, 156; Campbell, ...*Primitive...* 166-169, 409-410; Ross and Robbins, 69-74.

23. Graves, *White Goddess* 67-112; Young, 215-217, 348 FN 7.

24. Burkert, *Greek Religion* 109, 223 / ...*Necans* 246-247; Campbell, ...*Oriental...* 391 / ...*Primitive...* 226-227, 244-247; Graves, *Myths...* 15.4; Kerenyi, *Dionysos...* 119-125, 310 FN 121; Otto, 84-85; Winkler and Zeitlin, 136 FN 6; Young, 304.

25. Ross and Robbins, *passim*; Tierney, *passim*.

26. Campbell, ...*Occidental...* 28; Dodds, 244, 277; Guthrie, *Orpheus...* fig 18A, 267-271 & FNs; Turcan, 125-129, 262-265.

27. Kerenyi, *Dionysos...* 99-110; Otto, ch. 6, *passim*; Plutarch/Fuller, 24-25.

28. Campbell, ...*Primitive...* 408-411.

29. Dowden 76-79; Otto, 84-85.

30. Burkert, *Greek Religion* 85; Cornford 130-131, 183; Harrison, 620; Kerenyi, *Dionysos...* 70-71, 193, 329, 361 / *Heroes...* 213-214; Segal, 29, 215-271; Williams, 60; Winkler and Zeitlin, 65 & FN 65, 138 FN 6, 143, 153-154.

31. Burkert, *Greek Religion* 237-239 / ...*Necans* 217; Harrison, 33; Otto, 100; Plutarch, *Q. Symp.* III-VIII.

32. Burkert, *Greek Religion* 237-240 / ...*Necans* 238-239; Campbell, ...*Primitive...* 417; Harrison, 37; Kerenyi, *Dionysos...* 307 / *Gods...* 272.

33. Burkert, *Greek Religion* 240 / ...*Necans* 227-230, 238-239; Harrison, 35, 37.

34. Burkert, *Greek Religion* 6-73, 85, 240 / ...*Necans* 217, 233-289; Harrison, 37-38.

35. Burkert, ...*Necans* 241-243 & FNs; Kerenyi, *Dionysos...*156-160 and plates 94-96.

36. Burkert, *Greek Religion* 103-104 / ...*Necans* 228-230; Guthrie, *Orpheus...* 118, 147 FN 40; Harrison, 458-461 & FNs, 498 & FNs, 561; Tierney, 448; Winkler and Zeitlin, 24-25 & FNs, 27.

37. Burkert, *Greek Religion* 186; Harrison, 50-53.

38. Burkert, ...*Necans* 226-230.

39. Burkert, *Greek Religion* 186, 292; Harrison, 50-53.

40. Harrison, 51-53; Burkert, ...*Necans* 84-89.

41. Harrison, 37; Ross and Robins, 30-33, 165. Ceremonies conducted in swamps appear to recall human sacrificial rites.

42. Burkert, *Greek Religion* 73 / *...Necans* 239 & FN 4.

43. Burkert, *...Necans* 26-230; Harrison, 498; Tierney, 448.

44. Burkert, *...Necans* 225-230; Harrison, 53, 165-175.

45. *Pharmakos* means both "scapegoat" and "ambivalent drug." The wine imbibed at the Anthesteria must have been the very same entheogen-fortified beverage mixed by the Gerairai at the Lenaia, and the partaking of it during the ceremonies of the Anthesteria may have been a ritual re-enactment of those times when sacrificial victims were treated to the mercy of narcotic draughts; see Burkert, *Greek Religion* 82-84 / *...Necans* 149, 156; Harrison, 65, 68, 95-110; Hofmann, Ruck and Wasson, 106 FN 2; Ross and Robbins, 30, 90-97.

46. Harrison, 65, 68, 620; Ross and Robbins, 95-97; Tierney, 350.

47. Harrison, 105-110; Ross and Robbins, *passim*; Tierney, *passim*.

48. Harrison, 37, 589; Kerenyi, *Dionysos...* 303-304; Otto, 117.

49. Harrison, 86-95; Luck, 77.

50. Burkert, *Greek Religion* 170 / *...Necans* 4-5; Harrison, 56, 86-89; Nilsson, 75.

51. Guthrie, *...Gods* 221-222.

52. Burkert, *Greek Religion* 170; Harrison, 86-90; Luck, 77.

53. *Ibid.*

54. Guthrie, *...Gods* 221-222.

55. Burkert, *Greek Religion* 60, 70-84, 113, 200-205, 267 / *...Necans* 1-12 & FNs; Campbell, *...Primitive...* 99; Harrison, 1-39, 56-69, 84-95, 245-250; Kerenyi, *Dionysos...* 250; Sophocles *Oedipus Coloneus* 467-469; Tierney, 17-19.

56. Guthrie, *...Gods* 221-222.

57. Burkert, *Greek Religion* 60, 80-84, 113, 200-205, 267 / *...Necans* 9 & FNs; Harrison, 1-39, 56-69, 84-95, 245-250; Kerenyi, *Dionysos...* 250.

58. To tie the concept of *holocaust* into the Anthesteria (Harrison, 104), it must be noted that the "royal scapegoat" — whether human or animal or even a *pelanos* made of bread — would be burned after slaying, and his/its ashes collected in winnowing baskets (the *liknoi* of Dionysos, symbolic of the womb of rebirth; see Winkler and Zeitlin, 204 & FN 121) to be flung to the winds in offering. Such an action is reminiscent of the cannibalistic feast of the Titans on the flesh of the infant Dionysos (Guthrie, *Orpheus...* 80-85; Kerenyi, *Dionysos...* 242), who were subsequently reduced to ashes by the lightning of Zeus for the act; mythically, it was from those ashes that mankind was formed, again confirming Dionysos' role as *ultimate scapegoat* and *Sosipolis*.

59. Burkert, ...*Necans* 12, 37; Harrison, 14-24, 104; Kerenyi, *Dionysos...* 250.

60. Harrison, 34, 84.

61. Sophocles, *Oedipus Coloneus* 468; also found in Harrison, 91.

62. Guthrie, ...*Gods* 221-222.

63. Kerenyi, *Dionysos...* 67-68.

64. Burkert, *Greek Religion* 59-60, 80-82 / ...*Necans* 35-50; Jones and Pennick, 119; Harrison, 162; Tierney, 14; Young, 222.

65. Tannahill, 80, 370, 393.

66. Harrison, 61-64.

67. Eliade, ...*Sacred...* 51-52, 100-101; Tierney, 21.

68. Burkert, *Greek Religion* 60; Jones and Pennick, 119.

69. Harrison, 546-548.

70. Re: the cult of Cybele, see Turcan, 28-74; Wohlberg 338. Re; Christian beliefs deriving from Pagan practice, see Dodds, 244, 277; Guthrie, *Orpheus...* fig. 18A, 267-271 & FNs; Turcan, 125-129, 221, 223-234, 262-265.

71. Burkert, *Greek Religion* 80-82.

72. Burkert, *Greek Religion* 9 FN 41; Guthrie, ...*Gods* 221-222.

73. Burkert, *Greek Religion* 60, 71, 82, 113, 267 / ...*Necans* 5 FN 20, 9 FN 41, 48 FN 49; Harrison, 60-73; Keegan, 249.

CHAPTER FIVE

1. Burkert, ...*Necans* 265; Hofmann, Ruck and Wasson, 95.

2. Burkert, *Greek Religion* 260-295; Fierz-David, *passim*; Harrison, 572, 578-580, 640-641, 659; Kerenyi, 252-257 & FNs.

3. Campbell, ...*Occidental...* 28, 183; Kerenyi, *Dionysos...* 295.

4. Kerenyi, *Dionysos...*295.

5. Harrison, 559, 640; Hofmann, Ruck and Wasson, 95-108.

6. Burkert, ...*Necans passim*; Young, *passim*.

7. Burkert, ...*Necans* 264; Hofmann, Ruck and Wasson, 141-142.

8. Initiation as a symbolic re-enactment of a human sacrifice appears consistent between cultures (motifs found in all cultures which are relevant to the initiation/human sacrifice drama include the juxtaposition of water to fire, the

presence of the serpent, the use of or allusion to caverns, and some form of circle-dance; Burkert, *Greek Religion* 167, 293-255/ *...Necans* 46, 245, 270 FN 21, 281 & FN 36, 296; Campbell, *...Primitive...* 96-99, 101-103; Cooper, *passim*; Ferguson, see under *Baptism*; Harrison, 476-477, 576, 579-580, 589; Sutton, 89-91; Tierney, 23, 288, 377, 447; Willoughby, *passim*).

9. Burkert, *...Necans* 44 FN 39; Gimbutas, 182-183; Hofmann, Ruck and Wasson, 109 & FNs; Kerenyi, *Dionysos...* 26 & FN 42.

10. Mathews, 56; Otto, 188 and footnote #8, above.

11. Burkert, *Greek Religion* 76, 78, 286; Harrison, 498, 595; Turcan, 299. Mithraic initiation was similar to Orphic Dionysian initiation, but where the Dionysian lesser Mysteries inducted the dedicant into initiate status in one lengthy ritual — held either overnight or over several days — Mithraism divided the induction of a dedicant into seven distinct initiations (Campbell, *Occidental...* 264-267; Cooper, *passim*). This, I theorize, is where the modern neo-Pagan concept of many (dissimilar) "Degrees of Initiation" comes from (see Casavis, *passim* re: the origins of Freemasonry from the Mystery cults of Mithras, Attis/ Adonis, Orpheus, Dionysos/Demeter and, ultimately, Christianity. See also Dodds, 24, 277; Guthrie, *Orpheus...* fig 18A, 267 & FNs; Turcan, 125-129, 221, 223- 234, 262-265). Hellene Dionysian initiation had only two "degrees," the lesser Mystery of Agrai and the greater Mystery of Eleusis (Burkert, *...Necans* 12 FN 8, 295-296; Harrison, 559, 597; Hofmann, Ruck and Wasson, 53, 86 FN 6; Kerenyi, *Dionysos...* 262-270, 278). However, myesis might also be considered a "degree of initiation," even though it appears to be only a simple summary representation of the Agrai initiation, held just prior to the entry into the Telesterion at Eleusis. In Classical Greece, the nature of each initiation differed only in the magnitude of the ritual, not the presumed capacity of the initiate. The lesser Mystery initiation also exhibited commonalities with the tribal Mystery rites of Samothrace and Arcadia (Burkert, *Greek Religion* 281-282).

12. Burkert, *...Necans* 296; Campbell, *...Primitive...* 176-183.

13. A practice still in effect in many areas in the world; consider, also, the current and enduring function of flowers/floral wreaths placed on or in graves, relative to the wreaths used at Agrai. In either of these symbolic scenarios, the overriding theme that runs through such an initiatory rite is *hope for the perennial continuation of life* (Burkert, *Greek Religion* 167, 293-295 / *...Necans* 46, 245, 270 FN 21, 296; Harrison, 476-477, 576, 579-580, 589; Hofmann, Ruck and Wasson, 54, 62, 70 — hymn to Demeter — 127).

14. Quoted in Harrison, 559, 597 FN 1; see also Kerenyi, *Dionysos...* 267-272 and Turcan, 299.

15. Graves, *Myths...* 9.13, 31.C; Harrison, 526, 589; Head and Cranston 99-127.

16. Diogenes Laertius, VII; 77, also found in Harrison, 586-590, 673; Flavius Claudius Julianus, *Orations* Vol. III: *Letter to a Priest.*

17. Burkert, *Greek Religion* 281-285; Harrison, 588.

18. Guthrie, *Orpheus...* 96, 97, 184, 190, 237 & plates 8, 9 & 10; Harrison, 669-671; Meyer, *passim.*

19. Kerenyi, 267-272; Hofmann, Ruck and Wasson, *passim.*

20. I concur with several scholars regarding the theory that some myth is created from ritual action — or, that ritual actions are older than and take precedence over belief systems; see Harrison, xvii-xviii.

21. From Harrison, 436.

22. Burkert, *...Necans* 40; Dodds, 163 FN 44-45; Guthrie, *Orpheus...* 50, 208; Kerenyi, *Dionysos...* 267-272 & FNs, plates 110D&E, 139; Harrison, 125, 156, 593; Hofmann, Ruck and Wasson, 57, 64; Turcan, 309, 315; Young, 223-224, 349 FN 20. Some fragmentary pietistic literature suggests binding in the lesser Mystery initiation (Harrison, 590; Sutton, 91, 106. Other initiatory symbology vividly displayed in this hymn include the "thunder-cry" — Harrison, 479 — ostensibly of the drum, cymbal, or bullroarer used to sanctify the initiatory arena, the presence of snakes on the body, and the act of scourging using sacred Dionysian plants — Sutton, 90; Tierney, 377, 447). Many modern neo-Pagan initiations utilize the act of binding, and, since many Dionysian myths speak of the god himself being bound (see Kerenyi, *Dionysos...* 152, 167), such an action would not necessarily be out of place in a modern rendition of the Agrai. One late Classical artist's rendition of an Agrai ceremonial was preserved in Pompeii at the *Villa de Mysteri* (Burkert, *Greek Religion* 167, 260-295 / *...Necans* 271 FN 24; Harrison, 520-571; Kerenyi, *Dionysos...* 361-363. See Seaford's "The Mysteries of Dionysos at Pompeii," as found at *http: //www.stoa.org/ diotima.essays/Seaford.shtml* in Diotima. Materials for the Study of Women and Gender in the Ancient World, and/or Kerenyi, *Dionysos...* 106-112F for photo plates.)

23. Harrison, 587.

24. Athanassakis, 53; Campbell, *...Occidental...* 183-184.

25. Campbell, *...Occidental...* 183; Guthrie, *Orpheus...* 82-83; Kerenyi, *Dionysos...* 267-272.

26. Burkert, *Greek Religion* 78; Graves, *Myths...* 30.3; Harrison, 59-60, 64, 490-492, 513; Turcan, 309-315.

27. Harrison, 492-493.

28. Young, 180-181, 344-345 FN 19.

29. Kerenyi, *Dionysos...* 267-268 & FNs.

30. My thanks to Mr. Weidman and Mr. Yevcak of Western Technology's geotechnical laboratory for their help in determining this.

31. Kerenyi, *Dionysos...* 135, 259-260.

32. Kerenyi, *Gods...* 255-256.

33. Burkert, *...Necans* 146 FN 44; Kerenyi, *Dionysos...* 135.

34. Graves, *Myths...* 27.A, 27.G, 27.4; Guthrie, *Orpheus...* 196; Kerenyi, *Dionysos...* 52-55, 81-82, 110-111, 240-261 — see page 286 for comments on the same mud-daubing practice used in warfare; Otto, 131, 192.

35. Young, *passim*; Campbell, *...Primitive...* 95-112.

36. Harrison, 671-672.

37. Otto, 65.

38. Hofmann, Ruck and Wasson, 99-108 & FNs.

39. Burkert, *Greek Religion* 198, 284; Devereux, 72-74; Furst, 200; Hofmann, Ruck and Wasson, 129-130 FN 3; Sutton, 74 FN 16F.

40. Harrison, 670.

41. Burkert, *Greek Religion* 78-79, 277, 455 FN 10 / *...Necans* 40, 61, 288 FN 64; Flavius Claudius Julianus, *Orations* Vol. III: *Letter to a Priest* 170-184; Harrison, 127, 155-156; Hofmann, Ruck and Wasson, 62-65; Kerenyi, *Heroes...* 284.

42. Lines 9-20 as found in Harrison, 479 and Campbell, *...Occidental...* 183-184.

43. Babcock, *passim*; Burkert, *Greek Religion* 78, 291-292 / *...Necans* 40, 125, 272 FN 27; Campbell, *Occidental...* 184; Davis, N. Z., *passim*; Dodds, 276-278; Harrison, 56, 432, 481-491, 508-509; Otto, 132; Stallybrass and White, Ch. 1 *passim*; Turcan, 291-292; V. Turner, *passim*; Winkler and Zeitlin, 116 FN 59, 126 & FNs, 236.

44. Harrison, 537.

45. Furst, *passim*; Hofmann, Ruck and Wasson, *passim*; Hofmann and Schultes, *passim*.

46. Harrison, 418-419; Turcan, 77, 315-325.

47. Harrison, 419; Hofmann, Ruck and Wasson, 98 FN 5, 103, 107 FN 7; Kerenyi, 23-28 & FNs, 60.

48. Brown, 16-17; Devereux, 49; Hofmann and Schultes, 88.

49. Hofmann, Ruck and Wasson, 69, verses 5-17.3, 97 & FNs.

50. Proculus, *First Ennead...*; Schuré, 406; Harrison, 624-625.

51. Kerenyi, *Religion...* 30.

52. Furst, *passim*; Hofmann and Schultes, *passim*; Harner, *passim*.

53. See the chapter and accompanying footnotes detailing the Eleusinia for information regarding the contents of both *liknoi* and *kalathoi*, which were used in the *liknophoria* and *kernophoria* ceremonies. The inhalation of mind-altering substances using a pipe was not a method known to or employed by the Hellene people until the modern era; however, the thymaterion was utilized for this role, as it may have been by the Pythia of Delphi (see Devereux, 48, 80-85, Hofmann and Schultes, 86, and Graves, ...*Difficult*... 109 for more information on this topic). Regarding the Hellenic use of opium and other entheogens, see Burkert, *Greek Religion* 277, 455 FN 10 / ...*Necans* 281 & FN 36, 288 FN 64; Harrison, 419-422, 579-580; Hofmann, Ruck and Wasson, 49, 52, 96 FN 4, 102-107 & FNs, 115; Kerenyi, *Dionysos*... 24-26 / *Eleusis*...130-135, 144; Otto, 151.

54. Burkert, ...*Necans* 261-264 & FNs, 288 FN 64; Campbell, ...*Occidental*... 14-15, 264; Guthrie, *Orpheus*... 116-118; Harrison, 417-419; Hofmann, Ruck and Wasson, 49-52, 95-108 & FNs, 104 FN1, 115, 119, 126, 136; Kerenyi, *Dionysos*... 60 FN 26, 116-117, 288-289, 297, 362-363, 383 / *Eleusis*... 40 / *Heroes*... 282, 285; Otto, 116, 143; Turcan, 315-325. Hofmann, Ruck and Wasson note in *Road*... that the actions of Agrai mimic a "sacred hunt" and that *Agrai* itself means "spoils of the chase" (see *Road*... 104 as well as Pinsent, 28-29), inferring the presence of Zagreus "the hunter," who is often represented crowned with poppy capsules (*Road*... 107 FN 7). Harrison, (544) notes that Zagreus is "the son of Persephone," the goddess of the lesser Mystery.

55. As noted by Harrison, 441-443: "(worshippers of Dionysos) swarm like bees, their heads white with the pollen...of some intoxicant." It may alternately be inferred from this quote that *fresh sap* from opium poppies was used at Agrai, since the period just prior to grain harvest coincides with the ripening of the poppy capsule itself. Dionysos has been known from time immemorial as "(hermaphroditic Lord) of flowers" (*Anthos*, from which the title for the month of *Anthesterion*, when the Agrai itself is performed, was obtained; Kerenyi, *Dionysos*... 300-301).

56. Baum, 107; Elderkin, 212; Halliday, *passim*; Harrison, 595-596 & FN 4.

57. Burkert, *Greek Religion* 76, 78; Harrison, 498, 595.

58. Harrison, 588-595.

59. Burkert, *Greek Religion* 167, 260-295 / ...*Necans* 271 FN 24; Harrison, 520-571, 590; Kerenyi, *Dionysos*... 361-363 & plates 106-112F; Sutton, 90-91, 106; Tierney, 377, 447. See also Seaford's "The Mysteries of Dionysos at Pompeii" as found at *http://www.stoa.org/diotima.essays/Seaford.shtml* in Diotima: Materials for the Study of Women and Gender in the Ancient World.

60. Burkert, *Greek Religion* 48-49 / ...*Necans* 237; Dodds, 166 FN 60; Guthrie, *Orpheus*... 221-222; Harrison, 329, 559-560, 593; Kerenyi, *Dionysos*... 223-225; Plutarch, *Isis et Osiris* 364E. In the story of Demeter's search for Kore, Iambe/Baubo cheers Demeter at one point by lifting her skirts. Demeter was cheered by this act

because it showed the great goddess that she was in the presence of one who was well-versed in the Mysteries of life springing from death, for the vulva is a symbol of the sacred cave of initiation (as the Homeric Hymn states, "[Iambe knew] her duties." — See Clement 2,16-19; Kerenyi, *Gods...* 244, 274).

61. Burkert, *...Necans* fig. 9; Campbell, *...Occidental...* 184; Harrison, 520-522 & fig. 148, 532, 558 fig. 158, 559-560, 593; Kerenyi, *Dionysos...* 133-135, 223-225; Plutarch, *Isis et Osiris* 364E.

62. Burkert, *Greek Religion* 99, 294; Harrison, 309-311, 355-362, 532, 593, 621; Hofmann, Ruck and Wasson, 98 & FNs; Kerenyi, 371-372.

63. Campbell, *...Occidental...* 184, 264; Guthrie, *Orpheus...* 96-97, 111 & FNs, 114, 155, 194 & plates 8, 9 & 10; Harrison, 479, 487, 568, 595-599; Hofmann, Ruck and Wasson, 374; Otto, 34.

64. Burkert, *Greek Religion* 84-88, 144, 217.

65. Campbell, *...Primitive...* 101.

66. Harrison, 591.

67. Burkert, *Greek Religion* 76, 78; Harrison, 498, 595-596.

68. Harrison, 538, 621.

69. Burkert, *Greek Religion* 78, 108-109, 132-134, 259; Garland *...Life* 45-60; Kerenyi, *Dionysos...* 355-362 & plates 110C, 112F, 114.

70. Burkert, *Greek Religion* 76-78; Harrison, 498, 595.

71. Harrison, 593-597.

72. Kerenyi, *Dionysos...* 262-266.

73. Dodds, 163 FNs 44-45; Graves, *Myths...* 28.2; Guthrie, 50, 208; Turcan, 309, 315; Young, 223-224. See also *http: //www.logon.org/English/s/poo5.html.* Kerenyi, in *Dionysos...* (265) notes the importance of the "korybantic knife" used by the Titans in the dismemberment of Dionysos.

74. Kerenyi, *Dionysos...* 241-243.

75. Burkert, *...Necans* 181-182.

76. Regarding the ubiquitous use of drugs, initiatory symbols, and marshes or other bodies of water during rites of human sacrifice, see Ross and Robbins, 29, 59, 62, 71-72, 100, 129; Tierney, 53, 62, 95-97, 222, 350, 441, 446-450.

77. An ancient Orphic saying was *soma-sema*, or "the body, a tomb" (Campbell, *...Occidental...* 183).

78. Kerenyi, *Dionysos..* plates 138-141.

79. Kerenyi, *Dionysos...* 110D & 110E.

80. Burkert, 115; Harrison, 490-491, 517-534, 546-548.

81. Burkert, *Greek Religion* 186, 292; Harrison, 52, 475-477; Kerenyi, *Dionysos...* 373-374.

82. Harrison, 50-55.

83. Harrison, 163-223; Young, 180-181.

84. Harrison, 42-44, 166, 206-207, 230, 592, 634; Kerenyi, *Dionysos...* 359.

85. Burkert, *...Necans* 46; Dodds, 163 FNs 44-45; Graves, *White Goddess* 183; Guthrie, *Orpheus...* 50, 208; Harrison, 463 & FNs; Otto, 153; Partridge, 159; Redmond, 76-79; Turcan, 309, 315; Young, 223-224, 349 FN 20; Willoughby, *passim*. Both Young and Partridge note the similarity between the Latin *sacrificare* — to make sacred — and the Latin word for cutting or tattooing of the skin, *scarificare*.

86. Harrison, 463 & FNs.

87. Harrison, 454, 473, 600.

88. Burkert, *...Necans* 268-269; Dodds, 77-79; Guthrie, *Orpheus...* 118, 147 FN 40; Harrison, 498-500; Kerenyi, *Dionysos...* 262-272. As Burkert notes in *...Necans* page 39: "Underlying the practical use of bone-flutes, turtle-shell lyres, and the tympanon covered with cowhide is the idea that the overwhelming power of music comes from a transformation and overcoming of death."

89. Burkert, *Greek Religion* 293-295; Guthrie, *Orpheus...* 96, 79, 184, 190, 237; Harrison, 583-596, 659-673; Kerenyi, *Dionysos...* 252-256.

90. Guthrie, *Orpheus...* 96, 79, 184, 190, 237; Harrison, 583-584.

91. Burkert, *...Cults* 134-136; Campbell, *...Occidental...* 184, 264; Clement, *Exhortations...* 16; Dodds, 275-276, 281 FN 42; Harrison, 417-419, 423 FN 3, 430-431, 449, 534.

92. Campbell, *Occidental...* 27, 264; Dodds, 281 FN 42; Harrison, 326-331; Kerenyi, *Dionysos...* 288-289 and plate 143.

93. Burkert, in *Greek Religion* (295) notes that there were various sects among the Dionysian and Dionysian-syncretistic Mystery cults.

94. Campbell, *...Primitive...* 388-390 / *...Occidental...* 9, 15; Dodds, 275-276; Harrison, 12-23; Tierney, 222.

95. Campbell, *...Primitive...* 388-390.

96. Campbell, *Historical Atlas...* Volume 2, part 1, *passim*. The fish was likewise equated to the moon, due to lunar tide effects and the natural response of aquatic life to these effects.

97. *Ibid.*

98. Garland *...Life* 14-21.

99. Harrison, 49-50. Ginzberg (*passim*) bases his "witches' Sabbath" thesis on the idea that those caught up in the Inquisition who actually were "guilty" were, in fact, guilty of nothing more than continuing — in fragmentary and ultimately

exploitable fashion — the worship of Greco-Roman cthonic Deities. Religion, by its very nature, is conservative; when a Deity "dies," the death is likely to be an evanescent one.

100. Bremmer 71; Dodds, 281 FN 2.

101. Dodds, Chs. 5 & 7; Harrison, 506-534, 577, 586; Young, 17 & FN 17.

102. Excellent translation of the Petalia tablet in Harrison, 573, 659-660.

103. Burkert, *Greek Religion* (293); translation from the Hipponion-Vibo Valentia tablet, dated to 400 BCE.

104. Harrison, 660-661, from a tablet said to be from Eleutherai, Crete. A word which might possibly be *pais* is wedged between the Greek word for "[to be] parched (with thirst)" and "I am" on this tablet. It is by no means certain that the word in question is *pais*, but if it is, the translation might be altered to read: "I, child of the hearth of Eleusis, am parched with thirst." The *pais* of the greater Mystery ceremonies vicariously represented all people unable to attend the sacred rites. If the tablet is so translated, then it may have been one which was placed within the grave of an initiate who never personally obtained the blessings of the Eleusinia except for vicariously through the *pais* or — less likely — it may have been a tablet belonging to an individual who performed the role of *pais* as a child. Alternatively, the word in question may be *lais(s)*, possibly a poetic shorthand for "throat" — e.g., "my throat is parched," though I doubt that the limited space on such a minute and sacred object would be redundantly used for so fundamental a concept as "thirsty"; Harrison (663) notes the tendency to remove all redundancy, including non-accented letters and vast portions of common concepts, upon small inscribed amulets.

105. Harrison, 35; Kerenyi, *Dionysos...* plate 110C; Luck, 17.

106. Burkert, *Greek Religion* 292-295, 323; Campbell, *...Occidental...* 184; Harrison, 474-477, 487, 559, 563, 568, 574, 661; Otto, 34.

107. Hesiod, *Theogony* 135.

108. Burkert, *Greek Religion* 162; Guthrie, *Orpheus...* 111 & FNs, 114, 155, 194. Campbell, in *...Primitive Mythology* (21), comments on the paleolithic antiquity of the use of masks to simulate the immanent presence of a god. Harrison, (622-623, 628-629) notes that the Orphics had a penchant for revivifying paleolithic forms of worship in a moralistic format.

109. Burkert, *Greek Religion* 292-295, 323; Campbell, *...Occidental...* 184, 264; Harrison, 474-479, 487, 559, 563, 568, 574, 586, 598, 661; Hofmann, Ruck and Wasson, 374; Otto, 34.

CHAPTER SIX

1.   Hofmann, Ruck and Wasson, 142.

2.   Burkert, *...Necans* 255; Davis, *passim*; Hofmann, Ruck and Wasson, 19.

3.   Aristeides, quoted by Otto, (1955); Baum, *passim*; Cavendish, V. 6, 804-807; Cicero *Laws II* XIV, 36; Devereux, 80-90; Diodorus, *...Siculus* V, 48-49, 77; Hofmann, Ruck and Wasson, 47-127; Luck, 22; Plato, *Phaedrus* 248-250; Plotinius, *...Ennead* VI, 7; Schuré, 406-407.

4.   Furst, 200; Hofmann, Ruck and Wasson, 67.

5.   Aeschines 133; Beck, *History* section; Cavanaugh, *passim*.

6.   Beck, *History* section; Hofmann, Ruck and Wasson, 62, 86; Nigel and Pennick, 73; Norwich, 119-123.

7.   Burkert, *Greek Religion* 260-295 / *...Necans* 266; Graves, *White Goddess* 184; Harrison, 158-162, 520-571; Hofmann, Ruck and Wasson, 50, 53, 87 FN 6, 94-115, 119; Kerenyi, *Dionysos...* 376, 379-380.

8.   Brumfield, *passim*; Burkert, *Greek Religion* 67-68 / *...Necans* 260; Harrison, 29-31, 77-119; Hofmann, Ruck and Wasson, 117.

9.   Baum, *passim*; Euripides *Hypsipile*, quoted by Burkert, in *Greek Religion* 290; Pindar, *Fragment* 137A; Pinsent, 26; Plotinius, *First Ennead* VI, 7; Schuré, 406-407.

10.   Graves, *Myths...* forward to revised edition; Kerenyi, *Heroes...* 55; Ruck *...Hyperboreans passim*; Wasson, *Soma...* 108; Winkler and Zeitlin, 205; Wohlberg, *passim*.

11.   Burkert, *...Necans* 266; Harrison, 546-548; Hofmann, Ruck and Wasson, 15-116.

12.   Aristophanes, *Frogs* 361-362, cited in Beck.

13.   Graves, *Difficult...* 98, 126; Suetonius, *Nero* XXXIV, cited in Beck.

14.   Burkert, *Greek Religion* 89-92, 199-203 / *...Necans* 254, 265 FN 1; Harrison, 542; Williams, H. 40.

15.   Beck, *History*; Burkert, *...Necans* 253; Cavanaugh, *passim*; Harrison, 540-542; Hofmann, Ruck and Wasson, 199 & FNs; Kerenyi, *Dionysos...* 78-79.

16.   Mylonas, 284-285 / Beck, 1996.

17.   Burkert, *Greek Religion* 78-82, 286; Harrison, 156, 312, 546-548; Hofmann, Ruck and Wasson, 62-65.

18.   Athanassakis, *Homeric Hymn to Demeter* lines 45-50; Burkert, *...Necans* 40; Harrison, 127, 156; Hofmann, Ruck and Wasson, *Hymn...* 69-80, lines 45-50; also pages 57, 64.

19   Burkert, *Greek Religion* 78 / *...Necans* 258; Harrison, 312; Hofmann, Ruck and Wasson, 62, 115; Pinsent, 132; Williams, Hector 37.

20. Beck, *History*; Burkert, *...Necans* 269, 277-279, 283 & FNs; Harrison, 540-542; Hofmann, Ruck and Wasson, 94-95, 199 & FNs; Kerenyi, *Dionysos...*78-79.

21. *Ibid.*

22. Hofmann, Ruck and Wasson, 62-65; Martin, 80-89.

23. Beck, *History.*

24. Burkert, *Greek Religion* 287; Dodds, 30-31 & FN 8; Harrigan, 26; Harrison, 28-31; Winkler and Zeitlin, 271, 328.

25. Aristophanes, *Frogs* 361-362; also cited in Beck.

26. Athanassakis, *Homeric...* 4, lines 95-102.

27. Burkert, *...Necans* 257 FN 3, 269, 270 FN 20, 278, 283 & FNs; Hoffman, Ruck and Wasson, 90 & FN 4.

28. Regarding the sacred items found in the *liknon* and noted at Eleusis; Burkert, *Greek Religion* 78, 292, 295; Guthrie, *Orpheus...* 82, 98, 108, 120-123, 203; Harrison, 481-483, 508-509, 522-532. See also Graves, *Difficult...* 105 and Kerenyi, *Eleusis...* 240-242. Sophocles' *Antigone* from the quote found in Harrison, 541.

29. Hofmann, Ruck and Wasson, plate 5.

30. Burkert, *Greek Religion* 67-68, 78, 217 / *...Necans* 85-89, 185; Williams, Hector 37.

31. Burkert, *...Necans* 268 FN 16; Harrison, 511-516 & FNs.

32. Burkert, *...Necans* 165 fig. 9, 266-269 & FN 16; Harrison, 155-163; Hofmann, Ruck and Wasson, 115; Jewett 380-393; Taylor-Perry 2001, (Timothy White, illustrator/editor) 49; Williams, H., 37-38.

33. Burkert, *...Necans* 268; Harrison, 155-160; Hofmann, Ruck and Wasson, 62.

34. Plotinius; also found in Burkert, *Greek Religion* 283.

35. Harrison, 490 & FNs; Kerenyi, *Dionysos...* 262-272.

36. Apollodorus, V, 12; Stephen of Byzantium, as quoted in Harrison, 597 FN 1 & 559.

37. Apollodorus, V, 12; Aristophanes, *Clouds* 259-260; Burkert, *Greek Religion* 286; Harrison, 546-548; Plato, *Phaedrus* 348.

38. Burkert, *Greek Religion* 78; Harrison, 547; Hofmann, Ruck and Wasson, 115.

39. Harrison, 517-534.

40. Beck, *History...*; Bookidis, *passim*; Burkert, *...Necans* 275-280; Martin, 80-89.

41. Burkert, *Greek Religion* 161, 269, 276 / *...Necans* 68, 293-294; Hofmann, Ruck and Wasson, 94; Kerenyi, *Dionysos...* 33, 226, 247, 261, 293, 310 / *Eleusis...* 135.

42. Schuré, 406.

43. Harrison, 577-582 & FNS, 660, 672.

44. Schuré, 406.

45. Burkert, *Greek Religion* 289; Foucart, *passim*; Harrigan, 21-29; Harrison, 567-571.

46. Bookidis, *passim*; Buxton, 17-18; Kerenyi, *Eleusis...* 187; Knox, 75-90; Taplin, 167; Thucydides, 2.38-4; Winkler and Zeitlin, 5, 97-129 & FNs, 247. Mallory (129) suggests a similar "sound-alike (in English)" pseudo-philologenic error between the Indic *sabala* ('multicolored, dappled') and the Greco-Roman *Cerberus* — which might cause a non-linguist to come to the erroneous conclusion that the three-headed canine guard of Hades answered to the name 'Spot'! The website *About.com* contains many humorous examples of similar linguistic errata in its "Urban Legends" section.

47. Kerenyi, *Eleusis...* 27-28.

48. Hofmann, Ruck and Wasson, 46-47, 88-89; Martin, 80-89.

49. Winkler and Zeitlin, *passim.*

50. Burkert, *...Necans* 288 FN 64; Hofmann, Ruck and Wasson, 90.

51. Schuré, 407.

52. Bookidis, *passim*; Hofmann, Ruck and Wasson, 88; Martin, 80-89.

53. Devereux, 84-87; Hofmann, Ruck and Wasson, 93.

54. Burkert, *Greek Religion* 455 FN 10 / *...Necans* 287 & Strabo, 59; Furst, 193-200; Graves, forward to revised edition; Hofmann, Ruck and Wasson, *passim*; Hofmann and Schultes, 103.

55. Burkert, *...Necans* 274-275; Hofmann, Ruck and Wasson, 110 & FNs.

56. Bookidis, *passim*; Hofmann, Ruck and Wasson, plate 10; Taylor-Perry 2001, (Timothy White, illustrator/editor) 51.

57. Hippolytus, *Refutation...* V, 3.

58. Aristerios, *Engomion...*; Clement, *Exhortation.*

59. Kerenyi, voices the same concerns in *Eleusis...*; for a complete discussion of these scholars' reservations, please see Burkert, *...Necans* 251-253 & FNs.

60. Jones and Pennick, 73.

61. Aristerios, *Engomion...*; Burkert, Greek Religion 68, 72 / *...Necans* 54, 272, 285-286; Clement, *Exhortation*; Harrison, 149-150, 155-160 628; Hippolytus, *Refutation...*; Hofmann, Ruck and Wasson, 92-94; Kerenyi, *Dionysos...* 369; Plutarch, *...Symposium* II, 3; 1.

62. Guthrie, 10, 17; Harrison, 569-571; Hofmann, Ruck and Wasson, 94.

63. Athenaeus, *The Deisnosophists* X, 478D; Burkert, *...Cults* 94 / *Greek Religion* 286 / *...Necans* 269; Harrison, 158-160; Hofmann, Ruck and Wasson, 92-94 and plate 8; Pinsent, 50.

64. Burkert, *Greek Religion* 286.

65. Callimachus, *To Demeter* 1-7.

66. Burkert, *Greek Religion* 285.

67. Burkert, *Greek Religion* 286 / ...*Necans* 272-273; Hofmann, Ruck and Wasson, 92-95.

68. Furst, 256-265.

69. Burkert, *Greek Religion* 288; Dodds, 202 FN 77; Furst, 275-276; Harrison, xvii-xviii; Winkler and Zeitlin, 325; Turcan, 69.

70. Furst, 260.

71. The ringing of a gong ceremonially signified the nearness of a goddess; see Burkert, ...*Necans* 286 & FN 57; Luck, 69. This title is also translated as *torchbearer*.

72. The clerics of Eleusis came from only two families, the Kerykes and the Eumolpidae (Burkert, ...*Necans* 282; Luck, 131; Kerenyi, *Eleusis...* 29-35.) Sophocles, in *Oedipus Coloneus*, as quoted in Harrison, (553-554) alludes to the possibility of entheogenic sacraments in connection with the holy families of Eleusis:

    "Ablaze with light,
    The Holy Ones for mortals their dread rite
    Nurse, and on mortal lips the golden key
    is set of celebrant Eumolpidae."

    Harrison hastens to note that the Eumolpidae family, which supplied the Hierophant and often the priestesses to the rites, were never of native Attic derivation, but were known to be foreigners of northern (e.g., Thracian) descent.

73. Schuré, 406-407.

74. Athenaeus, *The Deisnosophists* X, 478D; Burkert, ...*Cults* 94 / *Greek Religion* 286 / ...*Necans* 269; Harrison, 158-160; Hofmann, Ruck and Wasson, 92-94 and plate 8; Pinsent, 50.

75. Harrison, 544-557.

76. Beck, *History...*; Diodorus, ...*Siculus* 48-49; Harrison, 563-567; Hofmann, Ruck and Wasson, 34, 50, 55, 118-120; Kerenyi, *Dionysos...* 83.

77. Aristerios, *Engomion...* 311-312.

78. Harrison, 564-567.

79. Burkert, *Greek Religion* 198, 284; Devereux, 72-74; Furst, 200; Hofmann, Ruck and Wasson, 129-130 FN 3; Sutton, 74 FN 16F.

80. Burkert, *Greek Religion* 288; Graves, *Difficult...* 97-98, 105-106, 110; Harrison, 545; Hofmann, Ruck and Wasson, 50, 119 & FN 4, 130-133, 136.

81. Harrison, 275; Hofmann, Ruck and Wasson, 110-113, 118-119; Kerenyi, *Dionysos...* 124/ *Eleusis...* 32.

82. Burkert, *...Cults* 94, 107; Tertullian, *To the Nations* 30. For a treatise on Sacred Marriage as part of Pagan Greek religion, see *http: //www.widdershins.org/vol5iss4/06.htm*

83. Burkert, *Greek Religion* 86-87.

84. These were the festivals of Anthesteria (*Limnaia*; Burkert, *Greek Religion* 109) and Eleusinia. Regarding the inversion morés to indicate sacred time or rites of passage, see N. Z. Davis, 97-123; Burke, 178-204; Burkert, *Greek Religion* 287; Harrigan, 26; Harrison, 28-31; Hyde, 336-338; Stallybrass and White, Ch. 1 *passim.*

85. Harrison, 620-621.

86. Burkert, *...Necans* 273-274; Harrison, 532, 545, 548-551.

87. Burkert, *...Necans* 284; Cavendish, V. 6 804-807; Hippolytus, *Refutation...* V, 3. The simple symbology of the figwood phallus within the *liknon* may, itself, have represented the consummation of the sexual act to the ancient Greco-Romans.

88. Harrison, 550-551. Considering the ease with which dried mushrooms are powdered, they may have been put into the sesame oblation cakes rather than the kykeon, making the libation itself a ruse; Robert Graves was the first to theorize this (*Difficult Questions...* 100, 106-107), and the theory assumes that such "cakes" were made from sesame paste and honey, like modern halvah, and not cooked.

89. Merillees, 1999.

90. Escohotado, 14.

91. *Archaeology Magazine* (featuring Hector Williams) July/August 1994, cover; Taylor-Perry 2001 (Timothy White, illustrator/editor) 55.

92. Ripinsky-Naxon, 160.

93. Ripinsky-Naxon, 159.

94. Hofmann, Ruck and Wasson, 110.

95. Kerenyi, *Dionysos...* 24-25; Ratsch, 1992, *passim*; Ripinsky-Naxon, 1993, *passim.*

96. Escohotado, 14.

97. Wasson, Ruck and Hofmann 100-110 and FNs.

98. Hofmann and Schultes, 13-14, 21.

99. Escohotado, 14.

100. Hofmann, Ruck and Wasson, 90; Martin 80-89.

101. See the *Agrai* chapter and footnotes for details and sources regarding this theory.

103. Ergot is a fungus that infects cereal and grass plants in a dual-stage life cycle. In its dormant phase, it appears as a fishy-smelling, spurlike, dark-purplish mass of spores growing on the ears of the grain/grass. In its active fruiting phase, the infected grains fall to earth and produce tiny mushrooms with incomplete clubbed caps and threadlike "roots" (Schultes and Hofmann, 103).

104. Hofmann, Ruck and Wasson, 68, 133 & FNs; Kerenyi, *Dionysos...* 365. See also *Agrai* chapter and footnotes (part II, FN 35).

105. Devereux, 76; Hofmann and Schultes, 103; Valencic, 330.

106. Hofmann, Ruck and Wasson, *A Challenging Question* section.

107. Bigwood, Ott, Thompson and Neely (1979), 147-149; Ott and Neely (1980), 165-166; Valencic, 328-333. However, according to Valencic (329), it is possible that "very small" (undefined) amounts of ergoline would seem to have a potentiating effect on other entheogens, possibly similar to that displayed by *P. harmala*. It may be possible that this is a further clue to one composition of kykeon, which would lend credence to the controlled use of ergot at Eleusis. To my knowledge, however, this theory has never been tested in a Western or modern Eleusinic setting, and cannot possibly be presented as more than intellectual conjecture until such experimentation has taken place.

108. Furst, 197.

109. Hofmann, Ruck and Wasson, plate 7.

110. Arora, 353-360; Ruck *...Hyperboreans, passin.*

111. Taylor-Perry, 2001 (Timothy White, illustrator/editor) 54.

112. Furst, 194; Graves, *White Goddess* 167; Hofmann, Ruck and Wasson, 75.

113. Festi and Bianchi, 10-30.

114. *Ibid.*

115. Festi and Bianchi, 15-38; Furst, 204-205; Hofmann and Schultes, 85; Wasson, *Soma...* 254-324; Wohlbert, 333-334.

116. There may, however, be one place in which it is inferred; see footnote 71, above.

117. Salzman, *et al.*

118. Burkert, *...Necans* 288 FN 64; Campbell, *Occidental...* 14-15, 264; Harrison, 417-419, 446-447; Hofmann, Ruck and Wasson, 50, 103, 99-103 & FNs,119, 136; Kerenyi, *Dionysos...* 59-60 & FN 26, 116-117, 288-289, 297, 362-363, 383; Otto, 116, 143. The Classical Greek concept of adding entheogens to wine may have derived from the use of entheogens as primary "carriers of the god," adapting

them over time by adding them to wine, ultimately ending with *only wine* as the "blood" of the god.

119. Cavendish, V. 14, 1908; Wohlberg, 336.

120. Wohlberg, 341.

121. Williams, C. K., 11, 14, 17, 20; Wohlberg, 339.

122. Cavendish, V. 14, 1908; Wohlberg, 334.

123. Hofmann and Schultes, 84-85; Salzman et al., 44; Wasson, *Soma...* 254, 281, 307, 324.

124. Arora, 358, 371, 373, 409, 895; Peele, color photo, 11.

125. Burkert, *...Necans* 271; Hofmann, Ruck and Wasson, 110 FN 7, 118.

126. Furst, 199-200.

127. Wasson, *Soma...* 108.

128. Hofmann and Schultes, 53, 66-67.

129. Pinsent, 136. Hermes Cthonios (psychopomp) was known to the ancient Greeks to be an epiphany of Dionysos, Lord of Entheogens. See Burkert, *...Necans* 237, 239; Campbell, *...Primitive...* 417; Kerenyi, *Dionysos...* 307 / *Gods of the Greeks* 272. Hades, too, was known as an epiphany of Dionysos (Hofmann, Ruck and Wasson, 98, 107, 119 FN 4).

130. Devereux, 40-49; Ott 247-254; Stafford 346-347.

131. DeKorne, 58; Hofmann and Schultes, 123.

132. DeKorne, 93-95; For methods by which the Eleusinic clerics may have prepared the psychoactive portion of the *kykeon*, see DeKorne, *passim.*

133. *Ibid.*

134. Turner, 25.

135. Callimachus, *Aetia* 10.

136. Callimachus, *To Demeter* 19-20.

137. DeKorne, 93-95; Salzman, et al. *passim.*

138. Hofmann, Ruck and Wasson, 57, 64. See information in the chapter on the lesser Mysteries for information regarding those foods most likely abstained from; also see Porphyry *On Abstinence...* IV.

139. DeKorne, *passim*; Furst, *passim*; Hofmann and Schultes, *passim.*

140. Harrison, 537.

141. DeKorne, 93.

142. *Ibid.*

143. Burkert, *...Necans* 288-289; Hofmann, Ruck and Wasson, 119.

144. Burkert, *...Necans* 288-289; Harrison, 525-529.

145. Burkert, *Greek Religion* 78, 289 / *...Necans* 293.

146. Burkert, *Greek Religion* 56, 66-68, 73, 298; Harrison, 11-12.

147. Harrison, 161.

148. Diodorus Siculus, V, 49.

149. Burkert, *Greek Religion* 58-59 / *...Necans* 258-259, 264, 289-296; Campbell, *...Primitive...* 151-225; Eliade *...Return passim*; Harrison, 452; Otto, *Dionysus* 142 / *...Mysteries* 20-21; Willoughby, *passim*; Young, 53-61, 135-139, 144.

GREEK-TO-ENGLISH GLOSSARY

αγων   (agon)   "Competition," either athletic, artistic, or intellectual in nature

Αγραι   (Agrai)   The lesser Mysteries performed in the month of Anthesterion (our mid-February), in preparation for the greater Mysteries of Eleusinia held during the month of Boedromeon (our mid-September)

αιωρα   (aiora)   "swinging ceremony" performed over half-buried, empty pithoi by young girls, during the Chöes phase of the Anthesteria; Representative of the life which follows death in cyclic progression

αμφιφωντεσ   (amphiphontes)   "Moon cakes": A delicacy made in honor of Artemis as *Potnia theron*, or mistress of animals. The linguistic roots of this word are no longer extant in modern Greek

ανακτορον   (anaktoron)   Eleusinian altar-room of the Hierophant, located within the Temple of Demeter at Eleusis (the *Telesterion*)

ανγοσ   (angos)   Metal vessel from which the Eleusinic *kykeon* was served

Ανθεστερια   (Anthesteria)   "Feast of souls" held by the ancient and Classical Athenians in our mid-February

171

απαρχεσθαι	(aparkhesthai)	The ceremonial cutting of the forelocks by newly-made ephebes (cadets) in ancient and Classical Attica; The roots of this word survive in modern Greek to describe things which are sanctified, inviolate, and/or essential
απορρητον	(aporrheton)	"Holy hidden (proscribed) secret"; Pertains to holy things which are forbidden (by law) to describe
αρρητον	(arrheton)	"Holy open (ineffable) secret"; Pertains to that which is divine beyond the ability of words to describe
αʃτοι	(astoi)	A freeborn Athenian citizen
βαθρον	(bathron)	The term for the steps leading up to the Delphic tripod, considered to be the grave or headstone of Dionysos; Together, the Apollonian tripod and Dionysian bathron were believed to connect the Olympic realm to the cthonic one. The word is related to *bothros*, the natural or man-made pits where offerings to the cthonic deities were placed
Βακχεια	(Bacchante)	Female follower of Dionysos, roughly equivalent to an Hiera or priestess of Demeter in status
Βασιλευʃ	(Basileus)	"[Ceremonial] king"; This title was lost to history after Diocletian ordered each city-state to be termed a *diocese*, and the Basileus of each city-state to be given the new title *vicar*
Βασιλιννα	(Basilinna)	Ceremonial queen, wife of the Archon Basileus
Βαυβο	(Baubo)	"Dwarf"; This mythic figure who made the sorrowing Demeter laugh was called *Iambe* by Orphics
Βουκολεον	(Boukoleon)	"Bull's stable"; The area within the Agora (marketplace) of Athens in which the Basilinna was united in Sacred

Marriage to Dionysos during the *Limnaia* portion of the festival of Anthesteria

Βουκολοι	(Boukoloi)	See *Hierophant*
βουπλεξ	(bouplex)	Double-bladed axe anciently used to sacrifice bulls; A similar axe known as a *pelekos* was associated with the worship of Dionysos
βωμοſ	(bomos)	Olympian-style raised stone, turf, or ash altar; The altar of the modern Greek Orthodox Church is still called a *bomios*
βωθροſ	(bothros)	Cthonic trench-or pit-altar; The use of this word has been lost to history
Γεραιραι	(Gerairai)	"Venerables"; The women who performed ineffable rites within the Dionysian temple *en limnais* (in the marshes) during the festivals of Lenaia and Anthesteria
γεφυρισμοι	(gephyrismoi)	See *Schommata/Eschralogia*
Δαδουκοſ	(Dadouchos)	"Torch bearer" and ringer of the Eleusinian gong during the greater Mystery rites, this priest was always a member of the Kerykes family; The Eleusinic Dadouchos also took part in other Mystery-related ceremonies, such as those held during the Dionysian festivals of Lenaia and Anthesteria
δεικνυμενα	(deiknymena)	The "things seen" in the greater Mystery rites
Δελφι	(Delphi)	The temple of Delphi was part of the sacred precinct of Apollo on the lower reaches of Mount Parnassos, where both the Omphalos and the "gravestone" steps of Dionysos were located, leading up to the Pythic tripod; Delphi proper was the town built up around the sacred district, composed primarily of the extended families of

Delphic clerics, who lived well from the offerings given at the Delphic temple, and of an extensive community of goatherders

δεμε	(deme)	See *phratrae*

διθυραμπ	(dithyramb)	A melodic theatrical interlude that Harrison (436-444) theorizes to be the remains of a Paleolithic ceremonial, the word *dithyramb* might be translated, concurrently, as "the summoning of the Bull" and "the hymn of the bees"; the *dithyramb* of Democratic Greece was a triumphal paean sung by elders and boys during Dionysian sacrifices and theatrical festivals

δρομενα	(dromena)	The "things done" in the greater Mystery rites

Ειρεσιονε	(Eiresione)	A branch decorated by children during the festival of Pyanepsia

Ελευσιϛ	(Eleusis)	Sacred precinct of Demeter where the clandestine greater Mystery rites were held; there were similar precincts in other parts of Greece. On Crete, the Mystery rites and the knowledge of how to perform them were not kept secret, but revealed to all who wished to know.

εναγισμωϛ (also termed εναγιζειν)	(enagismos)	Hellene cthonic spiritual rectification sacrifice

ενγυτριοτραι	(engytristrai)	Sanctified pourers of bloodied water in the ceremony of *Enagismos*

Εφεβε	(Ephebe)	"Cadet"; Refers to the group of youth for whom the Classical Katagogia ceremony was held, as a manhood ceremony in which Athens presented the orphans of its honored warriors with their first set of arms and armor

Εποπται/ Εποπτεια	(Epoptai/ Epopteia)	"With eyes open" or "those who [have] see[n]"; title given to initiates who have undergone the Eleusinia ceremony
εσχ'αρα	(eskhara)	An altar placed flat upon the ground, used by the Pagan Hellenes for worship of earth Deities and spirits
ευφεμειν/ ευφεμετε	(...euphemete)	"Be still," "remain silent," "say no unholy thing"; The pre-sacrifice command of an Hellene priest, this injunction is most often associated in surviving Hellenic literature with the Eleusinian Dadouchos
ευο'ι	(evohe)	"Rejoice!" Dionysian cry of praise
ζοε	(Zoë)	"Life of the Soul"
θανατοʃ	(thanatos)	"Death"
θεαται	(theatai)	"Observers" (in Athenian theater or political assembly)
Θεʃπιοι	(Thespioi)	Actors (also *komoi*)
Θιασοʃ	(Thiasos)	"Congregation"
θρωνοσιʃ	(thronosis)	Opening rite conducted during both the lesser and greater Mystery ceremonies
Θυιαδ	(Thyiad)	Female follower of Dionysos in a nurturant role, specifically mother or nursemaid
Θυειν	(Thyein)	"Raving [as a newborn infant]"; referent to the "zest for life" inherent in all living things, this word might be more accurately translated as "enflamed"
θυματεριον	(thymaterion)	"Censer"

Θυονε	(Thyone)	The reborn and immortalized Semele, mother of Dionysos
θυρσοʃ	(thyrsos)	Dionysian wand of fennel usually tipped with a pine cone, filled with ivy or other plants, or possibly used to carry fire
Ιακχοʃ	(Iacchos)	One Eleusinian aspect of Dionysos; the others include Triptolemos, Ploutos, and Brimos
Ιακχογωγοσ	(Iacchogagos)	Carrier of the object chosen to symbolize Iacchos in the procession to Eleusis from Athens just prior to the greater Mystery ceremony
Ιερεια	(Hiereia)	General household or Olympian sacrifice
Ιεροκηρυξ	(Hierokeryx)	"Herald of the Hierophant"; this Eleusinian priest was always chosen from the Kerykes family
Ιεροφαντηʃ	(Hierophant)	"[The one] Who shows the sacred things"; priest of Demeter at Eleusis. According to Burkert (Greek Religion, 98) the female form of this word is Ιεροφαντιʃ, alluding that the holders of this office were occasionally female, probably Bacchantes or priestesses of Demeter
ιΘυφαλλοι	(ithyphallic)	"Having an erection"; pertains to the satyrs or sileni of the Katagogia and other Dionysian festivals. Dionysos himself was often given the title *Orthos*, "rampant"
καδισκοʃ	(kadiskos)	A multiple-handled small storage jar; utilized ceremonially for the rites of *Dioskodion*, it appears that the *kadiskos* vessel itself, "enlivened" by whatever it contained, was a primitive *xoanon* designed to guard storage rooms

καλαθοʃ   (kalathos)   Sacred basket containing objects for use during the celebration of the greater Mysteries

καταβασισ   (katabasis)   "Going down into the abyss": An ancient Greek term referring to a form of apotheosis whose overtones can be reincarnative, resurrective, referent to physical conception or, in the case of the Mysteries, all of these at one time

Καταγογια   (Katagogia)   "Greater — or urban — Dionysia": A military and political festival held in early spring during the short period when Athens was a democracy (the word *katagogia* loosely translates as "those who come [back down] to tell stories")

κερνοʃ   (kernos)   "Separator" into which Eleusinic foodstuffs were placed during the central portion of the greater Mystery ceremony

κερυατιδ   (keryatid)   "Basket-bearing [nurse-]maid": Carved figures which held up the roof of the lesser Propulaia (porch) of the Telesterion at Eleusis, representing the myth of Baubo as the field through which joyous new life peers in the midst of sorrowful death

κιστη   (kiste)   "Chest" used during the greater Mysteries as a storage area for liknoi, kalathoi, and ritual objects

κολυμβηθρα   (kolymbæthra)   Mixed offering of grains and wild seeds given as a propitiation-offering to the souls of the ancestors on the final day of Anthesteria; modernly, this is a dessert of grains and fruits known as *kolyva*, often served on the last day of Lent by the Greek Orthodox Church

Κορυκιον Αντρον   "Natal cave of Bacchus" on the slopes of Parnassos, (Korykion Antron) above Delphi

Κορυβαντεʃ/ Κουρετε	(Korybant/ Kourete)	Mythic warrior (and/or) male follower of Dionysos, who carried a shield as liknon and a spear as thyrsos
κραδε	(krade)	"Figwood": What the Dionysian phallus carried in the *liknon* was composed of
κραδια	(kradia)	Katharevousa metaphor for the phallus, associated to the word for "heart" (καρδια)
κροταλοι	(krotaloi)	Finger-cymbals
κυκεων	(kykeon)	"Brew" or "admixture": referent especially to the sacred drink formulated for the greater Mysteries of Eleusis
λεγομενα	(legomena)	The "things said" in the greater Mysteries of Eleusis. *Legomena kai dromena* can be translated as "password of performance," a *synthema* (brief description of a ritual procedure) given by an initiate of the Mysteries to show that he was, indeed, an initiate: "I opened the chest; I took from the basket; I drank the *kykeon*; I worked; having worked, I replaced [the sacred items] back into the basket, then replaced the basket into the chest."
Λεναια	(Lenaia)	Theatrical midwinter festival in which the "nursemaids" of Dionysos care for him in a symbolic infantile state; Lenaia heralded the "Dionysian period" of the year for Hellenes, which would come to an end with the festival of Anthesteria, when Dionysos would attain adult form as Bridegroom and Lord of Souls
Λενοʃ	(lenos)	"[Wine] pressing-vat."
λικνον	(liknon)	A "winnowing basket" in which the sacra of Dionysian followers was stored; some mythographers (Harrison, et al.) theorize that this implement may originally have been a winnowing *fan* — a shovel-like implement, rather than a basket

λικνοφορια	(Liknophoria)	Consecration ceremony using the *liknon*
λιμναια/ λιμναισ	(Limnaia/Limnais)	*Limnaia* refers to the Anthesteric Sacred Marriage between the Athenian Basilinna and Dionysos, whose sacred temple *en limnais* (in the marshes) was open to worshippers only during the festival of Anthesteria
Λουτροφοροσ	(Loutrophoros)	"Water-bearer": A person, usually a young girl, chosen to carry and pour a libation of pure water upon or into an altar during Hellenic rites
Μαεναδεʃ	(Maenad)	"Mad one": Female follower of Dionysos, in a sacrificial role
Μυησιʃ	(Myesis)	Veiling and enthronement ceremony performed just prior to the greater Mysteries at Eleusis; Myesis represented a summary re-enactment of the primary or lesser Mystery initiation
Μυσταγωγοʃ	(Mystagogos)	"Those who guide the veiled": Individuals who attended the Eleusinia ceremonies for consecutive years in order to aid first-time initiates in the rites
Μυσται	(Mystai)	"With eyes closed (or veiled)": Pertains to first-time initiates in the greater Mystery rites of Eleusis
ναρθεξ	(narthex)	See *thyrsos*
νεβριʃ	(nebris)	Ceremonial deerskin worn by worshippers of Dionysos at festive rites. It is theorized by some scholars that the white spots of the fallow deer nebris represented the white spots of the mushroom Amanita muscaria, which is one entheogen scholars believe may have been used during Mystery rites
νυφαλια	(nephalia)	"Bloodless and wineless offerings": Cthonic sacrificial rites performed over a pit-altar

ξενοι	(xenoi)	Sacred statues or other physical representations of Deity
οικοͻ	(oikos)	"House": Mystery ceremonies were anciently held within the *oikos*, which might in fact have been a house, or which may also have been a cave or sepulchre renovated into a temple dedicated to cthonic divinities
ομφαλοͻ	(omphalos)	"Navel": The altar-stone of Delphi was known as the *omphalos*. Mythically, it is that place where the two eagles released by Zeus from the edges of the Universe met, and it was considered the center of the Attic world, the point at which Olympic and cthonic realms merged
Οποραλια	(Oporalia)	Classical Attic midsummer season, the beginning of which was defined by the rising of Sirius and the end of which was defined by the rising of the Pleiades
ορειβασια	(oreibasia)	"Procession [up the mountain]": Referent to Thyiadic rites, but not necessarily only those of Lenaia
οργιαζειν	(orgiazein)	"Celebration [of the physical expression of that energy which animates the soul]"
Οσιοι	(Hosioi)	"Unifiers [of realms]": Hellenic priests who mediated between those things considered profane or secular and those things considered pure or holy. These five select priests were ordained as young men or boys by the Pythia of Delphi, whose prophecies they were trained to interpret and whose temple they sanctified yearly; they lived at least a portion of each year at the Temple of Delphi, where both Apollo and Dionysos — the god of light and reason, and the *agathos daimon* of shadow and intuition — reigned. Plutarch remains the most famous of all *Hosioi* who ever served at Delphi

Παιϲ αφ 'εστιαϲ	(Pais...)	"Child of the hearth": One child, usually a boy, chosen to undergo lesser and greater Mysteries as a surrogate for, and a conduit of mystic blessings to, all individuals unable to attend that year's Eleusinia
παλινγεσια	(palingesia)	From *pali*, "again," and *gesia* "birth," this word might refer to reincarnation, resurrection, or metempsychosis, all common afterlife possibilities of the ancient and Classical Hellenic Mystery cults, as were concepts of reward and punishment as well as a hope for eternal union with the Divine after death. For a very thorough look at Pagan Greek afterlife beliefs, see Harrison, *passim*
Παρνασσοϲ	(Parnassos)	Mountain sacred to both Dionysos and Apollo; the Temple of Delphi is located in its foothills
παννυχιϲ	(pannychis)	"All-night festival": A standard event in the Hellenic Mystery rites, and during celebration of the Hellenic New Year
πελανοϲ	(pelanos)	An offering of unleavened bread or porridge; the mixed-grain offering given on the final day of the Anthesteria (*chytrogia*) was a pelanos
Πλουτοδοταϲ	(Ploutodotas)	"Bringer of wealth": An appelation of Dionysos invoked by the *Dadouchos* of Eleusis at the festivals of Lenaia and Anthesteria
πιθοι	(pithoi)	Large, conical, half-buried ceramic urns in which wine was fermented, grain was stored, or the remains of the dead were buried. In times of desperation — such as the invasion of the Persians in approximately 550 BCE — Hellenes hid, and even lived for a time, within the concealing pithoi
Πιθογια	(Pithogia)	"Festival of casks": The beginning of the festival of Anthesteria marked by the breaching of the pithoi in

which that year's wine had fermented after fortification and settling, and the racking of the wine for later use or for storage. No drinking of the vintage occurred on this day; drinking contests between the adult male heads of families, and the first drink of wine given to toddlers, occurred only on the second day of the Anthesteria

πλεμοχοαι	(plemochoai)	Enormous urns with wide mouths and narrow pedestals, in which the offscourings from the myesis ritual were collected and mixed with seed corn
ραμνοʃ	(rhamnos)	Buckthorn or hawthorn, symbolic of the Hellenic Anthesteria; its leaves were chewed and its flowered twigs used to garland doors on the second day of the festival
σαλπινξ	(salpinx)	Double-throated trumpet used to "call forth" Dionysos in rituals and, in war, to signal troop movement (Athena was also known as "she of the salphinges")
σατυρ	(satyr)	Mythical beings — or mummers — sporting the ears, tails, legs and randy habits of goats: Familiars of Dionysos
σχομματα/ εσχπαλογια	(schommata/ eschralogia)	Lewd gestures and lewd jokes performed as a form of purification and protection from maleficent spirits during rituals of *katabasis*
σιλενι	(sileni)	Mythical beings — or mummers — sporting horses' tails and, occasionally, hooves; not to be confused with centaurs, mythical beings whose upper anatomy is human and whose lower anatomy is equine

σφαγια	(sphagia)	"Offscourings": A cthonic sacrificial ceremony of rectification, designed to aid worshippers in the removal of impurity or guilt
συνθημα	(synthema)	See *legomena*
σταμνοʃ	(stamnos)	Ceremonial vessels from which wine was ladled for the rituals of Lenaia and Limnaia
τα Ιερα	(ta Hiera)	"The Sacred"
ταιναι	(tainai)	A fillet or band, representative of the swaddling clothes of the sacred infant, which was worn by worshippers and used to decorate ritual items, steles, sacred stones or herms — including the Delphic *omphalos* — and the bodies of sacrificial animals; Tainai were also displayed outside a house after the birth of a girl child (leafy branches were displayed when a boy was born)
Υελεστεριον	(Telesterion)	Temple of Demeter at Eleusis
τελετοʃ/ τελεσθεναι	(teletos/ telesthenai)	Actions, rites, or knowledge pertaining to Mystery initiations
τεμενοʃ	(temenos)	Consecrated boundary found around ancient and Classical Greek temples or other sacred areas, which separated hallowed ground from surrounding profane areas (the English word "profane" derives from the Greek *propulaea*, which means "porch [of the temple]")
τριετεριʃ	(trieteris)	The two-year festival period of Dionysos which was followed in many parts of the Hellenic world (Athens was an exception)

υεορται	(heortai)	Mandatory festivals put on and paid for by the Athenian government; individuals who shunned these festivals were labeled *asebia* (impious) by Athenian magistrates, and were fined
υδροφορια	(hydrophoria)	Fresh-water libation
υυε–κυε	(hye-kye)	"Rain and conceive!": The ceremonial cry given by the new *epoptai* on the final day of the greater Mystery rites, when *plemochoai* containing seed-corn and the offscourings from the *myesis* ritual were emptied by the Hierophant onto prepared ground on the Rharian Plain outside the Temple of Demeter
Φαλλοφοροʃ	(Phallophoros)	"Phallus-bearer": Refers to those who carried large carved phalloi or ithyphallic statues in Dionysian processions
Φρατραε	(Phratrae)	A familial clan: Several phratrae with equivalent social ties (usually occupational ones) made up a *deme*
χΘονιοʃ	(Cthonios)	"(The Dionysos) of the underworld." In later Hellenic religion, which tended toward linking all godforms into one complex and paradoxical god — a monotheism brought about by the influence of *philosophy*, a belief structure based upon observable phenomena, which was the forebear of modern scientific reasoning — this might be Hades himself, or the son of Hades and Persephone. *Cthonic* means "pertaining to the underworld (and its Deities)"
χερνιψ	(chernips)	This ceremonial washing of the hands or ablution of the body with water sanctified to ritual use prior to any liturgical act, entry into sacred space, or sacrificial rite, was taken into the purview of both Greek Orthodox and Roman Catholic Christian Churches, where a chernips basin may be found just inside the entry to any church or cathedral building

χοαι/χουϛ   (choĕ/chous)   1¼-liter jug from which wine was poured in libation to the gods and ancestors, as well as imbibed from, by individuals during Chŏes-day festivities; libation to any cthonic Deity is accurately called *choai*

χυθωϛ   (kythos)   A wine ladle

Χυτρογια   (Chytrogia)   "Feast of pots" or "feast of holes": The offering ceremony which ended the festival of Anthesteria

ωλουχυται   (olouchytai)   "In memory of ancient times": The practice of consecrating a hearth or altar by sprinkling it with grain, or a mixture of grain and salt, prior to use

ωμοφαγια   (omophagy)   The practice of eating raw meat; a sacramental rite in Dionysian cults

BIBLIOGRAPHY

Aoumiel. *Dancing Shadows; The Roots of Western Religious Beliefs.* St. Paul, Minnesota; Llewelyn World Religion and Magic Series, 1994.

Arora, David. *Mushrooms Demystified.* Berkeley, CA; Ten Speed Press, 1986.

Arthur, James. "Mushrooms & Mankind; Back to Ethno-mycology," @ *http: // www.Sirius.com/-holy/recipe.html.*

Athanassakis, Apostolos N. *The Homeric Hymns.* Baltimore, Maryland; Johns Hopkins University Press, 1976.

— — — — . *The Orphic Hymns; Text, Translation and Notes.* Atlanta, Georgia; Scholars Press for the Society of Biblical Literature, 1977, 1988.

Babcock, B. (editor). *The Reversible World; Symbolic Inversion of Art and Society.* New York; Cornell University Press, 1978.

Baum, Julius. *The Mysteries.* Princeton, NJ; Princeton University Press, ©1955, 1978.

Beck, Sanderson. "The Divine Mother and the Veil of Death; The Mysteries of Eleusis," @ http://www.san.beck.org/Eleusis-3.htm.

Bierlein, J.F. *Parallel Myth.s.* New York; Ballantine Wellspring, 1994.

Bigwood/Ott/Thompson/Neely. "1979 Effects of Ergonovine," *Journal of Psychedelic Drugs,* Volume 11 #1-2; January-June 1979.

Bookidis, Nancy. *The Sanctuary of Demeter and Kore; Topography and Architecture.* Princeton; American School of Classical Studies at Athens, 1997.

Bremmer, Jan N. *Greek Religion* (Greece and Rome; New Surveys in the Classics, #24). Oxford, England; Oxford University Press, 1994.

Brown, Deni. *Encyclopedia of Herbs and Their Uses.* New York; Dorling Kindersley Publishing, ©1995.

Bruit-Zaidman, Louise and Schmitt-Pantel, Pauline. *Religion in the Ancient Greek City.* Cambridge, Massachussetts; Cambridge University Press, 1992.

Brumfield, Allaire C. *The Attic Festivals of Demeter and their Relation to the Agricultural Year.* Philadelphia, PA; ©1976, 1983.

Burkert, Walter. *Ancient Mystery Cults* (Carl Newell Jackson Lectures). Cambridge, Massachussetts and London, England; Harvard University Press, 1987.

— — — — . 1986, 1988. *The Creation of the Sacred; Tracks of Biology in Early Religions.* Cambridge, Massachusetts; Harvard University Press, 1986, 1988.

— — — —. (Translated by John Raffian) *Greek Religion.* Cambridge, Massachusetts; Harvard University Press (Basil Blackwell, publisher) 1977, 1985.

— — — — . "Greek Tragedy and Sacrificial Ritual," In *Greek and Byzantine Studies #7,* (1966) 87-121.

— — — —. (Translated by Peter Bing.) *Homo Necans; The Anthropology of Ancient Greek Sacrificial Ritual and Myth.* Berkeley / Los Angeles / London; University of California Press, 1983.

— — — —. *Structure and History in Greek Mythology and Ritual.* Berkeley, California; University of California, Berkeley Press, 1979, 1982.

Buxton, R. G. A. *Persuasion in Greek Tragedy.* Cambridge, England; Cambridge University Press.

Campbell, Joseph. *Historical Atlas of World Mythology* (series). New York / Grand Rapids / St. Louis / San Francisco / London / Singapore / Sydney / Tokyo; Harper & Row Publishers, 1989.

Volume 1, part 1; "The Way of the Animal Powers; Mythologies of the Primitive Hunters and Gatherers."

Volume 1, part 2; "The Way of the Animal Powers; Mythologies of the Great Hunt."

Volume 2, part 1; "The Way of the Seeded Earth; The Sacrifice."

Volume 2, parts 2 & 3; "The Way of the Seeded Earth; Mythologies of the Primitive Planters. North, Middle, and South America."

— — — —. *The Inner Reaches of Outer Space; Metaphor as Myth and as Religion.* Novato, California; New World Library. ©1986, 2002 by the Joseph Campbell Foundation.

— — — —. *The Masks of God, Volume I; Primitive Mythology.* New York; Penguin Books, Arkana Edition, 1991.

— — — —. *The Masks of God, Volume II; Oriental Mythology.* New York; Penguin Books, Arkana Edition, 1991.

— — — —. *The Masks of God, Volume III; Occidental Mythology.* New York; Penguin Books, Arcana Edition, 1991.

— — — —. *Transformations of Myth Through Time; The Soul of the Ancients.* Volume I, Videotape 5. "From Darkness to Light; The Mystery Religions of Ancient Greece." William Free Productions and Mythology Ltd./Public Media Video in assoc. with Holoform Research, Inc., 1989.

Casavis, Jack N. *The Greek Origins of Freemasonry.* New York, NY, 1955.

Cavanaugh, Maureen B. *Eleusis and Athens; Documents in Finance, Religion, and Politics in the Fifth Century B.C.* Atlanta, GA; Scholar's Press, 1996.

Cavendish, Richard (Editor) *Man, Myth, and Magic; An Illustrated Encyclopedia of the Supernatural.* BPC Publishing Ltd. Italy; (LOC CC# 70-141143) 1970.

Cooper, D. Jason. *Mithras; Mysteries and Initiation Rediscovered.* York Beach, Maine; Samuel Weiser Publishing, Inc., 1996.

Cornford, Francis. *The Origins of Attic Comedy.* England; Cambridge University Press, ©1914, 1961.

Danielou, Alain (translated by K. F. Hurry). *Shiva and Dionysos; Gods of Love and Ecstasy.* London, England; East-West Publications, 1979, 1982, 1992.

Davis, N. Z. *Society and Culture in Early Modern Europe.* England; Oxford University Press, 1975.

Davis, Phillip H. *Some Eleusinian Building Inscriptions of the Fourth Century BC.* Geneva; W. F. Humphrey Press, 1931.

DeKorne, Jim. *Psychedelic Shamanism; The Cultivation, Preparation, and Shamanic Use of Psychotropic Plants.* Port Townsend, WA; Loompanics Unlimited, 1994.

Detienne, Marcel (translated by Arthur Goldhammer). *Dionysos at Large.* Cambridge, Massachusetts; Harvard University Press, 1986, 1989.

— — — —. (translated by Leonard and Mirielle Muellner). *Dionysos Slain.* Baltimore, Maryland; Johns Hopkins University Press, 1977, 1979.

Devereux, Paul. *The Long Trip; A Prehistory of Psychedelics.* New York / London / Victoria / Aukland / Toronto; Penguin Books, Arkana Edition, 1997.

Dioscorides (edited by Robert T. Gunther). *The Greek Herbal of Dioscorides.* New York; Hafner Press, ©1934, 1959.

Dodds, E. R. *The Greeks and the Irrational.* California; University of Berkeley Press, ©1951, 1984.

Dowden, Ken. *Death and the Maiden; Girls' Initiation Rites in Greek Mythology*. New York; Routledge Publishing, 1989.

Du Toit, Brian. *Drugs, Rituals, and Altered States of Consciousness*. Rotterdam; A. A. Balkema, 1977.

Durant, Will. *Our Oriental Heritage*. New York; MJF Books, 1994.

Edgerton, Robert. *Sick Societies; Challenging the Myth of Primitive Harmony*. New York; The Free Press, 1992.

Elderkin, George W. *Kantharos; Studies in Dionysiac and Kindred Cult*. Princeton, New Jersey; Princeton University Press, 1934.

Eliot, Alexander. *The Universal Myths; Heroes, Gods, Tricksters and Others*. New York; Meridian Books, 1990.

Eliade, Mircea. *The Myth of the Eternal Return*. Princeton, New Jersey; Princeton University Press, Bollingen Series XXI, 1951, 1969.

— — — — (translated by Willard R. Trask). *The Sacred and the Profane; The Nature of Religion. The Significance of Religious Myth, Symbolism, and Ritual within Life and Culture*. New York; Harcourt, Brace & Co. 1987.

Eschotado, Antonio (translated by K. A. Symington). *A Brief History of Drugs*. Rochester, Vermont; Park Street Press 1999.

Farnell, L. R. *The Cults of the Greek States*. Volumes One through Five. London, England; Oxford University Press, 1896, 1907, 1909.

Ferguson, E. (Editor). *Encyclopedia of Early Christianity*. New York / London; Garland Publishing, ©1990.

Festi, F. and Bianchi, A. "Amanita Muscaria; Mycopharmacological Outline and Personal Experiences." Taken from *PM&E* Volume Five, available @ *http: //diseyes.lycaeum. org/ fresh/amanmr.htm* (1-49; all page numbers taken from internet article).

Fierz-David, Linda. *Women's Dionysian Initiation*. Dallas, Texas; Spring Publications, 1988.

Finley, Moses. *Democracy Ancient and Modern*. New Brunswick, NJ; Beacon Press, 1988.

Flattery, D. and Schwartz, M. "Haoma and Harmaline." *Near Eastern Studies*, Vol. 21. Berkeley, California; University of Berkeley Press, 1989.

Fontenrose, Joseph. *The Delphic Oracle, its Responses and Operations, with a Catalogue of Responses* Berkeley, California; University of California Press, 1981. (Information pertinent to the oracles which I have paraphrased for use in this book may also be found at *http: // www.theosophy-nw.org/theosnw/world/med/me-elo.htm.*)

Foucart, Paul François. *Les Mystères d'Eleusis*. Paris; A. Picard 1914.

Foulkes, Christoppher (editor). *Larousse Encyclopedia of Wine.* New York; Larousse/VUEF, ©2001.

Fox, Robin L. *Pagans and Christians.* New York, NY; Alfred A. Knopf, Inc, ©1986, 1989.

Frazier, J. G. (translator). *Pausanias' "Description of Greece."* London, 1898.

Furst, P. T. (editor). *Flesh of the Gods; The Ritual use of Hallucinogens.* New York; Praeger, 1972.

Garey, Terry. *The Joy of Home Winemaking.* New York; Harper Resource/Quill (Harper Collins Publishers) ©1996.

Garland, Robert. *The Greek Way of Death.* Ithaca, New York; Cornell University Press, 1985.

— — — — . *The Greek Way of Life.* Ithaca, New York; Cornell University Press, 1990.

Gimbutas, Marja. *The Language of the Goddess.* New York; Thames and Hudson, 1989.

Ginzburg, Carlo (translated by Raymond Rosenthal). *Ecstasies; Deciphering the Witches' Sabbath.* Pantheon Press. Random House, U. S. A. ©1991; Penguin Books, New York, NY / London and Middlesex England / Victoria Australia / Ontario Canada / Auckland, New Zealand, 1992.

Grant, F. C. *Hellenistic Religions; The Age of Syncretism.* New York; Liberal Arts Press, 1953.

Graves, Robert. *Difficult Questions, Easy Answers.* Garden City, New York; Doubleday and Company, Inc., ©1971.

— — — — . *The Greek Myths; Complete Edition.* New York; Penguin Putnam, Inc., ©1955, 1992.

— — — — . *Food for Centaurs.* Garden City, New York; Doubleday and Company, Inc., ©1960.

— — — — . "Mushrooms, Food of the Gods." *Atlantic Monthly* 200 (2); 73-77.

— — — — . *The White Goddess; A Historical Grammar of Poetic Myth.* New York; Farrar, Straus and Giroux, ©1948, 1999.

Guthrie, W. K. C. *The Greeks and Their Gods.* Boston, Massachusetts; Beacon Press, 1955.

— — — — . *Orpheus and Greek Religion; A Study of the Orphic Movement.* New Jersey; Princeton University Press, ©1993.

Halliday, W. R. *The Pagan Background to Early Christianity.* London, England; Hodder and Stoughton, 1925.

Hanson, Victor Davis. *The Western Way of War; Infantry Battle in Classical Greece.* New York / Oxford; Oxford University Press, ©1989.

Harner, Michael J. (Editor) *Hallucinogens and Shamanism.* London / Oxford / New York; Oxford University Press, 1973.

Harrigan, Patrick. "Dionysus and Katagama; Parallel Mystery Cults." *The Journal of The Institute of Asian Studies*, Volume 14, #2; March 1997 (may also be found at; http: // www.katagama.org/research/dionysus.htm).

Harrison, Jane Ellen. *Prolegomena to the Study of Greek Religion.* Princeton, NJ; Princeton University Press, 1991.

Hatch, E. (F. C. Grant, Editor). *The Influence of Greek Ideas and Usages Upon the Christian Church* New York; Harper Publishing, 1957.

Head, Joseph and Cranston, S. L. *Reincarnation; An East-West Anthology.* Santa Barbara, CA; Aeon Publishing Company, ©1961 (©1999 by Caren M. Elin).

Heinrich, Clark. *Strange Fruit; Alchemy, Religion and Magical Foods, a Speculative History.* London, England; Bloomsbury Publishing, ©1994, 1995.

Henrichs, A. (edited by C. Houser). *Dionysos and His Circle; Ancient Through Modern.* Cambridge, Massachusetts; Fogg Art Museum, 1979.

Hignett, Charles. *A History of the Athenian Constitution to the End of the Fifth Century BC.* England; Oxford University Press, 1952.

Jaskloski, Helmut (translated by Michael Kohn). *The Labyrinth; Symbol of Fear, Rebirth, and Liberation.* Riverside, California; Shambala Press, 1997.

Jewett, Benjamin (Translator). *The Dialogues of Plato.* New York, 1927.

Jones, P. and Pennick, N. *A. History of Pagan Europe.* London / New York / Canada; Routledge Publishing, 1995, 1997.

Kakoure, Katerina I. *Death and Resurrection; Concerning Dramatized Ceremonies of the Greek Popular Worship.* Athens, Greece; University of Athens, 1965.

Keegan, John. *A History of Warfare.* New York, NY; Alfred A. Knopf Publishers, 1993.

Kerenyi, Karl (translated by Ralph Manheim). *Dionysos; Archetypal Image of Indestructible Life.* Princeton, New Jersey; Princeton University Press, Bollingen Series XV-2, 1976.

— — — — (translated by Ralph Manheim). *Eleusis; Archetypal Image of Mother and Daughter.* Princeton, New Jersey; Princeton University Press, Bollingen Series LXV-4, 1976.

— — — — . *The Gods of the Greeks.* London / New York; Thames and Hudson, 2000.

— — — — . *The Heroes of the Greeks.* London / New York; Thames and Hudson, ©1959, 1997.

— — — — . (edited by Joseph Campbell.) *The Mysteries; Papers from the Eranos Yearbooks.* Princeton, New Jersey; Princeton University Press, Bollingen Series XXX, Volume Two, 1955, 1996.

— — — — (translated by Christopher Holme). *The Religion of the Greeks and Romans.* Westport, Connecticut; Greenwood Press, 1940, 1962, 1973.

Knox, Bernard. *The Heroic Temper*. California; University of Berkeley Press, 1964.

Korshak, Yvonne. *Frontal Faces in Attic Vase Painting of the Archaic Period*. Chicago, Illinois; Ares Publishers, ©1987.

Lawler, Lillian B. *The Dance of the Ancient Greek Theater*. Iowa City, Iowa; University of Iowa Press, 1964.

Leadbeater, C. W. *Ancient Mystic Rites*. York Beach, Maine; Samuel Weiser Publishing, Inc. 1983.

Legg, Stuart. *The Barbarians of Asia; The Peoples of the Steppes from 1600 BC*. New York, NY; Dorset Press, ©1970.

Levi-Strauss, Claude (translated by John and Doreen Weightman). *The Raw and the Cooked; Introduction to a Science of Mythology, Volume I*. New York NY / Evanston, Illinois; Harper and Row Publishers, ©1969.

— — — —. (translated by John and Doreen Weightman). *From Honey to Ashes; Introduction to a Science of Mythology, Volume II*. New York NY / Evanston, Illinois; Harper and Row Publishers, ©1969.

Loeb Classical Library (Harvard University Press) for the following sources (some may also be found in Sanderson Beck's "The Divine Mother and the Veil of Death; The Mysteries of Eleusis" at http: //www.san.beck.org/Eleusis-3.html; and all may be purchased over the Internet at http: //www.hup.harvard.edu/ catalog/L344.html);

    Aeschines,*On the Embassy*

    Apollodorus,"Fragment" 36 and *The Library*

    Aristeides,Quote from page 20 of W.F. Otto's "The Meaning of the Eleusinian Mysteries" in *The Mysteries; Papers from the Eranos Yearbooks*. Also in Casavis 1953; 111.

    Artemidoros, *Oneirokritica*

    Asterios, *Engomion to the Saintly Martyrs*

    Aristophanes, *The Frogs* (also cited by Beck, Harrison, and Winkler and Zeitlin,).

    Athenaeus, *The Deipnosophists*

    Callimachus, *Aetia* and *To Demeter*

    Cicero, *Laws*

    Clement of Alexandria, *Exhortation to the Greeks*

    Demetrios, *On Style*

    Diodorus Siculus, *Diodorus of Sicily*

    Diogenes, *Diogenes Laertius* VII; 77

    Epictetus, *Disourses*

Euripides *The Bacchae, Cyclops, Hypsipyle* (quote from page 290 of Walter Burkert,'s *Greek Religion*) and *Ion*

Flavius Claudius Julianus, *Orations* Volumes I-III.

Hesiod, *Works* and *Days, passim* (may also be found at; http: //sunsite.berkeley.edu/OMACL/Hesiod/works. html), Theogony 135

Hippocrates, *Epidemics*

Hippolytus, *Refutation of all Heresies*

Isocrates, *De Pace*

Lucian, *Dialogues Meretrobia and Scholia..*

Nonnus, *Dionysiaca* books 1-38 in Volumes 1-3.

Pausanias, *Description of Greece*

Pindar, "Fragments" 102 and 137A

Plato, *Phaedrus*

Pliny, *Natural History*

Plotinius, *First Ennead*

Plutarch, *Isis and Osiris* and *Quaestiones Symposia*

Porphyry, *Cave of the Nymphs* and *On Abstinence from Animal Food*

Porphyrus, in Edouard Schuré's *The Great Initiates* 406.

Proculus, in Edouard Schurés *The Great Initiates* 407.

Seneca, *Quaestiones Naturalis*

Sophocles, *Antigone* (cited in Harrison, 541) and *Oedipus Coloneus* (cited in Harrison, 91, 553-554)

Strabo, *Geography* and *Iacchus*

Suetoneus, *Nero*

Synesius, *Oration*

Tertullian, *To The Nations*

Xenophon, *Kyropaida*

Loraux, N. (translated by A. Sheridan). *The Invention of Athens.* Massachusetts; Cambridge University Press, 1986.

Luck, Georg. *Arcana Mundi; Magic and the Occult in the Greek and Roman Worlds. A Collection of Ancient Texts Translated, Annotated, and Introduced by Georg Luck.* Baltimore, Maryland; Johns Hopkins University Press, 1985.

Martin, Thomas R. *Ancient Greece from Prehistoric to Hellenic Times.* New Haven, London; Yale University Press, 1996.

Mallory, J. P. *In Search of the Indo-Europeans; Language, Archaeology, and Myth.* London, Thames and Hudson, 1996.

Matthews, John. *The Winter Solstice; The Sacred Traditions of Christmas.* Wheaton, Illinois, Quest Edition published with Godsfield Press; Theosophical Publishing House, 1998.

McKenna, Terrence. *Food of the Gods.* New York, NY; Bantam Books, 1992.

Merilless, Robert S. "Opium for the Masses; How the Ancients Got High." *Archaeology Odyssey,* Winter 1999; 21-29.

Meyer, Marvin W. (Editor). *The Ancient Mysteries; A Sourcebook; Sacred Texts of the Mystery Religions of the Ancient Mediterranean World.* Philadelphia, Pennysylvania; University of Pennsylvania Press, 1999.

Mikalson, J. D. *The Sacred and Civil Calendar of the Athenian Year.* Princeton, NJ; Princeton University Press, 1975.

Morgan, Adrian. *Toads and Toadstools.* Berkeley, California; Celestial Arts Press, 1995.

Mylonas, George E. *Eleusis and the Eleusinian Mysteries.* Princeton, New Jersey; Princeton University Press, 1961.

Nilsson, M. P. *Greek Piety.* Oxford, England; Clarendon Press, 1948.

Norwich, John Julius. *Byzantium, the Early Centuries* (Book One). New York; Alfred A. Knopf, ©1988, 1989.

Oldfather, C. H. (Translator). *Diodorus of Sicily.* Cambridge, Massachusetts; Harvard University Press, 1993.

Osborne, Robin. *Dēmos; The Discovery of Classical Attika.* England; Cambridge University Press, 1985.

Ott, Jonathan. *Ayahuasca Analogues.* Kennewick, Washington; Natural Products Co. 1994.

— — — —. (Illustrated by Girvin and Torres). *Pharmacophilia of the Natural Paradises.* Kennewick, Washington; Natural Products Co. 1997.

— — — — . *Pharmacotheon.* Kennewick, Washington; Natural Products Co. 1993.

Ott, J. & Neely, P. "1980 Effects of Methylergonovine," *Journal of Psychedelic Drugs,* Volume 12 #20; April-June 1980.

Otto, Walter Friedrich (translated by R. B. Palmer). *Dionysos; Myth and Cult.* Bloomington / Indianapolis / London, England; Indiana University Press, 1965.

— — — — (edited by Joseph Campbell). "The Meaning of the Eleusinian Mysteries," in *The Mysteries*. Bollingen Series XXX, 2. New York; Pantheon Books, 1955.

Pahnke, W. N. "Drugs and Mysticism." *The International Journal of Parapsychology*, Vol. 8, no. 2; 295-320.

Papazian, Charlie. *The Home Brewer's Companion; The Essential Handbook.* New York; Avon Books, 1994.

Parke, Herbert. *Festivals of the Athenians.* New York; Cornell University Press, 1977.

Partridge, E. *Origins; A Short Etymological Dictionary of Modern English* (Second Edition). New York; MacMillan Publishing Company, ©1989.

Peele, Stephen L. (Editor/Curator). *The Mushroom Culture; The Journal of Mushroom Cultivation*, #46; April 2000 (photo 11).

Perdatto, J. & Sullivan, J. P. (edited by A. Cameron and A. Kuhrt). *Women in the Ancient World; The Arethusa Papers, Images of Women in Antiquity.* New York, London & Melbourne; Viking Press, 1983.

Pickard-Cambridge, A. (Revision of A. E. Haigh.) *The Attic Theater* 3rd Edition, England; Oxford University Press, 1907.

— — — — . *Dithyramb, Tragedy and Comedy.* London, England; Oxford University Press, ©1927, 1962.

— — — — . (Revised by J. Gould and D. M. Lewis) *The Dramatic Festivals of Athens.* London, England; Oxford University Press, ©1952, 1968.

Pinsent, John. *Library of the World's Myths and Legends; Greek Mythology* (New Revised Edition). New York; printed by Peter Bedrick Books and distributed by Harper and Row, ©1962, 1982, 1983.

Plutarch (Edited by Edmund Fuller). *Lives of the Noble Greeks.* New York; Dell Publishing/ Laurel Classics 1959, 1974.

Potter, T. W. and Johns, Catherine. *Roman Britain.* Barnes & Noble Books, Inc. 2000.

Radin, Paul. *The Trickster; A Study in American Indian Mythology.* New York; Shocken Books, Inc. 1956, 1972.

Ranke-Heinmann. *Eunuchs for the Kingdom of Heaven; Women, Sexuality and the Catholic Church.* New York; Doubleday, 1990.

Rätsch, Christian. *The Dictionary of Sacred and Magical Plants.* Bridport, England; Prism Press, 1992.

Redmond, Layne. *When the Drummers Were Women; A Spiritual History of Rhythm.* New York; Three Rivers Press, 1997.

Ripinsky-Naxon, Michael. *The Nature of Shamanism; Substance and Function of a Religious Metaphor.* Albany, New York; SUNY Press, 1993.

Robertson, John M. *Pagan Christs.* New Hyde Park, New York; University Books, Inc., ©1967.

Robins, Don and Ross, Anne. *The Life and Death of a Druid Prince; The Story of Lindow Man, an Archaeological Sensation.* New York / London / Toronto / Sydney / Tokyo / Singapore; Summit Books, 1989.

Rohde, Erwin (translated by W. B. Hillis). *Psyche; The Cult of Souls and Belief in Immortality Among the Greeks,* Volume I. New York; Pantheon Books, 1966.

Ruck, Carl A. P. "Mushrooms and Philosophers." *Journal of Ethnopharmacology* 4; 179-205. Reprinted in *Persephone's Quest* by R. G. Wasson, et al. New Haven, Connecticut; Yale University Press, 1981.

— — — —. "The Offerings from the Hyperboreans," *Journal of Ethnopharmacology* 8; 177-207. Reprinted in *Persephone's Quest,* by R. G. Wasson, et al. New Haven, Connecticut; Yale University Press, 1983.

Rudgely, Richard. *Essential Substances; A Cultural History of Intoxicants in Society.* New York; Kodansha International, 1993, 1995.

Ruspoli, Mario. *The Cave of Lascaux; The Final Photographs.* New York; Harry N. Abrams, Inc. ©1986, 1987.

Salzman Emanuel, Jason Salzman, Joanne Salzman, and Gary Lincoff. "In Search of Mukhomor, the Mushroom of Immortality," *Shaman's Drum; A Journal of Experiential Shamanism,* #41; Spring 1996.

Schultes, R. and Hofmann, A. *Plants of The Gods; Their Sacred, Healing, and Hallucinogenic Powers.* Rochester, Vermont; Healing Arts Press, 1992.

Schuré, Edouard. *Krishna and Orpheus; The Great Initiates of the East and West.* New York; Kessinger Publications Co. 1919, 1997.

Seaford, Richard. *Euripides' Cyclops.* England; Oxford University Press, 1984.

— — — — . "The Mysteries of Dionysos at Pompeii" as found at *http: //www.stoa.org/ diotima.essays/Seaford.shtml* in *Diotima; Materials for the Study of Women and Gender in the Ancient World* (re; photos and studies of Villa de Mysteries)

Segal, Charles. *Dionysian Poetics and Euripides' Bacchai.* New Jersey; Princeton University Press, 1982.

Sekunda, Nicholas V. (Plates by Angus McBride; Edited by Martin Windrow). *The Ancient Greeks.* London; Osprey Books (Military), Elite Series ©1986, 1996.

Siewart, P. "The Ephebic Oath in Fifth-Century Athens," 102-111, *Journal of Hellenic Studies,* Vol. 97, 1977.

Smith, Houston. *Cleansing the Doors of Perception; The Religious Significance of Entheogenic Plants and Chemicals* New York; Tarcher/Putnam, 2000.

Smith, Michael S. *http: //www.theforbiddenfruit.*com/articles/articles/Amanita.htm, article written October 1997, page 6. See also the following informative Internet articles by M. Smith;

http://www.theforbiddenfruit.com/articles/articles/aman.htm, and

http: //www.theforbidden fruit.com/articles/articles/mushrooms_and_religion.htm.

Stafford, Peter. *Psychedelics Encyclopedia.* Berkeley, California; Ronin Publishing, 1978, 1992.

Stallybrass, P. & White, A. *The Politics and Poetics of Transgression.* London, 1986.

Stevens, José. "A Journey in the the Selva Profunda; Dieting with Plant Teachers in Peru," in *Shaman's Drum; A Journal of Experiential Shamanism,* No. 49; 46-55.

Sutton, Dana Ferrin. *Papyrological Studies in Dionysiac Literature* (P. Lit. Lond. 77 and P. Ross Georg. I.11). Oak Park, Illinois; Bolchazy-Carducci Publishers, 1987.

Tannahill, Reay. *Food in History.* New York; Stein and Day Publishers, 1973.

Taplin, O. "Fifth Century Tragedy and Comedy; A Synkrisis." 160-180 *Journal of Hellenic Studies* Vol. 106, 1986.

Taylor, Thomas (Translator). *Iamblichus; On the Mysteries.* Wizard's Bookshelf, 1964.

Taylor-Perry, Rosemarie. (Drawings by Timothy White, Editor.) "Renewing *Ta Hiera,* the Holy Mystery Rites of Eleusis," 47-60; *Shaman's Drum; A Journal of Experiential Shamanism,* Vol. 60, Autumn 2001.

Thompson, Homer & Wycherley, R. E. *The Agora of Athens* (48-52). New Jersey; Princeton University Press, Edition 14.

Tierney, Patrick. *The Highest Altar; Unveiling the Mystery of Human Sacrifice.* New York / London / Victoria / Ontario / Auckland; Penguin Books/Viking Penguin, 1989, 1990.

Trippett, Frank. *The First Horsemen.* Alexandria, Virginia; Time-Life Books, Inc. ©1974.

Turcan, Robert (translated by Antonia Neville). *The Cults of the Roman Empire.* Massachusetts; Harvard University Press, ©1996, 1997.

Turner, D. M. *The Essential Psychedelic Guide.* San Francisco, California; Panther Press, 1994.

Turner, Victor. *Dramas, Fields, and Metaphors; Symbolic Action in Human Society.* Rochester, New York; Cornell University Press, 1974.

————. *The Ritual Process* Rochester, New York; Cornell University Press, 1969.

————. *The Forest of Symbols* Rochester, New York; Cornell University Press, 1969.

Valencic, Ivan. "Has the Mystery of the Eleusinian Mysteries Been Solved?" *Yearbook for Ethnomedicine and the Study of Consciousness,* Issue 3 (325-336) 1994. This article is also available @ Schaffer Library of Drug Policy/The Psychedelic LIbrary; http.//www. druglibrary.org/schaffer/lsd/valencic.html.

Vernant, J. P. & Vidal-Naquet, P. (translated by J. Lloyd). *Myth and Tragedy in Ancient Greece* Brighton, 1981.

Wasson/Kramrisch/Ott/Ruck. *Persephone's Quest; Entheogens and the Origins of Religion.* New Haven, Connecticut; Yale University Press, 1986.

Wasson/Hofmann/Ruck. *The Road to Eleusis; Unveiling the Secret of the Mysteries.* New York / London; Harcourt, Brace, Jovanovich, 1978.

Wasson, R. Gordon. *Soma; Divine Mushroom of Immortality* Harcourt, Brace, Jovanovich (Italy); Library of Congress Catalogue Card Number 68-11197.

Whitehead, D. *The Demes of Attica.* New Jersey; Princeton University Press, 1986.

Williams, C. K. *The Bacchae of Euripides.* The Noonday Press. New York; Farrar, Straus and Giroux, 1990.

Williams, Hector. "Secret Rites of Lesbos," *Archaeology Magazine.* July/August 1994; 34-40.

Willoughby, Harold R. *Pagan Regeneration; A Study of Mystery Initiation in the Graeco-Roman World.* Chicago, Illinois; Chicago University Press, 1900, 1983.

Winkler, J. J. and Zeitlin, F. I. *Nothing to do with Dionysos? Athenian Drama in its Social Context.* Chichester, West Sussex, England; Princeton University Press, 1990.

Wohlberg, J. "Haoma-Soma in the World of Ancient Greece." *Journal of Psychoactive Drugs,* Volume 22 #3; 333-342, 1990.

Young, Dudley. *Origins of the Sacred; The Ecstasies of Love and War.* New York; St. Martin's Press, ©1991.

INDEX